George Stoneman

George Stoneman

A Biography of the Union General

BEN FULLER FORDNEY

McFarland & Company, Inc., Publishers
Jefferson, North Carolina

The present work is a reprint of the illustrated case bound edition of George Stoneman: A Biography of the Union General, *first published in 2008 by McFarland.*

LIBRARY OF CONGRESS CATALOGUING-IN-PUBLICATION DATA

Fordney, Ben Fuller, 1931–
George Stoneman : a biography of the Union general / Ben Fuller Fordney.
p. cm.
Includes bibliographical references and index.

ISBN 978-0-7864-9549-8 (softcover : acid free paper) ♾
ISBN 978-0-7864-8346-4 (ebook)

1. Stoneman, George, 1822–1894. 2. Generals — United States — Biography. 3. United States. Army — Biography. 4. United States. Army of the Potomac — Biography. 5. United States — History — Civil War, 1861–1865 — Cavalry operations. 6. United States. Army. Mormon Battalion — Biography. 7. Governors — California — Biography. I. Title.
E467.1.S88F67   2014   973.7'33092 — dc22   [B]   2007043251

BRITISH LIBRARY CATALOGUING DATA ARE AVAILABLE

© 2008 Ben Fuller Fordney. All rights reserved

No part of this book may be reproduced or transmitted in any form or by any means, electronic or mechanical, including photocopying or recording, or by any information storage and retrieval system, without permission in writing from the publisher.

On the cover: *background* Battle of Chancellorsville, May 2, 3 & 4, 1863; *foreground* Maj. Gen. George Stoneman, officer of the Federal Army (Library of Congress)

Manufactured in the United States of America

*McFarland & Company, Inc., Publishers
Box 611, Jefferson, North Carolina 28640
www.mcfarlandpub.com*

To my wife, Betty Anne Martz Fordney,
for many hours of research, editing, travel,
encouragement, and constant support without which
this book would not have been possible,
and to my son, Craig Warren Fordney

Acknowledgments

There are a number of people who helped me complete this work. My wife, Betty Anne, not only encouraged me, but edited my work as well. Her assistance, patience, and support were invaluable. My son, Craig Fordney, was enormously helpful with computer and editorial assistance. The staff at Carrier Library, James Madison University, particularly the inter-library loan service, helped me acquire many sources. Mrs. Doris Waters, of the Norwich Guernsey Memorial Library, Norwich, New York, and the staff of New Berlin Library, New Berlin, New York, were very helpful with information about the early history of the Stoneman family. Ms. Dorothy Rapp, Archives Technician, U.S. Military Academy Archives, was of great assistance with Stoneman's West Point service, as was Ms. Judith A. Sibley, West Point Manuscript Librarian. Ms. Vivian D. Wellman, Reference Librarian of the Church of Jesus Christ of Latter-day Saints, provided very useful material on the Mormon Battalion. Mr. Norman Carlson, Historian, Town of Busti, New York, rendered invaluable assistance by providing background on the Stoneman family. The Manuscript Division of the Library of Congress and the National Archives staff, particularly Archivists Michael Musick and Michael Meir, were of great assistance. Ms. Susan Peters, of the Arizona Historical Society, provided very useful biographical material on General Stoneman, as well as Ms. Carol Downey, Reference Librarian of the State of Arizona, Department of Library, Archives, and Public Records. The staff of the Public Library of Saltville, Virginia, provided useful information on the Saltville Raid. The Rowan County Library at Salisbury, North Carolina, provided equally useful background on the Salisbury Raid. Mr. John D. Rhodehamel, Archivist of American Historical Manuscripts, The Huntington Library, San Marino, California, provided Stoneman correspondence. An old friend, Ms. Elinor Schmidt, of Corona Del Mar, California, helped greatly with research in the Los Angeles area. Joseph Gus Fitzgerald, a computer expert, was invariably patient and helpful answering my many questions. Winston Wine, an authority on the Battle of Brandy Station, contributed to the account of that engagement. I am especially indebted to Dr. George Beattie Stoneman, great-grandson of General George Stoneman, for his insight and willingness to share the diaries of Mary Oliver Hardisty Stoneman and family background. My friend and Civil War historian John C. Bonnell, Jr., prepared the maps depicting important engagements of Stoneman's career. Frances Pickin Florio, a descendant of George Stoneman's brother Byron Stoneman, made available to me copies of invaluable letters written by George Stoneman to his father. Lieutenant Colonel Sherman L. Fleek, U.S. Army (ret.), an authority on the Mormon Battalion, provided detailed information on their historic march. Andrew J. Potts made his extensive collection of Stoneman photos available to me. The late John Heatwole, as well as Eric Wittenberg, both noted Civil War historians, provided invaluable advice. Finally, my colleagues and friends in the History Department of James Madison University helped me immeasurably with my historical interests. All of these people gave invaluable help but any errors or omissions are entirely mine.

Ben Fuller Fordney
Harrisonburg, Virginia

Table of Contents

Acknowledgments vii
Preface 1

ONE. Stoneman in Command 5
TWO. West Point 11
THREE. With the Mormon Battalion 16
FOUR. From California to the Rio Grande 27
FIVE. With McClellan 35
SIX. Stuart Redux 48
SEVEN. Fredericksburg 54
EIGHT. The Bursting Shell 62
NINE. "We were whipped..." 81
TEN. Payment of a Debt 101
ELEVEN. Riots and Reconstruction 122
TWELVE. Arizona Territory 142
THIRTEEN. Governor Stoneman 156

Epilogue 171
Chapter Notes 175
Bibliography 189
Index 195

Preface

There is no lack of Civil War biographies on our nation's bookshelves celebrating those "larger than life" actors on the great stage of the nation's most traumatic, yet cathartic, event. Perhaps historical accounts of the most familiar Civil War heroes have reached the saturation point. Lee, Grant, and Jackson, for example, have been examined so thoroughly that one wonders if any more can be written to enlarge the places in history of these great commanders.

Historians are now moving down to the second echelon of Civil War figures. There are rich treasures to be mined by the historian researching the lives of those who played a significant, yet less flamboyant role in the war than the Grants and the Lees.

George Stoneman is one such figure. He directed the progress of Union cavalry from its dark days of humiliation early in the war to

Major General George Stoneman (Massachusetts Commandery Military Order of the Loyal Legion and the U.S. Army Military History Institute).

effectiveness on a par with the best the Confederates had to offer. The Federals reached equality on the fields of Brandy Station and Gettysburg. A stoical and brooding figure who resembled the haunted features of John Brown, or even those of a worn and troubled Abraham Lincoln, Stoneman has been largely ignored by Civil War historians. His life and career were marked by his inability to reach ultimate success in war, in politics, or in marriage, yet he led the first successful Union cavalry raid of the war at Chancellorsville, the first step in creating the eventual effectiveness and élan of Federal troopers.

Stoneman was ignominiously captured by Confederate regulars and militia during Sherman's Atlanta campaign, while on a highly dubious mission to free Union prisoners at Macon and Andersonville, Georgia. Exchanged after three months, he went on to redeem himself with another great raid in the waning days of the Confederacy. He destroyed the vital salt works in Virginia, thus depriving the desperate Lee of the means to preserve scant food supplies. The raiders then wrecked the Lynchburg and Bristol Railroad, eliminating Lee's last chance to join General Joseph Johnston's army in North Carolina and continue the war. While raiding in Southern Virginia and North Carolina, Stoneman missed capturing the fleeing Jefferson Davis by a matter of hours. Stoneman's North Carolina raid helped seal the fate of the Confederacy.

Although Stoneman is best known for his service in the Civil War, his life spanned an important era in our nation's history. He participated in one of the early expeditions to explore the West, the 2,000-mile march of the Mormon Battalion from Council Bluffs, Iowa, to San Diego, California, during the Mexican War. Stoneman was the Assistant Quartermaster of the battalion and vowed after the trek to someday return, little realizing that when he did, he would become California's 15th governor.

Stoneman's post–Civil War career was also historically significant. He was military commander in Memphis, Tennessee, following the war and did little to quell one of the worst race riots there. After succeeding his friend and supporter Major General John Schofield as military governor of Virginia, Stoneman supervised the reconstruction process and led Virginia back into the Union with a minimum of bitterness. His subsequent tenure as commander of the Department of Arizona was stormy. He grappled with the conflicting demands of the settlers who sought protection from the Apaches, while he tried to implement the peace policies of the Grant administration. Arizona was a frustrating end to his military career.

Stoneman's crowning civilian achievement was his term as governor of California, from 1883 to 1887. Winning the office as a Democrat, Stoneman took on the powerful railroad interests in California, demanding fair taxes and reasonable rates for farmers moving their crops to market. Stoneman's administration instituted prison reform, implemented progressive food and drug regulations, and championed riparian rights for farmers. According to a contemporary evaluation of California governors, Stoneman's administration was "the brightest period in the history of the office of governor during the last three decades of the nineteenth century."[1]

It would be impossible not to describe Stoneman's weaknesses both as a commander and as a politician. He was often frustrated by his lack of political skills. What impressed me the most about Stoneman was his rectitude and his sense of duty and service to his country. His was a sad life in a way, ending in Buffalo, estranged from his wife and apparently his children, living out his last days in the home of his sister, far from his adopted state of California. Researching this biography was difficult, as Stoneman's papers were destroyed twice, once in a train wreck in New York and finally when his beloved Los Robles was destroyed by fire. Nonetheless, I have done my best to bring George Stoneman to life. It is a life that deserves recognition.

ONE

Stoneman in Command

On a cold and windy day, President Abraham Lincoln sat astride his horse on Stafford Heights opposite the city of Fredericksburg and the Rappahannock River. The date was April 6, 1863, and the president, accompanied by Major General Joseph "Fighting Joe" Hooker, watched as the Army of the Potomac passed in review.

The occasion was an auspicious one for both men. The president was inspecting the reorganized Army of the Potomac at what had been the site of a major defeat the previous December. Morale of the Union army was low following the decisive Confederate victory at Fredericksburg, where Union assaults ordered by Ambrose E. Burnside cost over 8,000 casualties. After relieving Burnside, Hooker had brought an army of 100,000 men from a demoralized mob to an effective fighting force.

Hooker was criticized by his contemporaries and future historians for his conspiracies against Burnside and his failed leadership at the Battle of Chancellorsville. In the three months following his appointment as commander, however, his reorganization of the Army of the Potomac demonstrated great administrative ability. Rations and medical care were improved, additional clothing provided, and a reasonable system of furloughs adopted.[1]

Hooker's reorganization of the cavalry endeared him to both the cavalry officers and men. His General Orders No. 6, of April 5, 1863, specified, "The cavalry of the army will be consolidated under one corps, under the command of Brigadier General Stoneman who will make the necessary arrangements for detached duty."[2] George Stoneman was now responsible for 11,110 officers and men and was to lead the first major Union cavalry operation by an independent command in the Civil War.

Lincoln had kept in constant touch with Hooker and followed his progress in the revitalization of the Union army following the Battle of Fredericksburg. With the arrival of spring, Lincoln was ready to look for himself and urge Hooker to move against Lee's Army of Northern Virginia, which was quartered across the Rappahannock River awaiting developments.

President Lincoln informed Hooker on April 3 that he would arrive at Fredericksburg on a Sunday and stay until Tuesday morning. Lincoln left the Washington navy yard aboard the steamer *Carrie Martin* accompanied by his wife, his son Tad, Attorney General Edward Bates, Dr. Anson G. Henry, and Noah Brooks, a journalist and confidante. Bad weather forced the party to anchor in a small cove opposite Indian Head on the Potomac for the night.[3]

The following morning, Lincoln arrived at the Aquia Creek waterfront, which was packed with transports and government steamers unloading supplies. A cavalry escort took the president and his party to General Hooker's headquarters, where the two conferred. During the course of their conversation, Lincoln said, "If you get to Richmond, General..." but he was interrupted by Hooker, who interjected: "Excuse me, Mr. President, but there is no 'if' in this case. I am going straight to Richmond, if I live." Later on, Lincoln remarked to his friend Noah Brooks: "It is about the worst thing I have heard since I have been down here."[4] Lincoln had tried repeatedly to get his generals to understand that Lee's army, not the Confederate capital, was the Union objective. He commented to his secretary, "The hen is the wisest of all the animal creations because she never cackles until the egg is laid." Lincoln was already reacting to the bravado of Hooker, who called his army "the finest on the planet" and said, "My plans are perfect." He was ready for his confrontation with the Confederates. "May God have mercy on General Lee, for I will have none."[5]

Stoneman's troopers formed a major part of the grand review on April 6. The air was raw and windy, typical for an early spring day in Northern Virginia. The ground was soft and the mud flew as the president and his superbly confident commander reviewed the cavalrymen. Stoneman, who was now a brevet major general, was in full dress with a yellow silk scarf over one shoulder. He and his staff galloped to position at the center of the line and faced the front. The president and General Hooker, accompanied by a retinue of about 300 officers and men, took up their positions across from the cavalrymen.

Major General Hooker rode an elegant white horse and was "the personification of a military leader who, by his presence, inspired enthusiasm in his troops."[6] Lincoln and his party rode up to General Stoneman, who was introduced to the president.

The cavalry corps was so large that it took half an hour for the president and General Stoneman to ride along the lines. Another hour and a half was required for the columns of cavalry and four batteries of artillery to march past the reviewing officers. The historian of the 9th New York Cavalry noted: "Thus ended a notable review of the newly organized cavalry corps which, in the next two years, proved to be a powerful factor in defeating the Confederate armies and compelling their surrender."[7]

President Lincoln had reviewed the infantry corps of the Army of the Potomac on April 5. A participant with the V Corps reported that "Mr. Lincoln had, whether intentionally or inadvertently, been furnished with a small pony-built, bay horse, about 14 hands high. The President's legs looked longer than ever, and his toes almost seemed to touch the ground. He wore the same solemn suit of black that he always assumed — a tall silk hat, a little worse for wear, with long full-skirted black coat." The soldier went on to observe that the president had neglected to strap down his pants leg while riding so that eventually his "white drawers of leg began to be conspicuous.... Altogether he presented a very funny picture, calculated to provoke laughter along the entire length of the line, had it not been for the sad, anxious face that peered forth from his shaggy eyebrows."[8]

Major General George Stoneman (U.S. Army Military History Institute).

Although rumors of poor morale may well have been one of the reasons the president visited the army, he must have been pleasantly surprised at the apparent good condition of the troops. Whatever Hooker's shortcomings, his reorganization of the army, which abolished Burnside's unwieldy Grand Divisions, improved sanitation, living conditions, and rations and gave credence to Hooker's boast that the army was "the finest on the planet." By April 1863, the Army of the Potomac numbered close to 130,000 men, including Stoneman's newly created cavalry corps of over 10,000. At a dinner attended by all corps commanders that concluded the president's visit, Lincoln spoke to Hooker and Major General Darius Couch, Hooker's second-in-command. He offered advice, later recorded by Couch, that anticipated a fatal weakness in the Union command strategy: "'I want to impress upon you two gentlemen in your next fight, put in all your men.'"[9]

George Stoneman may have concluded as he rode next to the president of the United States that his command was on the verge of a major expedition against the enemy that would be the pinnacle of a long military career. There was little in his background that appeared to presage his present position. But George Stoneman was descended from a remarkable American family of pioneers who had settled in the state of New York. His grandfather was Richard Stoneman, an Englishman who had come from Exeter shortly after the turn of the century. Following the American Revolution, he came to the village of New Berlin in Chenango County seeking a new home. In the course of his wanderings, he purchased a few acres of land from Artemas Herrick "on the northwest corner of his lot 74 and made to himself a dwelling in that secluded nook, where he lived a retired life the rest of his days, seeking but little intercourse with society" according to an early historian of the town.[10] The same description of Richard Stoneman referred to his "intellectual accomplishments of a superior order" and observed that "it was supposed that in his native land he had occupied a higher station in Old England's aristocratic society than is to be found among our New England Yankee equality folk."[11]

Life in New Berlin during the early 1800s was a rough, frontier existence. Virgin forest covered the land, and all implements and household tools were made at home, except for a few manufactured items brought in by traders. The women of the family made the clothing. Money was hard to come by and barter was the means of most daily transactions. Shipping of locally produced goods was difficult, and it took about two weeks for potash and grain to be shipped to the nearest mill.[12]

The first immigrants to New Berlin often lacked necessary provisions until land was cleared and crops put in, causing many new settlers to depend on neighbors for food. The first requirement was to build a log house, usually in close proximity to a spring or running brook. The pioneers cut trees for logs that formed the body of the building, and poles were cut for rafters. Elm bark was used for shingles and basswood logs were split into slabs for the rough cabin floors.[13]

A "house warming" was the traditional introduction for newcomers. Mutual assistance was a strong feature of New Berlin society. The celebration was often mixed with the singing of patriotic songs such as "Hail Columbia, Happy, Happy Land."

Planting crops was accomplished with primitive tools. A hoe was used to prepare the ground for corn, and grain was sowed by means of a two-pronged wooden tooth harrow and harvested by a reaper's sickle. Grass was mowed with a scythe, raked by hand, and carried to the barn on a sled. Stumps and roots prevented farmers from using a plough to prepare the land for crops.

Because cotton was not available in New Berlin, flax was raised for clothing. Wool was produced from sheep for winter clothing and children were clothed in coarse, loose dress which, a local historian noted in 1876, permitted the free use of their limbs. "No steelspring carriages [were used] to weaken the muscles and enfeeble the body. Girls and boys were early taught in the school of industry, acquiring habits of prudence and economy; success in after life was the result."[14]

Richard Stoneman met Mary Perkins, whose family had relocated to New York from Rhode Island. Mary "possessed a fine amiable manner and fine character" and "reared their children well following the decease of her husband, Mr. Stoneman."[15]

The eldest son of Richard and Mary Stoneman was named George after his uncle, who was killed while serving with the British army at the Battle of the Nile.[16] When young George came of age in 1810, he moved to Chautauqua County in New York. He lived in Ellery and Jamestown and eventually moved to the town of Busti, later incorporated as the village of Lakewood, near the western border of New York state. He was apparently seeking new opportunities. He soon married Catherine Chaney Aldrich from Baltimore and the couple had ten children, eight of whom survived the rigors of frontier conditions and grew to adulthood.[17] George, named after his father, was born on August 8, 1822, the eldest son of an accomplished American family.

George was not the only member of the family to achieve fame. His brother John was a state senator and judge in the Superior Court of Iowa. George's sister Kate was the first woman to be admitted to the New York State Bar, despite male opposition. Another sister, Charlotte, married New York State Senator Benjamin H. Williams of Buffalo. Rebecca and Mary Jane, called Jenny, were teachers. Rebecca eventually joined the Stoneman family in California, where she tutored the Stoneman children. Byron Stoneman was a farmer who not only educated his own family but assisted his brothers as well. His daughter, Bertha Stoneman, was a distinguished botanist. She traveled to South Africa in 1897 and was in charge of the Botany Department at the newly founded Huguenot College. She not only taught botany but philosophy and psychology as well.[18]

Busti was named after Paul Busti, general agent of the Holland Land Company that was formed in 1823. George Stoneman, Sr., must have found life there every bit as rigorous as at the home he left behind in New Berlin. Busti was covered with dense forest, especially pine trees, and there were chestnut groves near the lake that have disappeared over time. The early pioneers eked out a living by growing corn, often by making gashes in the roots of tree stumps and placing the seed. Bags of grain had to be taken over long distances on horseback to a gristmill. Families and their possessions were moved by ox team. The principal cash crop for farmers was black salts of lye that came from burning hardwoods. At the ashery, black salts were converted into potash through burning in ovens.[19]

The history of the area is closely intertwined with Chautauqua Lake, said to be the highest body of navigable water in the United States. The lake has long been a summer resort, but to the early settlers of Chautauqua, it was a means of transit for both settlers and commerce. Household goods were conveyed in canoes with pioneer families while the men cut their way through the wilderness with horses and wagons. The lake was an important route for trade between Lake Erie and Western Pennsylvania, as salt and other provisions were transported in canoes and other watercraft.[20]

Horse-boats were developed in 1824 and were considered to be a major improvement in lake transportation, but they were superseded by steamboats in 1828. The first steamboat on Chautauqua Lake was a side-wheel steamer called the *Chautauqua* which was built at Jamestown. George Stoneman, Sr., built *The Twins* in 1852. The boat plied the waters of the Chautauqua from 1849 to 1852. It was an unusual design and its pioneer was the object of some ridicule by his neighbors. However, it was noted that it met with some success:

> Mr. Stoneman constructed a horse-boat, built upon two huge dug-out canoes. These canoes were placed several feet apart and decked over from one to the other, catamaran style. An immense horizontal wheel extended across the deck upon which the horses travelled. The under surface of this wheel was geared to the shaft of a paddle wheel in the center of the boat — the motive [of] power, a horse on each side of the boat. Upon assuming command of this quaint craft, his friends dubbed him Commodore Stoneman ... in those easy-going times, this means of transportation was quite liberally patronized.[21]

The father of the future general was a justice of the peace and a lumberman, but his sawmill was also an object of local amusement and speculation. It was built "within a few rods of the lake shore with no visible water power." There was speculation over how Stoneman expected to run the mill after it was built. The dilemma was solved when a race was constructed to the lake and corn baskets were used to transport water to the mill. The "corn basket or dry saw mill" was operated with a modest profit and "was a great convenience to farmers and lumberman."[22]

Two

West Point

George Stoneman attended Jamestown Academy until he was 18. His headmaster, E.A. Dickinson, reported that Stoneman was a student "in good standing as a scholar and has ever made exceedingly good proficiency in those branches to which he has directed his attention." He studied arithmetic, algebra, and some higher math at this school, which, although it served a rural and remote area, provided Stoneman with a good classical education that served him well in later years. The headmaster also noted that Stoneman developed good habits "both in application and perseverance. He has the confidence of all those who know him as a correct moral man."[1]

Stoneman made the rather surprising decision to seek an appointment to West Point following his graduation from Jamestown Academy. His interest in a military career was piqued by an old magazine article written by a woman he later met in Chicago, en route to his first assignment in the West after his graduation from West Point.[2] A competitive and highly sought-after appointment to West Point was not an unusual ambition for a boy from a prominent and influential family, but Stoneman's chances for success must have seemed remote to both him and his family. In an era when political influence and social standing determined appointment to West Point, Stoneman's family had no influential connections.

West Point accepted its first class in 1802, despite opposition from President Thomas Jefferson, who was suspicious of a professional military that he felt might be an instrument of tyranny. The academy had rapidly progressed in the quality of its curriculum under Sylvanus Thayer, who was appointed superintendent in 1817. Academic standards were upgraded and outstanding faculty recruited. By 1842, the academy had achieved prestige and national recognition. Stoneman's class of 1846, with 225 cadets, was the highest enrollment at the academy to date.

Undeterred by his family's lack of standing, Stoneman wrote directly to the secretary of war, the Honorable Abe Bell, applying for an appointment. Writing on July 26, 1841, Stoneman presented his case with directness and eloquence:

> It is with greatest diffidence that I approach you feeling as I do the vast difference in our situations but with your permission I will and introduce my business at once. A military life has

ever comported with my inclination. But to make a military man he wants a proper education. I have therefore concluded to apply for the privilege of becoming a Cadet at West Point. My age is eighteen and besides the necessary qualifications I have considerable of a knowledge of Algebra, Geometry, Chemistry and Philosophy, six books in Virgil and have gone part way through Charles Twelfth in French, these by my own exertions. If you will take the trouble you will please to cause my name to be registered and in due time I will send in my certificate and recommendations from my parents, etc....[3]

Stoneman's application was supported by letters from citizens of Chautauqua. Four community leaders wrote Secretary Bell stating that they were "acquainted with this applicant and with his family connections and can very cheerfully say that a more appropriate selection cannot be made.... He is of that class which forms the independence of our country and from which we must expect its defenders." In a reference to his background, they described his "very respectable attainments and knowledge considering the circumstances in which he has been placed."[4]

Regulations of the Military Academy of 1839 established physical requirements for admission. No cadet "who is below five feet in height, or who is deformed, or afflicted with any disease or infirmity" was to be admitted. Nor would he be if he had "any diseases of an infectious or immoral character."[5] The Stoneman family physician, Dr. L. Hazeltine, found that no "defect or deformity exists which would render him inadequate for military service." The doctor went on to write in his report that he was well acquainted with Stoneman's family "and knew them to be healthy and of strong constitution."[6]

Congressman Staley N. Clarke did not find a typical plethora of candidates to support for admission to West Point in 1842. In fact, he had nominated his own son because of the lack of other candidates. One additional appointment was unfilled. Clarke asked the secretary of war to send Stoneman's name forward to the U.S. president. On May 9, Stoneman accepted an appointment to the Corps of Cadets at West Point.

The young man from Busti was about to enter a world ruled by discipline, and there was little in his experience on his father's farm to prepare him for the four years that followed. Cadets arrived at West Point by means of a boat trip up the Hudson River from New York. They landed at a pier below a high bluff that must have looked gray and forbidding. Stoneman arrived on June 10, 1842, at an institution that served as an important fort during the Revolutionary War. The roll of plebes, or first classmen, who reported in the summer of 1842 contained some of the most illustrious names in the history of the American military. Less than 20 years later, they would form the highest ranks of both the Union and Confederate armies in the Civil War: George B. McClellan, A.P. Hill, Thomas J. Jackson, George E. Pickett, Darius Couch, Jesse Reno, George H. Gordon, and Stoneman were among those who began their military careers that summer.

The West Point of 1842 was not an egalitarian institution, but class distinctions were not formed on a sectional basis. George McClellan, the son of a socially prominent Philadelphia physician, wrote his brother that he greatly preferred Southerners to Northerners, although he had little to do with the Virginian Thomas Jackson, who came from a humble background. McClellan's roommate was another Virginian, A.P. Hill, and one of his closest friends was Virginian Dabney Maury. It is unlikely that George Stoneman's very modest circumstances enabled him to mix easily with cadets like McClellan. The Description List of New Cadets recorded the "Circumstances of Parents of Cadets." Stoneman's father was listed simply under "agriculture."

Stoneman's classmate, Darius Couch, wrote in 1895 that Stoneman's West Point years were "uneventful" but noted that he was "esteemed by his personal associates as a generous-hearted, whole-souled companion." Couch wrote that Thomas Jackson was one of his friends and noted that "they were a great deal alike in some respects and very different in others." Roommates in their junior year, they both had "unobtrusive, meditative dispositions, not putting themselves forward, rather thinkers than talkers, and never saying a word that would wound a comrade's feelings."[7] Stoneman and Jackson may have found a common bond in their modest backgrounds in contrast to their socially prominent and wealthy classmates. The two cadets would play prominent, but opposing, roles in the coming Civil War, particularly at the Battle of Chancellorsville in 1863. Stoneman would lead a major cavalry raid, and Jackson, following a brilliant campaign that was a major factor in one of the greatest Confederate victories of the conflict, would suffer wounds resulting in his death.

Cadets were given an examination to ensure that they could "read and write well and ... perform with facility and accuracy the various operations of the four ground rules of arithmetic—of reduction, of simple and compound proportion, and of vulgar and decimal fractions."[8] Mathematics was the most important subject because of its relevance to other subjects necessary for a military education. Infantry tactics, French, drawing, natural philosophy, chemistry, and mineralogy formed an important part of the curriculum. Artillery tactics, engineering and the science of war, geography, history, and ethics were also studied. Practical instruction included "the use of the small sword, cut and thrust ... and sword exercises of cavalry."[9] Examinations were given in January and June that caused great stress to the cadets, as the year's work depended on these evaluations.

For cadets such as George McClellan, who had been educated in Philadelphia's best schools, good marks came easily, but academic studies must have been more difficult for cadets like Stoneman and Jackson who did not have the advantage of elite schools. During Stoneman's second year, he ranked 16th out of 83 cadets in the "Order of Merit in Their Respective Classes" as determined by general examination. He slipped to 27th in 1844 and dropped to 30th in 1845.[10] Stoneman graduated 33rd in his class of 60 cadets in 1846, behind his future adversary Thomas Jackson, who fought his way up to graduate 17th.[11]

Life at West Point was spartan and steeped in discipline that controlled every activity of the young cadets. The academic board, which set instruction and standards of conduct, noted in 1841 that "a cadet enters the institution at an early age, with perhaps loose habits, owing to a bad system of domestic training.... For the first six months or year, falls into daily errors and finds himself at the end of the first year, burthened with a load of demerits."[12]

Discipline was rigorously enforced; regulations were prefaced with the dictum that "obedience and subordination are essential to the purposes of this institution." Any refusal to obey an order was cause for dismissal. No cadet could drink or have "in his room or tent, or otherwise in his possession, wine, porter, or any other spirituous or intoxicating liquor." Card playing was forbidden, as was the preparation of any food in their rooms. No cadet could "keep a waiter, horse, or dog." Any cadet who behaved "indecently or irreverently while attending divine service, or shall use any profane oath or execration, or profane the Sabbath shall be dismissed or otherwise severely punished."[13]

The cadets were summoned and marched to every activity by the signal of a drum. Reveille was at 5 A.M. in the summer and 6 A.M. in the winter. The signal for breakfast was "Peas-upon-a-Trencher" and was beat at 7 A.M. "Roast-Beef," the drum for dinner, was at 1 P.M. Tattoo was at 9:30 P.M. and taps at 10 P.M., when all lights were extinguished. There was military drill every day from March to November. The cadets lived in drafty stone barracks with a bare minimum of furniture and comfort.[14]

Despite this austere regimen, Stoneman appeared to cope well with life at the Point, if a letter to a friend dated October 29, 1842, is any indication. He complained, however, to his friend back in Chautauqua County that he would go through "more different scenes in a week" at home than he did in six weeks at the Point as "every day here is alike." He gave his friend a description of a typical day "and from that you can judge of every day as they are all alike except Saturday afternoon when we can go as we see fit." In the morning "beds must be folded up and put at head of the bedstaff." Stoneman wrote his friend that "Our duties are not arduous but what we do here has to be done with promptness and exactness." Nevertheless, the cadets of the time had some help:

> There are about a hundred laborers on the Point who are constantly employed making repairs. Our boots and shoes are taken from our rooms and blacked, rooms swept out and slop tubs emptied daily and rooms washed out once a week and our fires are made whenever it is requisite they should be. Our washermen come and get our clothes and bring them back to us twice a week.[15]

Any infraction of the rules meant demerits that could lead to dismissal. A Register of Delinquencies and punishments was kept, and the records reveal that Stoneman's transgressions were of a trivial nature. In 1842, he accumulated eight demerits: dirty water in quarters, falling in ranks without bayonet, and late at evening parade. During his second year, he was penalized for tardiness at recitation in grammar, supper mess parade, and "marching his Sect. in a careless and disorderly manner." His shoes were not blacked at "guard-mounting" and his floor was not swept under the "bedsteads." The most intriguing infraction of regulations in Stoneman's record was noted on August 14 when he earned four demerits for "highly unmilitary conduct allowing the guards and guard tent to be made use of for the amusement of ladies."[16]

Stoneman apparently was somewhat rebellious at church as he was cited for not answering to roll call more audibly at services and again for leaving church on January 4, 1846. However, his record appears to be above average overall in comparison to the records of some of his classmates. One such classmate, Thomas Jackson, earned similar demerits for "trigger rusty at company inspection" and several for tardiness: "late at roll call," "late at breakfast," and "late at church."[17]

The class of 1846 was electrified by the news of the coming war with Mexico over the disputed Texas border. To the cadets, war meant that all of their military training could be put to good use, especially since promotions were given out much faster during wartime. When President James Polk delivered his war message to Congress, Stoneman's classmate George McClellan wrote his sister Frederessa and exuded: "Hip! Hip! Hurrah! War at last sure enough! Ain't it glorious...."[18]

No doubt the newly commissioned Stoneman shared McClellan's enthusiasm for the fight with Mexico, but Stoneman's service in the Mexican War would prove to be unusual and somewhat indirect. While many of his classmates went off to the Rio Grande to join General Zachery Taylor, Stoneman, immediately upon graduation, joined Company "G" 1st Dragoons. They were commanded by General Stephen Watts Kearny at Fort Leavenworth, where he was assembling the Army of the West to drive the Mexicans from California.[19]

General Kearny had been ordered to organize the 1st Missouri Mounted Volunteers, a group of hard-fighting, hard-drinking, largely undisciplined troopers who were enthusiastic, but untrained. Stoneman's first duty was to help drill the Missourians and create a semblance of military order. By June 5, Company G was marching down the Santa Fe Trail ready to do battle with Mexicans, Comanches, and Apaches.

With the Mormon Battalion

After four rigorous years at West Point, George Stoneman, armed with his brevet second lieutenant's commission, was ready for his first real assignment.¹ Although he was still assigned to the 1st Dragoons, he was detailed to the famous "Mormon Battalion" as assistant quartermaster for that expedition.

The circumstances surrounding the creation of the Mormon Battalion form a controversial chapter in the record of relations between the Church of Jesus Christ of the Latter-day Saints and the United States Government. George Stoneman was about to serve in one of the unique units in U.S. military history, members of which marched nearly two thousand miles from Council Bluffs, Iowa, to San Diego, California, in 1846–1847.

The chain of events that led to this epic march began in Washington, D.C., when Mormon Elder Jesse C. Little was authorized by church president Brigham Young to proceed to Washington for the purpose of negotiating an agreement with the Polk administration. Young and a large colony of his followers were in desperate straits following their departure from the Mormon settlement at Nauvoo, along the Mississippi River, about 50 miles north of Quincy, Illinois. The Mormons were moving west and Elder Little was in Washington to solicit possible U.S. government support. The Mormons had learned that the government was considering the construction of a string of forts and block houses along the Oregon Trail to the Columbia River in anticipation of the migration of settlers along that route. The Mormons hoped for a commission to build these forts. The Mormon mission took place at an opportune moment, as Congress had declared war on Mexico, acting on President Polk's war message of May 11, and the Mormons were a potentially valuable asset in the western campaign.

President James K. Polk had mixed feelings concerning the Mormons in general and any part they might have in military operations against the Mexicans. His diary of June 3, 1846, noted that he met with Mr. Amos Kendall, a Washington "in-sider" and ex-postmaster general who had been influential in the Jackson administration. Elder Little also wished to see the president and "learn the policy of the government towards them."² The president was aware that a large group of Mormons was moving toward California, but he wished to assure the Mormon leaders that he held no prejudice against them:

> I told Mr. Little that by our constitution the mormons would be treated as all other American citizens were, without regard to the sect to which they belonged or the religious creed which they professed, and that I had no prejudices towards them which could induce a different course of treatment. Mr. Little said they were Americans in all their feelings, & friends of the U.S....[3]

The President asked if 500 or more of the Mormons on their way to California would be willing to serve in the U.S. Army in the war against Mexico, under the command of a regular officer. Elder Little said that he was sure they would and said he would overtake the emigrants now in transit and would make the necessary arrangements. The president decided not to inform him that an expedition under General Stephen Kearny to California was planned with the expectation that the Mormons would make up no more than ¼ of Kearny's command. The president also noted in his diary that enlisting the Mormons might prevent them from "assuming a hostile attitude toward the U.S. after their arrival in California."[4]

The president met with Kendall and Little a second time on June 5. He told Elder Little that he had consulted with the secretary of war and that it had been decided that a battalion of Mormons:

> could not be received into the service of the U.S. until they reached California, but that on their arrival there (if the war with Mexico still continued) they would to the number of 500 be mustered into the service of the U.S. as volunteers for 12 months, placing themselves under the command of a U.S. officer who would be there ready to receive them....[5]

The agreement in Washington between President Polk and Elder Little led to an order from Colonel Kearny to Captain James Allen to proceed to the Mormon camps. Allen was ordered to "raise from among them four or five companies of volunteers to join me in my expedition to [California], each company to consist of any number between seventy-three and one hundred and nine...."[6] On June 26, Captain Allen and three dragoons, soon to be George Stoneman's comrades, rode into the Mormon camp at Mt. Pisgah, a camp east of the growing Mormon settlement at Council Bluffs. At first, the Saints did not understand the nature of Captain Allen's mission. The following day, June 27, would be the second anniversary of the murder of their leader, Joseph Smith. The alarm was sounded as the dragoons approached and the Saints were understandably anxious and apprehensive. Captain Allen was allowed to address the people in the camp after his peaceful intentions had been established.[7]

Allen's proposition to form a battalion was met with disbelief. This government, which had done nothing to prevent mobs from driving them from their homes and assassinating their leader, now wanted help in fighting a war with Mexico. Not a few of the Saints hesitated to respond to Captain Allen's proposition. "It was not from a lack of courage, either," reported Sergeant Daniel Tyler, a participant in the meeting and later a member of the Mormon Battalion:

> The danger of such an expedition would never have caused them to shrink or falter; but they had been deceived so many times by those who held authority in the nation that they looked upon this new requisition with distrust.[8]

The situation faced by the Mormons, if not desperate, was at best tentative. Many Mormons, sick and helpless, were left back in Nauvoo and expected the advance guard to eventually rescue them from hostile Illinois and Missouri "mobocrats." An unknown and dangerous wilderness and perhaps hostile Indians were in front of them. The young men were concerned about the safety of the women and children who would be left behind.

Captain Allen made his proposal to President Young on July 1 at a mass meeting at Council Bluffs. Young did not hesitate to endorse the formation of the battalion, but referred to it as a "requisition" rather than a proposal to be accepted or rejected. He told the meeting, "If we want the privilege of going where we can worship God according to the dictates of our consciences, we must raise the battalion."[9]

Young advised the brethren "to enlist and make up a battalion and go and serve your country and if you do this, and live your religion, I promise you in the name of Israel's God that not a man of you shall fall in battle."[10]

Another consideration may have induced Young to agree to the battalion. It was an article of faith among the heavily persecuted Mormons that Thomas Hart Benton of Missouri, father-in-law of John C. Fremont, had extracted a pledge from President Polk that if the Mormon battalion was not raised, volunteers from Missouri would be used against them. Since Benton represented the hated Missourians, this report was probably given considerable credence.[11] There is no historical evidence to support the charge that either Polk or Benton intended to attack the Mormons if the battalion was not raised.

On July 16, 1846, four companies of over 400 men, and part of a fifth, were mustered into the service of the United States at Council Bluffs, Iowa. Before their departure, Brigham Young counseled the members of the battalion:

> Captains, act as fathers to your companies. Manage your men and control yourselves by the power of the Priesthood. Keep yourselves neat and clean in appearance. Observe strict chastity.... Take with you your Bible and Book of Mormon, but do not seek to impose your views or religion upon others. Card-playing should not be allowed. Burn any cards you may find.... If you keep these counsels, no blood shall be shed.[12]

The Mormons held a farewell ball where church authorities, officers, men and the women of the community danced to the music of Captain William Pitt's brass band until "the sun dipped behind the sharp skyline of the Omaha hills." Then silence was called and a young girl named Susan Divine[13] sang a song of lament before the silent community of Saints. "By the rivers of Babylon we sat down and wept. We wept until we remembered Zion." This brought tears, but the evening ended with a prayer from one of the Elders, who "asked the blessing of heaven on all, with purity of heart and brotherhood of spirit had mingled in that society, and then all dispersed to cover from the falling dews."[14]

To the tune of "The Girl I Left Behind Me," the battalion began its epic march on July 20, passing through St. Joseph on July 29. They crossed the Missouri River and arrived at Fort Leavenworth on August 1. It was here that the Mormons drew their arms from the fort armory, U.S. Model 1816 flintlock muskets with a few percussion locks for sharpshooting and hunting. The men were anxious to examine their weapons and crowded around the arsenal, prompting Colonel Allen to say: "Stand back, boys, don't be in a hurry to get your muskets; you will want to throw the damn things away before you get to California."[15]

Colonel James Allen, who had impressed the Mormons with his fairness and sincerity, became seriously ill while the battalion was outfitted at Fort Leavenworth. On July 12, the orders were given to the four companies to begin the march to Santa Fe, where Stoneman would join them, although the battalion did not depart Fort Leavenworth until August 13. Despite fervent prayers for his recovery, Allen died on August 23, much to the dismay of the Mormons, who considered Allen to be a gentleman in every sense of the word. They were also concerned that a "more tyrannical man" might take command.[16] Although Allen had promised Brigham Young that Captain Jefferson Hunt, captain of Company A and the senior Mormon officer, would be given command of the battalion, Lieutenant Andrew Jackson Smith was given command. Both Smith and his future comrade in arms George Stoneman were to become major generals in the Union army during the Civil War.

The Saints were convinced that Lieutenant Smith's appointment and his subsequent harsh behavior towards them was yet another example of a Gentile conspiracy. Sergeant Tyler wrote in his journal that "the appointment of Smith caused a greater gloom throughout the command than the death of Colonel Allen had."[17] Mormon Henry Bigler wrote that "the honor had been conferred on Smith simply because he was a West Pointer."[18] Smith caused immediate resentment by ordering sick Mormons out of the wagons because they had not reported to the battalion physician, Dr. George B. Sanderson, another hated Missourian, who had been named "Captain Death." Sanderson prescribed calomel, a purgative, and arsenic for any complaint and the Mormons were convinced he was trying to poison them. Calomel was a very common treatment at the time, but Bigler noted that "before we would take Doctor Sanderson's medicine, we would leave our bones to bleach on the prairie first."[19]

Despite dissension, temperatures of over 100 degrees, and numerous families accompanying the battalion, the march to Santa Fe continued. Lieutenant Smith and a group of the 2nd Missouri Mounted Volunteers under command of Colonel Sterling Price were ordered by Kearny to take the shorter Cimmarron branch of the Santa Fe Trail. The Mormons remembered that Price had commanded the Missouri jail where Prophet Joseph Smith had been imprisoned.[20]

The Missourians did nothing to help the Mormons, who were now down to half-rations. Some of the families and the sick were separated from the battalion on September 17 after they crossed the Arkansas River. They were sent to Pueblo in present-day Colorado while the able-bodied pushed on to Santa Fe to meet the October 10 deadline imposed by Kearny or the battalion would be discharged. The vanguard of the battalion arrived in Santa Fe on October 9, 1846, where they were greeted by Colonel Doniphan, the commander of the post, as Kearny had departed for California. Doniphan ordered a 100-gun salute in honor of the Mormons, who were delighted to learn that no such honor had been given to Price's 2nd Missouri, which had arrived a few days earlier. Back in 1838, Doniphan commanded the militia in Missouri and had been ordered to shoot Prophet Joseph Smith and other Mormon leaders for treason. Doniphan had refused to carry out the order, calling it "cold-blooded murder." The order was changed and the prisoners were turned over to civil authorities.[21]

The Mormon Battalion had survived the first leg of the journey to California, and they were now to receive a new commander. Kearny had placed Philip St. George Cooke in command with the rank of lieutenant colonel. Lieutenant A.J. Smith was appointed quartermaster, and Cooke announced that "Brevet Second Lieutenant George Stoneman, 1st Dragoons, will perform the duties of Assistant Quartermaster on the expedition to Upper California...."[22] Colonel Cooke duly noted in his journal that Smith and Stoneman reported for duty at 9:00 A.M., October 21.

George Stoneman's appointment to the battalion three months after graduating with his brevet commission was an honor, although it is unlikely he considered it so at the time. Both he and his commander, no doubt, sought the glory and honors of combat in the recently declared war with Mexico.

The Mormon Battalion began its march to the Pacific on October 18. It departed Santa Fe with 25 government wagons: six wagons for equipment, 15 mule wagons for company supplies, and four mule wagons. In addition, there were four or five private wagons.[23]

Cooke, a hawknosed, profane man, recorded in his journal that the battalion was paid and that salt pork, beef cattle, and pack saddles had arrived, 60 days' rations in all. Cooke "reluctantly consented to take five women, the wives of officers and servants" but noted that they were traveling at their own expense.[24]

Although the Mormons found Cooke to be a strict disciplinarian, they also recorded in their diaries that he was fair and impartial. Tyler noted that his discipline differed from that of Lieutenant Smith, who was accused of preferential treatment of officers. The first man punished under Cooke was an officer. "Captain Jesse D. Hunter was put under arrest and made to march in the rear of his company for remaining overnight in Santa Fe without the knowledge or consent of the Commanding Officer."[25]

Cooke's misgivings about the Mormons were recorded early in his journal of the march. "The battalion were never drilled, and, though obedient, have little discipline; they exhibit great heedlessness and ignorance and some obstinacy."[26] On top of these weaknesses, the battalion began the march from Santa Fe with the same worn-out and broken-down mules and ox teams that had begun their service at Fort Leavenworth or even Council Bluffs.

The battalion began its march down the Rio Grande and turned on a southwestern course along the Chihuahua Road on November 13. They were now marching due south and Cooke, riding at the head of the column with his scouts, suddenly ordered his men to turn west. Bigler reported that Cooke swore "he would be G-d damned if he was going all around the world to get to California."[27] Cooke was determined to march west to the Gila River, although neither the pilots nor the guides had ever traveled that route.

The Mormons attributed Cooke's decision to divine intervention. Religious leaders among them had urged the men to pray for the Lord to inspire Cooke to lead the column away from the southern route which would not only take them away from their destination but would take them closer to the Mexicans as well.

Diarist Tyler recorded that Cooke, who observed the trail company turning south, instead of west, exclaimed: "This is not my course. I was ordered to California and I will go there or die in the attempt." Private David Pettegrew, also known as Father Pettegrew because of his white hair, one of the religious leaders, exclaimed "God bless the Colonel!" Cooke's stern face softened and showed signs of satisfaction.[28]

Cooke had two privately published commercial maps to guide the western march, but noted in his journal that they were next to worthless. However, he had recruited a guide and an interpreter to search for a road. The battalion was traversing Apache country, but fortunately the interpreter, Dr. Stephen Foster, had lived in the area and knew the language, customs, and habits of the Indians. Antoine Leurox, a mountain man for 20 or 30 years, also knew the area and aided the expedition.[29]

Lieutenant Stoneman was having problems obtaining fresh mules and oxen from small Mexican towns located along the battalion's route. Mexicans of mixed blood were hostile toward the band of armed men and sold them little except some feed and perishable vegetables. Stoneman was able to exchange 30 worn-out mules for some fresh ones, a feat greatly appreciated by the Mormons who were beginning to form a favorable opinion of the young man from New York. Their words of praise were not always used to describe non–Mormon officers:

> Quartermaster Stoneman, who was a gentleman in all that word implies, used every effort to obtain a larger supply of good animals before leaving the last Spanish-Indian settlements. He was several times highly insulted by Mexicans, who contemptuously refused to trade with him. He could hardly seem to realize that he was endeavoring to deal with a whipped, though as yet unconquered foe.[30]

The battalion's route led it along a sandy road, extremely difficult for the wagons to traverse. The men, carrying blankets, knapsacks, cartridge boxes, and muskets, living on half rations, had to help the teams by pulling the wagons with long ropes. Despite the hunger of the men, Cooke issued strict orders to kill for food only those animals too weak to work. In the rare instances when this was done, no part of the animal that could possibly be used for food was thrown away. Hides, tripe, and entrails were eaten, and the marrow bones were considered a luxury.[31]

Sickness continued to plague the battalion, and Cooke reported that 22 men were on the November 9 sick list. The breakdown of mule teams was equally discouraging. On November 10, a detachment of 55 sick men under the command of Lieutenant Willis was sent back to Pueblo through Santa Fe to spend the winter.

The route of the battalion toward Tucson forged a new wagon road between the Rio Grande and the Gila River and was a major contribution to the development of the Southwest. General Kearny, who had preceded the Mormon Battalion, followed a trail suitable for mules but not for wagons. Cooke created a passable trail for loaded wagons that would be used by settlers, railroads and gold-seekers in future years.

The Rocky Mountains were reached on November 28 and preparations were made for descending the mountains to the valley below. Again, it was hard work, as the wagons were lowered with long ropes. Stoneman was ordered to construct a path over the cliffs with a crew of 21 pioneers and, using his two-mile road, the battalion reached the ruins of the ranchero San Bernardino, where they rested and traded with the Apaches.

When the battalion continued, Cooke noted that the weather was exceedingly cold, ten degrees below zero Fahrenheit.[32] Another hazard now appeared as the men encountered herds of wild cattle that menaced the battalion. At Cooke's order, muskets were loaded as wild bulls attacked the wagons near the San Pedro River. The "Great Bull Fight" or "Battle of the Bulls," as it is also called in Mormon legend, turned out to be the only real fight in which the battalion engaged during the expedition. A few bulls had mingled with the beef cattle and were killed, but as the wagons stopped to water the teams, bulls charged the column. Pandemonium reigned as the soldiers fired at the bulls from behind their wagons. Even mules were attacked, and wagons were damaged by the enraged beasts.[33]

Although the scene had its comical elements, there were serious injuries. Amos Cox was thrown ten feet in the air and gored in the thigh. A quartermaster sergeant, Albert Smith, was run over and suffered broken ribs. George Stoneman was one of the casualties. One of the balls misfired in his rifle and ripped off the upper part of his thumb.

One man, Lafayette Frost, was the genuine hero of the melee. An enraged bull ran directly at him and Cooke yelled "Run, run, God damn you, run" but the intrepid Frost stood his ground and dropped the bull in his tracks, ten paces from the Mormon marksman. Cooke was impressed and swore that he would be "God damned if that man wasn't a soldier." Estimates of the number of animals killed vary, but accounts of the incident report anywhere from 60 to 80 bulls were dispatched.[34]

After butchering the bulls, the battalion continued on, following the San Pedro River towards Tucson on a trail found by the scouts. Tucson was garrisoned by 140 Mexican troops who wanted the Mormon Battalion to circle east of Tucson to the Gila River, but to avoid Tucson would add a hundred miles to the march. Determined to enter Tucson, Cooke ordered the battalion to overcome all resistance but reminded them that "the American soldier ever shows justice and kindness to the unarmed and unresisting; the property of individuals you will hold sacred: the people of Sonora are not our enemies."[35]

At a point about 16 miles from Tucson, Cooke sent word to the Mexican commander proposing that the American troops enter the town for trade. He asked the Mexicans to surrender a few arms and agree not to fight against the United States. The Mexican commander refused Cooke's terms and the battalion was ordered to load muskets and prepare for an engagement. Mexicans came out from town, however, and told the Americans that the Mexican troops had fled. On December 16, the battalion entered the town and found it to be nothing more than a small outpost to oppose the Indians, but it had fruit trees, green wheat, and water — all luxuries to the exhausted Mormons. It was a chance for Stoneman to purchase flour, fruits and vegetables, such as beans and corn.

All was peaceful until the evening of December 17 when the battalion pickets spotted about 20 men riding towards Tucson. This was enough for the pickets to race into camp and report the arrival of a large Mexican force. The troops were turned out and a battle line formed, but there were no signs of attacking Mexicans. Cooke then ordered Stoneman to take ten men and reconnoiter the town, but nothing untoward was observed. Apparently, citizens who had left the town when the Americans arrived were returning home after ascertaining they had nothing to fear.

After assuring the governor of Sonora, Don Manuel Gandara, that he was en route to the Gila River and that he had not come "as an enemy of the people whom you represent: they have received only kindness at my hands,"[36] Cooke resumed the march.

The 80-mile march from Tucson to the Gila River was extremely difficult. Heat and desert terrain caused terrible suffering and led to a breakdown of order and discipline, but the march continued.[37] They passed Pima and Maricoda Indian villages on their route. The Indians were a graceful people and even Cooke was charmed by them, so much so that he suggested to the Mormons that they settle in the vicinity. Stoneman was able to buy 70 or 80 bushels of corn, 600 hundred pounds of flour, and to exchange mules.

Cooke had been reluctant to take women along on the march, but he noted in his journal entry of January 1 that "Mrs. M. was happily delivered of a fine child two days ago." She was of hardy stock, as Cooke also noted on the same day that "she traveled ten miles on horseback."[38]

The battalion reached the Gila River on December 21. Their route was along the river, crossing sandy bottoms that became quick sand. The going was hard and made doubly difficult by the lack of rations as the beef from the bullfight was gone, and the sheep and oxen that were slaughtered were so thin that little sustenance was gained. Dr. Sanderson tried to get the men to broil or fry what little meat there was, but the Mormons continued to boil it to make soup. Entrails were hung over sticks and boiled. Even the hide was eaten as the hair was singed off and the meat boiled.[39]

As men and beasts weakened due to exposure and hunger, Stoneman proposed a daring plan to Cooke. Remembering his experiences with his father on Lake Chautaugua, Stoneman suggested that two wagon bodies be lashed to pontoons to float a substantial quantity of supplies down to the Colorado River crossing. It was a bold plan with substantial risk, as food was in short supply and, if it was lost, disaster could be the result for the battalion. Cooke agreed, although he was now anxious not only over Stoneman's plan, but also over reports that General Kearny had engaged the Californians and the outcome was in doubt:

> I have determined to send Mr. Stoneman at first in charge of the boats; they have been fresh pitched, but one of them still leaks tonight. Perhaps in the morning it will not. It appears that the most authentic information leaves General Kearny engaged with a superior force, strongly posted in a fortified defile defended by one or more twelve pounders. This gives me much anxiety; I do not doubt our success; but what valuable lives may have paid for it, who can tell?[40]

Spurred on by reports of battle and anxious to expedite the Battalion's march to re enforce Kearny, Cooke proceeded with Stoneman's plan:

> I separated about 2,500 pounds of provisions, corn, etc., for Stoneman's flotilla; it consists of pork, about thirteen days' rations (to which quantity two of the companies had been before reduced) and flour, about eighteen days' rations, and seven or eight bushels of corn, some tools, part of my own baggage, etc.[41]

Not all the men welcomed the plan. Tyler noted that "This move cast a gloom over the men generally, as they took the view that with our already scanty supplies no further risk of loss should be taken."[42] As the boats were loaded on January 1, Cooke proceeded with most of the battalion southwestward. The Gila was a rapid river about 150 yards across and appeared to be three or four feet deep. Unfortunately for young Stoneman, the improvised boats ran into trouble almost immediately. There were shallow sand bars throughout the river and the boat was continuously delayed.

Cooke had marched ahead but, having received no word from the flotilla, began to worry about the success of the venture. On January 2, he wrote: "It is now after sundown. Stoneman is not here. I fear much he has failed from the shallowness of the river...."[43] Cooke still hoped for news on the following day and, although no word was forthcoming, he left six pack mules with a note to Stoneman to lighten his load, if necessary. By January 4, Cooke wrote in his journal that he had reason to be exceedingly uneasy, although Stoneman was finally able to get a message to Cooke informing him that he would stick to it until he got to the mouth of the river, or until he overtook him. Cooke now worried that Tonto Indians, who had a reputation of attacking sleeping men, might attack Stoneman and his party, who were lightly armed.

Cooke now ordered Stoneman to abandon everything but 500 pounds of flour and rejoin the main party, but Stoneman was forced to abandon his entire load about 20 miles from the last camp. Cooke was particularly concerned about the loss of flour since he had enough for just 14 more days. To the great dissatisfaction of the men, rations were again reduced, to nine ounces a day. Stoneman's popularity no doubt suffered as well.

The Stoneman expedition was a disaster, and it can only be surmised what the exasperated Cooke must have said to the bedraggled lieutenant when he finally rejoined the battalion empty-handed. The entry in Cooke's journal, marking the end of the affair, was a mild rebuke considering the magnitude of the loss of vital supplies:

> If Mr. Stoneman had done as I particularly wished and urged, have got off before I did (we were twenty-one hours in that camp), corn and flour would have been saved; for the experiment would have shown itself a failure at once. I had put in but three days' ration of flour, until in the last hour his assurances induced me to add three more. Mr. S. spoke of his experience in rafting or boating.[44]

Tyler wrote that "several of the men had fainted or fallen to the earth through hunger and exhaustion as the march continued. The reduction of one ounce to the man was noted with comment that further reductions would reduce rations to practically nothing."

The battalion finally reached the mouth of the Gila River and the junction of the Colorado River. Lieutenants Smith and Stoneman led a pioneer party to prepare a road that traversed ridges and gullies around a mass of rocks aptly named "Devil's Point." The rugged terrain and the reduced rations caused great suffering and the diaries carry a note of desperation. There were nine days' half-rations remaining and they estimated they were at least 12 days' march from the nearest California settlement.

On January 10, at least part of the supplies that were lost as a result of the Stoneman boat fiasco were retrieved. The men who had been sent back to recover the provisions left on the Gila returned with about 400 pounds of flour. The battalion crossed the Colorado River on January 10 with much difficulty, losing a wagon in the process.

The battalion was now marching from well to well, finding some of them dry, forcing them to dig new ones. The water that was found was of poor quality. Cooke decided to take a route north of Cerro Centinela to a well called Pozo Hondo, where Stoneman and a party of 25 armed men were dispatched, to prepare the well for the rest of the battalion.[45] Cooke led the battalion along a clay flat where seashells and salt were found, leading the Mormons to conclude that the Gulf of California must have covered the entire area at one time.

The water was also of poor quality at Pozo Hondo, and the climatic conditions of the region added to the suffering of the men. The days were burning hot and the nights were well near freezing. While at Pozo Hondo, Cooke received letters informing him of Kearny's engagement at the Battle of San Pasqual and the loss of his fellow officers, Captains Benjamin Moore and Abraham Johnston:

> What a loss to my regiment. Ah, who but loved Johnston — the noble, sterling, valued Johnston. And who had warmer friends than poor Moore. Peace to their ashes! May their country honor the memories of its heroic champions; who serving her, have found their graves in distant and desolate regions![46]

The march after Pozo Hondo was the most difficult of the journey. Cooke considered abandoning the wagons, but he had been ordered by General Kearny to make a road and he was determined to accomplish his objective. There was no water and little food for five days as the men and animals struggled through thick sand. Many of the men were nearly barefoot and were using strips of animal skin for "boots." Tyler noted that words were inadequate to describe their condition. The men began to straggle and all except five wagons had broken down and were abandoned. Cooke ordered the battalion to march at night to escape the heat and "end this terrible state of things." On January 15, they marched ten miles "through dreaded sand" with great suffering. They finally reached the Carrizo, a small creek known as "first running water," the first they had seen since leaving the Colorado. The men staggered in, stumbling from fatigue, and Cooke halted the march for a day to give the men rest and a chance to clean their weapons. He was surprised to see them playing the fiddle and singing after a brief respite from the rigors of the march.

On January 21, the battalion reached John Warner's Ranchero, the first house they had seen since entering California. The ranch had developed into an important way station for the settlers taking the southern trail to California. Four pounds of fresh beef, but little else, were issued to each man, but Cooke, ever the disciplinarian, noted that he would "reduce it by half if they do not eat it, which I shall ascertain."[47]

The weather was fine, if cold, and the grass was green at the ranchero. Hot water came from a boiling spring and Cooke observed that the country was "verdant." Although it started to rain before the battalion departed, spirits soared as the trail was easy and the end was in sight.

Cooke had decided to march to Los Angeles to assist General Kearny in capturing that important center. On January 25, however, a dispatch was received from Kearny, who assumed Cooke was headed for San Diego as originally planned. Kearny and Commodore Robert Stocton defeated the Californians at San Pasqual on December 6, 1846, a short but bloody action in which 18 Americans were killed and Kearny was wounded. This was followed by dual victories by Commodore Stocton at the San Gabriel River and La Mesa. Lieutenant John C. Fremont met the retreating Californians and accepted their surrender, and Los Angeles was back in American hands.[48] The war in California was over. Although many of the Saints did not think the treaty would last, Mormon Robert Bliss expressed the sentiments of many when he exulted: "God be praised for his protection over us according to the Word of his Servant the Prophet."[49]

The battalion marched through the San Luis Valley, through tall grass and wild mustard, which was eaten with beef, their only other food. On January 27, the battalion passed a deserted Catholic Mission called Luis Rey and ascended a bluff. There, before them, the great Pacific Ocean appeared in the distance. The Saints were overwhelmed, cheered, and gave thanks. Sergeant Tyler wrote that, prior to leaving Nauvoo, the Saints had heard of the "great Pacific Sea" and its beauty "far exceeded our most sanguine expectations."[50] Their joy, Tyler recorded, was mixed with sorrow, as they pondered the fate of family members left behind in the wilderness or in Nauvoo. They comforted themselves with the thought that the Lord had provided for the Saints.

For Cooke, and his lieutenants Smith and Stoneman, who had survived their first test on a truly historic endeavor, the ordeal was over. Cooke lauded the Mormons in his Order No. 1, issued at the mission.

> History may be searched in vain for an equal march of infantry.... Without a guide who had traversed them, we have ventured into trackless prairies.... With crowbar and pick and axe in hand, we have worked our way over mountains.... The garrisons of four Presidos of Senora concentrated within the walls of Tucson gave us no pause.... Thus, marching half naked and half fed, and living upon wild animals, we have discovered and made a road of great value to our country.... Lieutenants A.I. Smith and Geo. Stoneman, of the First Dragoons, have shared and given valuable aid in all these labors.[51]

After camping at a Catholic mission four miles from San Diego, Philip St. George, Cooke rode by moonlight and reported to the general in San Diego.

FOUR

From California to the Rio Grande

General Stephen Kearny issued a proclamation to the people of California under his titles of Brigadier General, USA, and Governor of California. Published in the *California* on March 6, Kearny expressed his "ardent desire to promote ... the interests of the country and the welfare of its inhabitants."[1] Kearny maintained that the United States was forced to occupy California before it was seized by a foreign power. While he admitted that there had been excesses by the American army, he urged everyone to work for the peace and quiet of the land.[2] Lieutenant Colonel Cooke was in command of the southern military district and Company "C" of the 1st Dragoons, which included the California Volunteers and the Mormon Battalion.

George Stoneman was now part of the occupying army of California, a somewhat tattered force of which he, as a West Pointer and cavalry officer, was one of the more impressive members. The officers gathered at the "Ciudad de la Los Angeles" decided to celebrate the first Fourth of July to be marked in this newly acquired territory in as grand a style as possible. The band of the 7th Regiment of the New York Volunteers, who had arrived aboard the American ship the *Susan Drew*, played the "Star-Spangled Banner" before a host of invited dignitaries, followed by a Federal Salute given by the Dragoons. Stoneman and his fellow officer, Lieutenant John McHenry Hollingsworth, decorated the ballroom with lights, evergreens, and with an appropriate military theme of stacked cutlasses and sabers.[3]

Stoneman must have accumulated several months of back pay from his long march with the Mormons, which he imprudently stored in his trunk. On August 4, his quarters were broken into and the money was stolen. Lieutenant Hollingsworth was sympathetic. "I am truly sorry for poor Stoneman — It is hard to lose money so far from home." Private John Smith, of the 1st Dragoons, was soon apprehended and tried for the crime. Part of the money was later recovered, but Smith tried to take his own life.[4]

Despite these tribulations, Stoneman was enamored with the scenery and countryside in the Los Angeles area, especially the country close to a post called El Monte. He resolved to return and make the area his home if he was able to do so. He did, in fact, return after his retirement from the military in 1871.

While on duty in Los Angeles, Stoneman was developing into a good officer, admired by his men. A civilian living in Los Angeles reported that Stoneman was "an unusual favorite with all the officers and likewise beloved by the private soldiers at Los Angeles." It was noted that when a detachment was ordered to conduct a scouting operation, the men all wanted to go if Stoneman was in command.[5]

The discovery of gold in 1848 led to an influx of miners and the need for control by an army already overtaxed by frontier duty. After being engaged in scouting and participating with occasional skirmishes along the frontier, Stoneman was placed in command of 40 hand-picked men who acted as a police force in the newly discovered gold mines. In 1849, Stoneman commanded an escort for T. Butler King, a confidential agent of the federal government, who set out to gauge the views of the new settlers. King's extended tour led him to report that they wanted to form a state government as soon as possible. The settlers felt that slavery was a question they should settle themselves, but pro-slavery sentiment was strong. Many Southerners had migrated to California and King himself held pro-slavery views, even though he was a Northerner from Pennsylvania. A Constitutional Convention was held in September at Monterey and, although many delegates favored slavery, no objection was made to a Bill of Rights outlawing slavery in California.[6]

While the political future of California was under debate at Monterey, Stoneman was ordered back to frontier duty. He helped to enforce the prevailing view of the government and settlers that destiny had awarded California to white settlers and that Indians would not contribute to the development of the territory and should be pushed aside. The newly formed state government authorized military campaigns against Indians who were alleged to have committed atrocities against whites, and the state treasury was authorized to pay for these campaigns.[7] One observer, Horace Bell, wrote, "We will let those rascally redskins know that they have no longer to deal with the Spaniard or Mexican, but with the invincible race of American backwoodsmen...."[8]

Frontier service in the regular army was characterized by poor food, danger, and spartan living conditions. Probably the worst feature of army service was the monotony of long periods of duty away from family and friends. There were health hazards due to disease, poor diet, and the possibility of enemy action. Slow promotions, low pay, and strict and often brutal discipline were the lot of the professional military on the frontier. It was no wonder that desertion frequently thinned the enlisted ranks.[9]

Severely restricted by a lack of funds and personnel, the regular army lacked the resources to play a significant role in the confrontation between Indians and whites, following the California gold rush. Nevertheless, there were clashes between the army and Indians in which Stoneman was directly involved. In September 1849, Pit River Indians ambushed an army exploration expedition near Goose Lake in Northeast California. Captain William H. Warner of the Topographical Engineers was killed. In 1850, General Persifor Smith, commander of the Pacific Division, sent a force of dragoons and infantry, including Stoneman, to Clear Lake, where 400 Indians were encamped. Between 60 and 100 Indians were killed in the ensuing attack. The troopers then marched to Russian River, where an additional 400 Indians had also fortified an island. What followed was described by the commander of the expedition, Captain Nathaniel Lyon, as "a perfect slaughter pen," as between 75 and 150 Indians were killed.[10]

Stoneman's duty with the 1st Dragoons took him to the newly established Fort Orford in Southern Oregon in 1851, where Coquille Indians were attacking the ever-increasing numbers of miners and farmers. A mixed force of dragoons and infantry defeated the Indians in an engagement that took place in October. Stoneman's duty in Oregon continued during the winter of 1852 and into 1853, opening new roads for settlement.[11]

Command of an escort for a railroad surveying expedition followed, from 1853 to 1854. Jefferson Davis, then secretary of war, had encouraged the Pacific Railroad Survey's search for the most feasible routes to the American West.[12] Stoneman was assigned in July 1853 to the topographical party of Lieutenant R.S. Williamson, who was looking for feasible passes through the formidable Sierra Nevadas and Coast Range that would connect California with Oregon and Washington. The expedition explored five passes in the Sierras, of which only two were recommended as practical, the Tehachapi Pass and the Canada de las Uvas.[13]

In December of 1853, Lieutenant John G. Parker, who had assisted Williamson on the California surveys, was ordered to resurvey the Gila River route between the Pima village and the Rio Grande with an escort commanded by Stoneman. The route of the expedition took Stoneman back to the route of the epic march of the Mormon Battalion in 1846–1847. The party traveled to Tucson through the Chiricahua Mountains to a junction with Cooke's Wagon Road, where it proceeded south after leaving the Rio Grande. Parker found a more direct route through the town of Molino near El Paso. The level terrain in Arizona and Texas argued for this route along the 32nd parallel, despite the lack of timber and water.[14]

Following this duty, Stoneman was assigned as aide-de-camp to Major General John E. Wool, commander of the Department of the Pacific. Wool was a demanding and contentious 42-year veteran of the army who disliked the citizens and political officials of the Northwest. He felt they were exploiting the Indians, killing them if necessary. He did not hesitate to speak his mind in public, a practice which eroded his support from civilians in the territory.[15] Stoneman's assignment must have taxed his political and administrative skills, as he served the cantankerous general.

Stoneman was now one of the more experienced frontier officers in the service. An incident occurred that would present him with an opportunity to join some of the best officers in the U.S. Army, including then Lieutenant Colonel Robert E. Lee. In midsummer 1854, while Stoneman was assigned to General Wool, Indians ambushed Lt. John L. Gratlan's patrol near Fort Laramie, Wyoming. Only one man escaped alive, and he died shortly after the engagement. Alarmed by the threat of further attacks, Secretary of War Jefferson Davis urged Congress to authorize the formation of two new cavalry and two infantry regiments for service on the Western Frontier.[16]

The new 2nd Cavalry was assigned to the Texas border and Davis, a West Point graduate, personally selected its officers. It was a rare collection of military talent. Albert Sidney Johnston was named colonel in command, Robert E. Lee, lieutenant colonel, while

William J. Hardee and George H. Thomas were appointed majors. The captains assigned to the 2nd included Earl Van Dorn, E. Kirby Smith, N.G. Evans, I.N. Palmer, R.W. Johnson and George Stoneman. Many of these officers achieved senior rank in either the Union or Confederate armies. Hardee, Van Dorn, Smith, Evans, and even the young lieutenants, John B. Hood, Charles W. Field, Charles W. Phifer, and William P.Chambliss, rose to the rank of general in the Confederate army. In addition to Stoneman, Thomas, Palmer, Johnson, and Lieutenant K. Garrard were generals in the Union Army.[17] By 1855, the four company captains were all veteran soldiers. Stoneman, Van Dorn, and Charles J. Whiting were West Pointers. Van Dorn had fought in the Mexican War and was decorated for valor. Whiting had served in the Florida Seminole War and had taken part in the American-Mexican border survey in 1849. The regiment even had a poet: Captain Theodore O'Hara, who had also fought in the Mexican War, and was the author of "The Bivouac of the Dead" and other poems.[18]

Robert E. Lee was ordered to Jefferson Barracks, St. Louis, Missouri, in April 1855, and was temporarily in command, as Sidney Johnston was not immediately available. Lee drilled the troopers and waited for requisitioned clothing and other supplies to arrive. Stoneman joined the regiment in August.

In October, Johnston led the 2nd Cavalry, now consisting of 35 officers and 365 men, through the Ozarks into Indian Country in Texas.[19] The regiment marched in a southwesterly direction over the mountains, following the Pacific Railway Surveys, through Missouri to Arkansas, and then southwest into Indian territory. The regiment reached Tahlequah, the capital of the Cherokee Nation, and were surprised to find brick houses and a seminary, as well as other signs of an advanced civilization.

Continuing their march, the regiment crossed the Neosho and Arkansas rivers in December and began to suffer from freezing temperatures and storms called "Northers." The Red River was crossed on December 15 and the troopers passed through Preston, Texas, shortly afterwards, en route to Fort Belknap. The temperature fell below zero, accompanied by six inches of snow. Horses froze to death on the picket lines. They finally reached Fort Belknap on December 27, with temperatures remaining below zero.[20]

Lee returned from court-martial duty in March 1856 and was ordered by Johnston to command two squadrons of the regiment at Camp Cooper, a remote outpost in the Comanche Reserve about 170 miles north of Fort Mason. Stoneman led one of the squadrons attached to Lee's command. Lee had a conciliatory, as well as a military, role to play with the Comanches, who were becoming increasingly hostile as white settlers moved into their reserve, depleting the herds of deer, elk, and buffalo. The government was trying to "humanize" the Comanches through free clothing and food, and Lee called on the Comanche chief, Catumseh, shortly after his arrival to foster good relations between the soldiers and the Comanches. Lee voiced his distrust of Catumseh, and Comanches in general, in letters to his wife. "These people give a world of trouble to man and horse and, poor creatures, they are not worth it."[21]

Life at Camp Cooper was bleak. There were no buildings at the camp as lumber was not available. The area was infested with snakes, and Lee reported the death of his pet rattlesnake in a letter to his youngest daughter, Mildred. There were blistering heat, choking dust and isolation to contend with, and boredom, which was broken only by an occasional foray into Comanche territory. One such expedition was ordered by the department commander, General Persifor F. Smith, who instructed Lee to take four companies of the 2nd Cavalry, two from Camp Cooper and two from Fort Mason, to prevent Indian depredations under a chief named Sanaco. Lee selected captains Van Dorn and O'Hara to lead their companies from Camp Cooper against the Indians north of the Brazos River, but little came of the operation. Other sweeps were carried out, but there was practically no contact, which led Lee to conclude that the Indians transited, but did not remain in the country near the upper waters of the Colorado and the Brazos. The 2nd Cavalry's long march of 40 days, covering over 1600 miles, accomplished very little.[22]

Stoneman found service in Texas trying and tedious, and he longed for California. He expressed his frustration to a friend living in San Diego:

> This is a god forsaken country and the lord only knows when I shall get out of it again. I shall embrace the first opportunity to get to California and it is altogether probable that when once there I shall never again leave it.[23]

Despite the rigors of the Texas frontier, Stoneman bragged to his friend about his troopers. "We have a very good Rgt., as good material and as well disciplined as any I ever saw, far ahead of the 1st Cavalry," he observed.[24]

Stoneman endured the hard life of the Texas frontier until March 1858, when he was given a leave of absence for one year for a European tour. It was common for an army officer to do a European "grand tour" if he could manage it, but there is nothing in the historical records to indicate where he went or whether his excursion had a professional purpose. Stoneman's characteristically brief biographical notes that he prepared from time to time simply mention the tour, but offer no details as to its purpose. In any event, it must have been welcome after three years in the dust of the Texas outposts.

Stoneman returned to Texas and the 2nd Cavalry in April of 1859. His task now was to interdict the raids of Juan Nepomuceno Cortinas, who claimed to be a citizen of both Mexico and the United States, and who dealt in cattle, either purchased or stolen. Cortinas traveled with armed henchmen, who protected him from arrest, although he had been indicted for murder in 1850 and horse theft in 1859. He was a hero to the Mexicans, however, who saw him as a defender of their rights against the gringos. On September 28, Cortinas occupied Brownsville, threatening to kill all Americans. The marauder played hide and seek with the American authorities, including the Texas Rangers and the Mexican militia, and actually captured two field pieces from this irregular force. On December 5, 1859, Major S.P. Heintzelman, a colleague of Stoneman, rallied the demoralized Texas Rangers and soundly defeated Cortinas's band at Brownsville, but Cortinas, once again, escaped.[25]

Stoneman was in command of Company "E" and, after participating in scouting expeditions around the Horse Head crossing of the Pecos and in the Guadalupe Mountains, joined Heintzelman's campaign against Cortinas. Stoneman engaged Cortinas on December 14 and again on December 27. The latter encounter was a significant one when, according to 2nd Cavalry records or returns, the Mexicans suffered a loss of 40 to 50 killed.[26]

Stoneman's men dismounted and drove the enemy across the Rio Grande so successfully that the company was cited for "gallant and distinguished services" in the report of the engagement by Major Heintzelman.[27]

Heintzelman's squadron, of which Stoneman's company formed a part, was responsible for guarding over 100 miles of the Rio Grande. The men were frustrated by Cortinas' ability to cross the river at will after raiding on the U.S. side. In March, Stoneman saw an opportunity to strike a mortal blow against Cortinas and his men, having received intelligence that Cortinas had established his headquarters in the town of La Mesa, a scant three miles from Stoneman's camp. Stoneman and his subordinate Lieutenant Kimmel decided to take matters into their own hands.

Acting on their own authority, the two officers led two companies, reinforced by 75 state troops, across the river and assaulted the town on March 15. Several Mexicans were killed and wounded and 300 armed men were captured. The cavalrymen's elation at apprehending Cortinas and his men turned to dismay as they learned that they had captured a garrison of Mexican soldiers. There was nothing to do except apologize and free the prisoners, but 400 Mexican infantry appeared on the scene to repel the invaders. The Mexicans demanded that the Americans withdraw, but Stoneman reasoned that as he had grievously violated international law, he might as well make the most of it. He refused to leave the area and continued his search for Cortinas, marching over twenty miles into the interior. He remained in Mexico until March 20, when he was ordered by his superiors to return to his camp across the Rio Grande.[28]

Stoneman apparently was not reprimanded for his actions. The regimental return for March 1860 quietly reported the affair as follows:

> Company G arrived at Fort Brown on the 7th inst, and proceeded to establish a camp above Captain Stoneman on the Rio Grande, and on the 15th inst. joined him and proceeded into Mexico on a scout for the purpose of arresting Cortinas. The companies returned on the 20th inst. after a long and tedious march.[29]

Lieutenant Colonel Robert E. Lee was in temporary command of the Department of Texas following court-martial duty. This pleasant interlude had been interrupted when he commanded the U.S. Marines who put down John Brown's raid at Harpers Ferry, Virginia, on October 18. Upon his return to Texas, Lee decided to see how the campaign was going against Cortinas. Lee was attended by a single company that was probably Stoneman's, as later correspondence from Stoneman indicated he was "ordered on the Brownsville Expedition against and engaged in fights with Cortinas and his band" about this time.[30] The cavalry made for the Rio Grande near Eagle Pass, but failed to find Cortinas. Fort Brown was reached on April 11 after an inspection of the lower Rio Grande Valley. About 400 troops were now stationed along the Rio Grande, of which 50 dragoons commanded by Stoneman scouted between Brownsville and the border. The *Dallas Herald* reported on April 4, 1860, that Cortinas had gone into the interior of Texas and noted sarcastically that "he has pillaged the Rio Grande settlements till there is scarcely any property left to pay him for further depredations."[31]

As the fateful year of 1860 drew to a close, events were swirling around Texas and the nation. John Brown's raid the previous year had inflamed passions that were fanned further by Abraham Lincoln's election in November. Many southern sympathizers in Texas were flying the "Lone Star" flag, and support for secession from the Union was high. On December 26, Colonel Robert Anderson, whose brother Charles was an army officer in Texas and a close friend of Robert E. Lee's, ordered his troops to evacuate Fort Moultrie and occupy Fort Sumter opposite Charleston, South Carolina.

Lee was waiting to be relieved as commander of the Department of Texas by General David Emanuel Twiggs, who had distinguished himself in the Mexican War in the battles of Palo Alto and Reseca de la Palma, commanding the 2nd Dragoons. Twiggs was a Georgian and was married to Elizabeth Hunter, a Virginian.[32] He was a strong "states' rights man," and was 70 years old. He relieved Lee on December 13, 1860, delaying his departure from his command of the Department of the West as long as he could until the results of the November presidential election were known. Upon his arrival in Texas, Twiggs told Lee that he thought the Union would be dissolved within six weeks. Lee still hoped for peace as he departed for Washington, struggling with his conscience, dreading the decision he would soon have to make to follow his native state of Virginia and resign his commission from the United States Army.[33]

George Stoneman, stationed on the Rio Grande, watched these events with increasing apprehension. Although he was a relatively junior officer, he had taken it upon himself to do what he could to prevent the capture of Union military assets by the secessionists. He had written four former commanders of the Texas Department, as he credited himself with "having peculiar facilities for obtaining information in regard to the intentions of the secessionist movement," including those of General Twiggs.[34] After the war, Stoneman revealed that he had tried to enlist Robert E. Lee in his plan to oppose the Texas secessionists:

> I also wrote to R.E. Lee then Col. of CAVLY and second in command of the Department urging upon him the propriety of a concentration of all the troops in the state and the assumption by him, Lee, that he would be recognized by us all as our Commanding Officer.[35]

It was not to be. On February 1, 1861, the Texas Convention passed an ordinance of secession by a vote of 106–7. The ordinance called for a referendum but the secessionists were confident it would be approved, as indeed it was, and they began to organize their forces. On February 4, Lee was ordered to Washington and he reported to General Winfield Scott, General in Chief of the War Department. For Lee and his comrades-in-arms, the fateful choice was upon them. David E. Twiggs was about to earn the stigma of "Traitor Twiggs" from his subordinates who remained loyal to the Union.

Twiggs had written General Scott on the day he assumed command, seeking guidance:

> I think there can be no doubt that many Southern states will secede from the Union. The State of Texas will be among that number, and, from all appearances at present, it will be an early day, certainly before the 4th of March next. What is to be done with public property in charge of the Army?[36]

Scott was ill, so Colonel George W. Lay responded saying that the situation in Texas was "political" and instructions must come from civilian authority. Lay told Twiggs that

Scott had confidence in Twiggs's discretion, firmness, and patriotism and that he "leaves the administration of your command in your own hands...."[37]

On January 15, Twiggs sent a more urgent appeal to the Assistant Adjutant General at Army Headquarters in New York. "The crisis is fast approaching, and ought to be looked at in the face. What disposition is to be made of public property and the troops now in this department?"[38]

At this point, Twiggs made his true intentions known to Scott. He wrote and said he was a "Southern man" and that the states were certain to secede. Like Lee, Twiggs would follow his native state but, unlike Lee, he was about to surrender his posts and equipment while still wearing the uniform of a United States Army officer. On February 19, Twiggs complied with the demand of Colonel Ben McCulloch, a Texan who commanded an armed body of over 1,000 state troops, to "deliver up all military posts and public property" to the Texans. The commissioners of Texas agreed that the United States troops "should march out of [San Antonio] taking with them their arms, clothing, camp and garrison equipage, and all the necessaries for a march out of Texas."[39] This agreement was not upheld by the Texans, and many U.S. Army men were eventually held and released on parole.

Stoneman's regiment was able to begin its evacuation in February 1861. He led his company to Brazos, Santiago, at the mouth of the Rio Grande, by steamboat and then sailed to Indianola, a port on the Gulf of Mexico. Marching to Green Lake, he joined six other companies of his regiment who then returned to Indianola and embarked on the steamship *Coatzacoalcos* on March 31. The steamer proceeded to Key West and Havana and then on to New York.[40]

Other ships sent to evacuate loyal Union troops were not that successful. The ill-fated *Star of the West*, which had been fired on at Charleston Harbor while attempting to reinforce the beleaguered Fort Sumter, was captured by Confederate forces in late April off the coast of Texas as last-minute efforts were made to evacuate Union forces.[41] Stoneman was resourceful enough to avoid the fate of being paroled and therefore becoming unable to take up arms against the Confederacy, which happened to a number of his comrades who remained loyal to the Union.

Twiggs had agreed to surrender the equipment and supplies of U.S. Army forces in Texas, but the men, who numbered 2328, were to be allowed to leave Texas. Stoneman's former comrade-in-arms, Earl Van Dorn, now a colonel in the Confederate Army, was ordered on April 11 to "intercept and prevent the movement of United States troops from the State of Texas."[42] Officers and men were to be considered prisoners of war. The commissioned officers were permitted to be released on parole if they swore an oath not to serve against the Confederacy. In the end, 815 officers and men were captured. Many of the enlisted men were confined for two years.[43]

George Stoneman escaped to fight another day. He made his way to Carlisle Barracks in Pennsylvania and joined the staff of his West Point classmate, General George McClellan, on May 9. For Stoneman, the war was about to start in earnest.

With McClellan

George Stoneman entered the war in Washington, D.C., a city in a high state of anxiety as Confederate campfires began to appear across the Potomac River in Virginia. President Lincoln issued a proclamation calling on each state to provide 75,000 militia who would serve for 90 days. Until the militia arrived, the capital was defenseless.[1]

Militia units began to arrive in the city by mid–April, and Federal forces moved to secure Arlington and Alexandria and end the immediate threat to the capital. Following his promotion to major on May 9, 1861, Stoneman received his first assignment. He commanded a cavalry advance across the Long Bridge connecting Washington to Alexandria on May 24.

Federal infantry formed on the Washington end of the bridge at 2:00 A.M. on the 24th and took possession of the Virginia end of the bridge before an alarm could be given by the Confederates. The infantry of the 1st Michigan and the 1st New York Zouaves swept into Alexandria, capturing a few Confederate cavalrymen. About 700 Confederate infantrymen escaped on the Orange and Alexandria railway, burning the bridges behind them. The Union troops advanced on the Columbia Turnpike as far as Fort Albany. The movement was basically unopposed, and Colonel O.B. Wilcox of the 1st Michigan reported that "Alexandria is ours" by 5:30 A.M.[2] Apparently, the role of cavalry in the affair, and Stoneman's participation in it, was not significant, as Major General Heintzelman, the commander of the operation, did not mention either in his official report.

Stoneman would soon join the staff of his West Point classmate, General George B. McClellan, who had been placed in command of the Department of the Ohio on May 3. Ohio, Indiana, and Illinois originally formed the department, and Western Pennsylvania, West Virginia, and eventually the state of Missouri were added.[3] McClellan had requested several officers for his staff while he was in Cincinnati organizing his forces. He was able to have his way with a few, as in the case of Stoneman, but he failed to get Fitz-John Porter or West Point classmate Jesse Reno.

Various plans for quickly delivering a decisive blow to the Confederacy occupied Union strategists during this early stage of the war but, no matter where an offensive would begin, it was clear that western Virginia would soon be an area of conflict. The region was different culturally, economically, and geographically from eastern Virginia and the people had more in common with Ohio and Pennsylvania than they did with other Virginians. Few were slave owners and most opposed secession of Virginia from the Union. As McClellan organized and trained his forces, Virginians prepared to vote on the secession referendum.

Virginia, under the leadership of Governor John Letcher, had been one of the fence-sitting states on the issue of secession when the Confederacy was formed. Lincoln's proclamation for militia, however, pushed Virginia out of the Union. The vote was heavily in favor of secession everywhere east of the Blue Ridge, but Unionist sentiment remained high in the west as the majority voted against secession.[4]

Stoneman joined McClellan on June 20, just after the young general ordered the troops of the Ohio to "cross the frontier and enter upon the soil of Virginia. Your mission is to restore peace and confidence, to protect the majesty of the law, and to restore our brethren from the grip of armed traitors."[5]

By the time Stoneman joined McClellan's staff as an acting assistant inspector-general, the latter had occupied the town of Grafton after assuring the Union men of Western Virginia that all their rights would be "religiously respected." McClellan also reassured slave owners that they would not be interfered with. "Not only will we abstain from all such interference but we will, on the contrary with an iron hand, crush any attempt at insurrection on their part."[6] It was clear that McClellan was not coming to liberate slaves.

McClellan now provided the North with a badly needed victory which shored up Union morale. Shortly after Grafton was occupied, McClellan's troops routed the southerners at the village of Philippi. The Northern press called the Confederate retreat the "Philippi Races," and McClellan was the man of the hour. On June 11, delegates from the western counties of Virginia met and established a provisional state government, naming Francis H. Pierpoint as governor.[7]

McClellan had his eye on Kentucky, a state that duplicated western Virginia in its Union sentiment to build on. McClellan wrote Lincoln on May 30, 1861, and informed him of his proclamation to Union sympathizers in western Virginia. He would not interfere with slavery and this had a "happy effect" in Kentucky.[8] McClellan was convinced that a similar policy would help to keep Kentucky in the fold. McClellan also advised Lincoln that he was "preparing to seize the ... Great Kanawa Valley." On June 25, McClellan issued a proclamation to his troops and, in the bombastic tradition of the day, said that he expected "the highest and noblest qualities of soldiers — discipline, courage, and mercy." His only concern was that his men would "not find foeman worthy of your steel."[9]

Stoneman joined McClellan's staff in time for the campaign at Rich Mountain, an early Northern victory that propelled McClellan to his appointment as Commander in Chief of the Army of the Potomac. McClellan commanded some 20,000 men in West Virginia, also including 18 Ohio regiments, nine from Indiana, and two from West Virginia. McClellan faced Confederate Brigadier General Robert S. Garnett, whom Lee had ordered to the town of Beverly with 4500 men. Garnett was supposed to recruit as many regiments as possible from the local populace, but this proved to be difficult. "The West

Virginians," he reported, "are thoroughly imbued with an ignorant and bigoted Union sentiment."[10]

Garnett believed that the two passes through the Rich and Laurel mountains held the key to control of the west. Accordingly, he positioned 1300 of his men at Rich Mountain, which he considered the easiest to defend, while he remained in command of his troops at Laurel Mountain. McClellan divided his army as well. One force held Garnett in place while Brigadier General William S. Rosecrans took some 1,850 infantrymen and used a local trail to reach the Confederates' left flank. Rosecrans was scheduled to begin his attack by midmorning on July 11, and it was agreed that when firing was heard indicating Rosecrans's attack had begun, McClellan would begin a frontal attack with two brigades of infantry.[11] As Rosecrans began his attack, McClellan heard the sound of battle and readied his troops to attack the Confederates in front of Rich Mountain, commanded by Brigadier General John Pegram. McClellan had close to a five-to-one advantage with his 7,000 troops to Pegram's 1,300.[12] Faced with uncertainty, McClellan did nothing. It was obvious that Rosecrans had engaged the enemy, but it was not clear where he had done so. Because of the sound of the firing, McClellan knew Rosecrans had not attacked the rear as planned. Faced with these unknowns, McClellan chose to wait for further information. Rosecrans had, in fact, successfully driven the Confederates from their position and forced most of Pegram's men to surrender. Garnett was forced to evacuate his position at Laurel Hill and was killed while directing a rear guard action at the Cheat River, the first general on either side to be killed in action. While the battle was of relatively minor importance, McClellan displayed qualities of indecisiveness and hesitation that would cost the Union dearly in coming months.

Cavalry did not play a significant role in the battle. Burdsal's Ohio Dragoons and Baker's Illinois cavalry were present, but in all probability were used for courier and administrative duties. McClellan realized that he was hampered by a lack of sufficient cavalry for scouting purposes and, on June 11, asked the Adjutant General's office for six companies of cavalry from Fort Leavenworth, but no expansion of his cavalry arm was reported.

McClellan viewed the results of all elements involved with satisfaction. "I am more than satisfied with you," he told his troops. "You have annihilated two armies, commanded by educated and experienced soldiers, and entrenched mountain fortresses fortified at their leisure.... You have proved that union men, fighting for the preservation of our government, are more than a match for our misguided and erring brethren...."[13]

For the moment, McClellan was a hero of the Union. He was called to Washington, proceeding through adoring crowds en route to the capital, where he met Lincoln, who presented him with his new command as head of the Division of the Potomac, responsible for the defenses of Washington. McClellan moved rapidly to restore order and instill rigid discipline. Training of the troops, who were pouring into Washington in response to Lincoln's call for 400,000 volunteers, was established.

George Stoneman was appointed a Brigadier General of Volunteers on August 13, 1861, and named Chief of Cavalry of the Army of the Potomac the following day. Although he had reached the pinnacle of his career, his command was limited by his commanding officer's concept of the employment of cavalry. McClellan was a superb organizer and logistician and he skillfully organized the infantry into brigades and divisions as the untrained troops poured into Washington. His organization of the cavalry was a different matter. Mounted regiments were assigned to infantry divisions. Once five corps of infantry were formed, cavalry regiments were assigned to each corps. Although a "Cavalry Reserve" was formed under Stoneman's old commanding officer, General Philip St. George Cooke, the failure of independent command for the cavalry prevented an effective use of mounted troops until the organization was changed just before the Battle of Chancellorsville.

Stoneman's appointment as Chief of Cavalry of the Army of the Potomac gave him authority in name only. In March 1862, each infantry corps was also assigned a chief of cavalry, so Stoneman and his cavalry corps commanders were "ornamental staff officers."[14] Stephen Starr, in his definitive work on Union cavalry, pointed out that McClellan may have felt that the cavalry did not have the training or leadership to conduct independent operations, but his subordination of the cavalry to inexperienced infantry commanders led to an ineffective use of this element of the forces available to him.[15]

The Confederacy did not make this mistake. A cavalry brigade was formed in October 1861 under Brigadier General J.E.B. Stuart. One North Carolina and four Virginia regiments soon followed. Within a month, Stuart had a cavalry division of four brigades with five batteries of horse artillery. The Confederates continued this organization in the west where the cavalry was organized under two brigadiers, Nathan Bedford Forrest and Joseph Wheeler.[16]

McClellan was appointed General-in-Chief of the Army on November 1, 1861, replacing the aging and ill Winfield Scott. For the next three months, the army and the nation wondered what McClellan would do. One of his first moves was to send Stoneman "with a large body of cavalry with some infantry"[17] to reconnoiter along the Orange and Alexandria Railroad in Virginia and determine the position of the enemy. The plan was to force the Confederates across the Rappahannock, if possible. Stoneman's report of the raid indicated that, while it was not a success in meeting the inflated objectives established for it, the raid did provide some information. Rains caused Bull Run to rise, making it impassable. Stoneman, however, made it to Warrenton Station, where he felt the enemy "cautiously" and discovered two regiments of cavalry and three bodies of infantry on the other side of Cedar Run. "Had we crossed, should not have been able to get back for high water."[18] Stoneman gave a litany of woes; three men of the 5th Cavalry were wounded driving in the enemy's pickets, two men of the Pennsylvania Cavalry were shot through the foot by their own carbines, one man was wounded by his own bayonet. Stoneman did report that the Confederates had burned the bridges up to Warrenton Junction.[19] Thomas F. Thiele, in his work on the evolution of cavalry, described the raid as a failure: "unaggressive, feeble and it had not accomplished its full mission."[20] A biography of Stoneman in a history of the 5th Cavalry describes the raid in more flattering terms:

> General Stoneman made a reconnaissance on the 14th of March, 1862, with a large force of cavalry and some infantry ... but the roads were in such bad condition and the streams so flooded that having obtained the desired information, he halted upon reaching Cedar Run, where he had a skirmish with the enemy, after which his command bivouacked on a hillside nearby until the next morning, when he offered battle, which was declined, whereupon he returned without serious molestation to Union Mills.[21]

McClellan used Stoneman's report to inform Secretary of War Stanton that the Confederate force seen near Warrenton "did not come from Aquia, but that it is the rear guard of the troops who left Manassas."[22]

Lincoln, impatient with McClellan's inactivity, had previously issued War Order No. 1, which directed the Army of the Potomac to engage General Joseph E. Johnston's army encamped in winter quarters near Manassas. McClellan, who held Lincoln in low regard, opposed this plan. He had submitted a counter-proposal on February 3, which listed his opposition to a land campaign against Johnston and the consequent long overland route to Richmond the army would have to follow. Instead, McClellan proposed moving the army over water, down the Chesapeake Bay to Urbanna, on the mouth of the Rappahannock River. If Urbanna proved to be unsuitable, McClellan proposed landing the army at Fort Monroe. This would force the Confederates out of their position for one chosen by the Federals. Lincoln, who was distracted by the serious illness and eventual death of his son Willie, held a series of meetings with McClellan and his generals. He reluctantly approved the plan with the condition that enough troops remain in Washington to defend the capital.[23]

On March 9, prior to Stoneman's reconnaissance, Lincoln learned that the Confederate army had departed Manassas. At the same time, the generals decided to use Fort Monroe as the advance base on the peninsula. A vast armada was organized to move the army to Fort Monroe: 400 vessels transported 121,500 men, 44 artillery batteries, 1,500 wagons, and 15,600 horses and mules.[24] Stoneman's cavalry forces totaled 24,110.[25] The troops began to embark on March 17. Starr records that the voyage to Fort Monroe for the cavalry was "anything but pleasant."[26] The horses were transported on open decks of the steamers and there was no protection from bad weather. The men had little space to sleep and there were no bunks. Despite these hardships, the men were anxious to get away from the dull routine of the camps surrounding Washington and they cheered McClellan whenever they saw him.[27]

McClellan referred to the Peninsula as "terra incognita," as there was little known about the area. The Union planners were familiar with the York and James rivers and there was some knowledge of the Chickahominy, but existing maps were inaccurate and close to worthless.

The assignment of cavalry to infantry corps continued in the Peninsula Campaign except for Cooke's cavalry reserve, which seemed to be under Stoneman's supervision at times, but operated independently on occasion as well.

The organizational structure of the cavalry was not the only problem. Then-Colonel William Averell, who commanded the First Cavalry Brigade, noted that the "topography and soil of the peninsula campaign presented a most difficult field for cavalry operations. From Fort Monroe to Hanover Court House there was hardly a field with sufficient scope for the maneuvers of a single regiment of cavalry."[28]

McClellan later complained that "the cavalry operations remained unchanged, and were sadly deficient in that important arm, as many of the regiments belonging to the Army of the Potomac were among those which had been retained near Washington."[29] Starr observed that he probably could have taken as much cavalry as he needed and in fact misused what he did have. "Had he organized his nine and a half regiments of cavalry into a three brigade division, properly led at the brigade and division level and properly used, the cavalry could conceivably have had a decisive effect on the course of the campaign."[30] Divided and inexperienced as it was, the cavalry contributed little to a generally dispirited campaign.

The Peninsula Campaign commenced on April 4, when the Federal forces moved to Yorktown. Just as the campaign started, McClellan learned that he would not have McDowell's corps of 35,000 men, as Lincoln decided they should remain in the Washington area to defend the capital. McClellan greatly overestimated the Confederate forces opposing him and was convinced that he faced 100,000 men. Relying on the faulty intelligence of Allan Pinkerton, he thought that the Confederate army under Johnston had arrived at Yorktown when in fact it had not.

Much to the amazement of the Confederates who expected an imminent attack, McClellan laid siege to Yorktown, allowing the Confederate forces under Brigadier General John Magruder to be reinforced. Magruder was known as a great actor, and he lived up to his reputation, moving his 11,000 men back and forth in front of the Union lines to give the impression that he had many more men in place than was actually the case. Heavy rains also hindered Union movements. Convinced that he unexpectedly faced a large Confederate force, McClellan reacted, predictably, as he had at Rich Mountain. He besieged Yorktown because it was the safest course. Blaming the loss of McDowell's troops and "treason" in Washington, McClellan brought up the siege trains and determined that he would not attack until the Confederate forces were pulverized by siege guns. Lincoln, exasperated by McClellan's lack of aggressiveness, wrote: "I beg to assure you that I have never written you, or spoken to you, in greater kindness of feeling than now, nor with a fuller purpose to sustain you ... but you must act."[31]

Aided by McClellan's dilatory tactics, Confederate General Joe Johnston had reached Yorktown and assumed command. On May 4, the Confederates abandoned Yorktown. McClellan had spent a useless month preparing for a siege but the Confederates now fell back to Williamsburg. The French volunteer assisting McClellan noted: "The Confederates had vanished and with them all chances of a brilliant victory. We had spent a whole month in constructing gigantic works that were now worthless. The Confederates fell back, satisfied with gaining time to prepare for the defense of Richmond."[32]

George Stoneman led the cavalry advance toward Williamsburg on May 4 to prod and harass retreating Confederates. There was little opposition until he reached the outskirts of the old Virginia capital, 12 miles from Yorktown, Virginia. The Confederates had constructed fortified positions. The stage was set for Stoneman's first major engagement. The York and James rivers form a narrow isthmus where the roads leading from Yorktown to Williamsburg merge. The Confederates had built Fort Magruder and 12 other redoubts, positioned so the rivers guarded the flanks on either side. McClellan's aide, Prince de Joinville, reported that Stoneman, seeing that the enemy occupied the fork of the roads, "undertook to dislodge them by a powerful blow."[33] All horse artillery units were employed and the 6th Federal Cavalry was ordered to charge. De Joinville observed that the Union cavalry met the Confederate cavalry but the enemy had the advantage of position and numbers. Major Lawrence Williams, who led the charge of May 6, saluted Stoneman with his saber and reported that he had lost 31 men. "We will go at it again but it's no use." Stoneman ordered a retreat and fell back to wait for the promised infantry making its way up the road from Yorktown. Heavy rain and the late arrival of infantry support ended the engagement, but the Battle of Williamsburg had begun.

Stoneman's official report of the initial clash with the Confederates on the outskirts of Williamsburg mirrors the confusion surrounding Union cavalry organization during the Peninsula Campaign. Stoneman, commander of the advance guard, Army of the Potomac, consisting of the 8th Illinois, 3rd Pennsylvania and 1st U.S. Cavalry accompanied by horse artillery, was instructed to "pursue and harass the rear of the retreating enemy, and if possible to cut off his rear guard."[34] Two divisions of infantry, commanded by Brigadier Generals Joseph "Fighting Joe" Hooker and William F. Smith, were supposed to follow close behind the cavalry by a forced march.

Stoneman's old commanding officer of the Mormon Battalion, General Philip St. George Cooke, was actually at the head of the cavalry advance when it reached the junction of the Yorktown and Williamsburg road and Lee's Mill Road. Commanding part of the First Cavalry and an element of Gibson's battery, Cooke found a strong Confederate earthwork surrounded by redoubts occupied by a regiment of cavalry, a battery of artillery, and three regiments of infantry.[35] Stoneman ordered up the remainder of the 1st Cavalry and Gibson's battery when he overtook Johnson's rear guard and encountered J.E.B. Stuart's cavalry.

Hooker, in his report, explained the failure of Union infantry to support Stoneman. "I left my command and galloped to the front to see what disposition it would be necessary to make of my force on its arrival," Hooker reported. He learned that Smith's division had moved into the road, preventing his troops from moving forward. Hooker was delayed by a burning bridge until May 5, when he and Smith engaged Confederate troops under Major General James Longstreet. By May 6, Union troops occupied Williamsburg, as Longstreet moved up the Peninusula after sharp fighting.[36]

Stoneman ended his report to McClellan on the engagement with the comment that when the division commanders arrived on the scene "my command was split up into fragments by the commanders, and I remained an idle spectator until the arrival of the general commanding."[37]

The Battle of Williamsburg was essentially a draw, although the Confederates claimed victory, as Johnston was able to proceed up the peninsula. Stoneman's performance received mixed reviews from contemporary accounts of the battle. Major H.B. McClellan, who was on the staff of J.E.B. Stuart and a first cousin of the Union commander, wrote that "a more vigorous pursuit" by Stoneman's troopers might have captured the Confederate rear guard.[38] However, Governor Sprague of Rhode Island, who had observed Stoneman's advance, testified before the Committee on the Conduct of the War that the pursuit of Union cavalry was "all that could be asked — the men moving so rapidly that when Stoneman stopped to write a dispatch, he had to gallop to keep up."[39] Stoneman also sent General William Emory, with the 3rd Pennyslvania and Barker's squadron, supported by a battery of artillery, to cover the road upon which Stuart was operating. Stuart was forced to divert to the James River and march to Williamsburg along the beach.[40]

Although Union cavalry units held their own against J.E.B. Stuart in the first test of the Peninsula Campaign, coordination between Federal cavalry units was poor, as it was between Union cavalry and infantry. Major Lawrence Williams, commander of the 6th U.S. Cavalry, reported he was confused as to who was his immediate commander. "Both Generals Cooke and Stoneman gave me orders."[41] Cooke, who was senior to Stoneman in age and experience, may have resisted subordination to Stoneman, but there is no question that whatever the reason, the Union assault was conducted in a confused and inefficient manner.

Once again, the Confederates failed to engage in a decisive battle. Confederate units under Joe Johnston retreated toward Richmond on May 6, leaving the historic capital of Virginia in Federal hands. McClellan cautiously moved his army up the Chickahominy River. The terrain was swampy and difficult and the Union movement was hampered by almost constant rainfall. Stoneman referred to "constant skirmishing with the enemy, particularly at Slatersville on May 9 and White House on May 13 and 14, at New Bridge May 23 and at Mechanicsville on May 27. From that time until after the Battle of Gaines Mill June 27 [I] was in command of cavalry of A of P" [Army of the Potomac].[42]

Stoneman was involved in a series of engagements as he led the advance guard in the tracks of the retreating Confederates. Weather and terrain severely hampered movements of troops and horses as rain made roads nearly impassable and trails had to be cut through woods. On May 9, the Confederates opposed Stoneman at Slatersville, but were silenced by horse artillery.

McClellan's army now moved along the south side of the Pamunkey River, led by gunboats. Stoneman's cavalry was assigned to escort topographical officers, who made maps of the area. Rain continued to impede all operations, combined with hot weather that produced fever and associated medical problems. Despite these difficulties, Stoneman reached White House Plantation on May 15, the home of Colonel W.H.F. "Rooney" Lee, Robert E. Lee's son. The plantation formed part of the Custis estate, and Mrs. Robert E. Lee was still there. A guard was placed around the property at her request. McClellan respected the history of the White House, as it had been the residence of Martha Custis when she married George Washington at nearby St. Peter's church. However, the circumstances of war prevailed as McClellan established his headquarters and a huge new supply base at the plantation landing.[43] It was here that McClellan also reorganized his command. He retained his three senior corps commanders, but reduced their commands by two divisions each. Two new army corps were created under Generals Fitz-John Porter and William B. Franklin.

McClellan now placed his cavalry in action. Stoneman was ordered to operate against the railroads. On May 23, he reached Brandy Run on the Chickahominy River about a mile from New Bridge. Confederate cavalry positioned on the bank of the river opened fire on the Union cavalry, and in the ensuing skirmish, the Confederates were beaten back from the Chickahominy.

Stoneman made use of one of the more adventurous assets in the Union arsenal in the Peninsula, the observation balloons of Professor Thaddeus Lowe, the "aeronaut of the Army of the Potomac."[44] The balloon had been used at Yorktown in the beginning of the campaign, when General Fitz-John Porter was almost dumped behind Confederate lines when the balloon went adrift. McClellan was appalled at this near catastrophe and wrote his wife on April 1: "You may rest assured of one thing: you won't catch me in the confounded balloon nor will I allow any other Generals to go up in it."[45] Professor Lowe observed afterwards that he "found it difficult for a time to restore confidence among the officers as to the safety of this means of observation on account of this accident."[46] Undaunted, Stoneman went up at Gaines Mill on May 21 to an altitude of 500 feet, which afforded a beautiful view of Richmond. With the aid of an eyeglass, he spotted Confederate troops on the road to Bottoms Bridge.[47]

On May 25, Stoneman and Lowe ascended to 1000 feet where they spotted Confederates near New Bridge, concealed in order to watch Union movements. Commanding from the balloon, Stoneman directed the fire of two batteries, causing the Confederates to retreat for a mile and a half. Lowe remained in the balloon after descending, and Stoneman went to Mechanicsville and drove the enemy from their position. Lowe remarked that Stoneman "is too keen an observer and too able an officer to be insensitive of the advantages of so superior and accurate means of observation as that afforded by the balloon."[48]

The Army of the Potomac began to move across the Chickahominy, where it faced Joe Johnston and his army of 53,688 men. The Confederates wanted to prevent McDowell's Union corps at Fredericksburg from joining McClellan in the Peninsula. The left wing of the army crossed the Chickahominy at Bottoms Bridge, a movement which was unopposed by the Confederates, despite the presence of the troops spotted by Stoneman. McClellan sent his right wing northward as far as Mechanicsville, where his troops forced the Confederates across the Chickahominy at the Mechanicsville Bridge. If McDowell, who was still kept in reserve by Lincoln to protect the capital, could join McClellan, the Army of the Potomac would number 140,000 men.[49]

Thomas "Stonewall" Jackson, a West Point classmate of both McClellan and Stoneman, moved to prevent this juncture of Union forces. Jackson's brilliant Shenandoah Valley campaign drove Union General Nathaniel P. Banks from Front Royal and Strasburg down the valley and defeated him at Winchester. Banks's demoralized troops did not stop until they crossed the Potomac at Williamsport. Jackson's offensive had the desired effect. Lincoln telegraphed McClellan on May 14 and informed him that McDowell would not be sent to the Peninsula because of this new threat to Washington. McDowell was ordered to the Valley by forced march and General John C. Fremont proceeded to Harrisonburg as Lincoln set a trap to snare Jackson. If the two Union armies could move fast enough, Jackson could be trapped at the upper end of the valley like a cork in a bottle and prevented from joining Confederate forces on the Peninsula. Jackson, however, escaped following his twin victories at Port Republic and Cross Keys. A combination of bad luck, poor weather, and less than skillful Union leadership failed to spring the trap.

McClellan's army was now in two wings astride the Chickahominy River, and the Confederates moved to take advantage of this division of Union forces. On May 31, Joe Johnston struck the corps of Keyes and Heintzelman, who composed the Union left flank, in an attempt to destroy McClellan's forces on the left bank of the Chickahominy. The Battle of Fair Oaks, or Seven Pines, was poorly fought by inexperienced commanders and was expensive for the Confederates, who lost 6,100 men, 1000 more casualties than the

Union army suffered. In the end, little was changed. Perhaps the most significant outcome of the battle was that it led to the appointment of Robert E. Lee as Commander of the Army of Northern Virginia to replace the wounded Joe Johnston.

Lee turned to J.E.B. Stuart for information and directed him to take four regiments of cavalry, which included Fitz Lee's 1st Virginia and Rooney Lee's 9th Virginia, reinforced by the 4th Virginia and two squadrons from the Jeff Davis Legion.[50] Beginning near Richmond, he turned toward Hanover Court House where they met the first Union cavalry encountered on the raid, but the 150 Federals were no match for a reinforced regiment and they quickly departed. Continuing on their circular route that would eventually take them around the entire Union army, Stuart's horsemen ran into 100 Union cavalrymen about a mile from Totopotomoy Creek. After a Confederate cavalry charge, the Union force was scattered. Later, Stuart reached the village of Old Church, where the 5th United States cavalry was encamped. Quickly overcoming the Federals, Stuart's men carried off all the supplies that they could and burned the rest, an exercise enjoyed by Fitz Lee, who had served with the regiment when it was the old 2nd Cavalry before the war.[51]

At this point, Stuart knew that the Union right flank was lightly defended and he now had to get the information to Lee. The raiders continued to Tunstall Station, overwhelmed the small Federal infantry garrison guarding the village, and, on the third day of the raid, crossed the swollen Chickahominy River and crossed to safety while a Federal patrol fired a few parting shots. Stuart and his command were soon in Richmond.[52]

The raid confirmed what Lee had suspected and provided little that was new, but its primary effect was the humiliation of Union cavalry and its officers, particularly Stuart's father-in-law, Philip St. George Cooke. Cooke did not know that Stuart was unsupported by infantry until late on June 13 when Stuart was deep in Federal territory. It took Cooke seven hours after Stuart attacked the 5th Cavalry at Old Church to send elements of the 5th and 6th Cavalry in pursuit. He later wasted more time around Tunstall Station, until he learned that Stuart had safely crossed the Chickahominy.

While Cooke was ineffectually trying to deal with Stuart's marauding cavalry, Stoneman was assigned to protect the vital Union supply depot at White

Stoneman near the Fair Oaks battlefield during the Peninsula Campaign, June 1862 (U.S. Army Military History Institute).

House landing. Fortunately for Stoneman, Stuart decided that it was too risky to attack a facility guarded by infantry as well as cavalry. Stoneman was suffering from the cavalryman's affliction of a severe case of hemorrhoids, a condition that grew steadily worse as the campaign continued. Stoneman's suffering was noted by his subordinate, Colonel William W. Averell, who wrote after the war that Stoneman had infirmities "that would have kept a man of lesser fortitude in the hospital."[53]

Despite his extreme discomfort, Stoneman continued with his duties, although his was a peripheral role in the next stage of the Peninsula Campaign, the Battle of Gaines Mill. Confederate Brigadier General John Magruder, known as "Prince John" because of his theatrical talents, was ordered by Lee to demonstrate against Union forces south of the Chickahominy River, a repeat of his Yorktown performance. The diversion was equally effective. McClellan reported that he had repulsed several attacks and that he was outnumbered everywhere. Fitz-John Porter was in command of the Union troops north of the Chickahominy, and it was here on June 27 that Lee struck after a heavy bombardment. McClellan was a passive observer of the battle, waited for events to control his actions, and never personally visited his battle lines.[54] McClellan finally responded to Porter's request for reinforcements by sending Slocum's division, although his forces were committed piecemeal to close holes in the Federal lines.[55] During the critical hours of the fighting, McClellan kept 60,000 men on the left bank of the Chickahominy facing Richmond, thanks to Magruder's theatrics.

Although cavalry did not play a major role at Gaines Mill, Stoneman's cavalrymen did make a significant contribution to the Union cause. Stoneman's troopers informed McClellan two days before the battle that Jackson, with a force of 18,500 men, was at Frederick's Hall and was on his way to participate in the Confederate assault. This was useful information as it informed McClellan of the danger faced by his right flank. He sent Porter to Beaver Dam, a creek Southeast of Mechanicsville, where a strong position was established. Lee planned to send the divisions of Longstreet and A.P. Hill against the Union position there while Jackson, who was making his way down from the north, would outflank Porter and force him to evacuate his main position on the east bank of the creek. Major General D.H. Hill's troops would also cross Beaver Dam creek in support of Jackson. Stoneman's troopers scouted Jackson's movements, occasionally running into Stuart's cavalry, who were operating on Jackson's left. A.P. Hill impetuously opened the Confederate attack without waiting for Jackson, who was delayed by fatigue, bad roads and skirmishes with Union cavalry. While an impatient Lee waited for Jackson, wave after wave of Confederate infantry attacked the entrenched Union position only to be thrown back with heavy casualties.[56]

While Stoneman commanded the cavalry assigned to the Union right flank, the left flank of Porter's line was supported by General Cooke. He commanded five companies of the Fifth United States, four under-strength companies of the First United States, and six companies of the 6th Pennsylvania.[57] Confederate attacks had been beaten off all day, but at sunset, General John B. Hood's Texans broke the Union line. Seeing the Federal line waver, Cooke, who was protecting Union artillery on a ridge above the Confederate assault, ordered Captain Charles J. Whiting, who commanded the 5th United States, to charge the advancing Confederate infantry. It was a suicidal assault. Whiting lost 150 killed, wounded or captured out of his force of 250 men. Only one officer of the seven in command was unhurt. This action was the subject of an acrimonious debate between Fitz-John Porter and Cooke that continued long after the war.[58]

McClellan, who had not visited a single corps of his army that had been engaged at the Battle of Gaines Mill, now accepted defeat. Fitz-John Porter's command now carried out a well-conducted retreat and joined the main army on the Richmond side of the river. McClellan moved his headquarters several miles east on the Chickahominy to Savage Station, where he held a council of war with his commanders. Any hope of taking Richmond was now lost. McClellan was determined to absolve himself of the defeat as he sent his famous telegram to Secretary of War Stanton: "If we have lost the day we have yet preserved our honor.... I have lost the battle because my force was too small. I again repeat that I am not responsible for this...."[59] McClellan concluded with what amounted to a charge of criminal conspiracy: "If I save this army now, I tell you plainly that I owe no thanks to you or any other persons in Washington. You have done your best to sacrifice this army."[60] The message was received on the morning of June 28. The military supervisor of telegrams, Edward S. Sanford, found the last sentence so scandalous that he ordered it deleted.[61]

Cavalry was now relegated to scouting and reporting on Confederate movements and escorting retreating Union columns and trains. Approximately 2,500 wounded men in a federal field hospital were left to the Confederates. Stores were burned and trains of heavy equipment were organized. Stoneman, still operating on the army's far right flank with 2,000 cavalry, including the 17th New York and the 18th Massachusetts, and two regiments of infantry, was at Tunstall Station on the York River, cut off from Porter's Corps.[62] The Confederates were advancing with a large force from Dispatch Station. Stoneman ordered his troops to White House landing where they embarked by steamer to Harrison's Landing, after burning all that could not be taken.[63] The final act was the burning of the ancestral home of Colonel W.H.F. Lee. General Casey, the infantry commander, said this act of vengeance was done without his knowledge.[64] Stoneman's role, if any, in this destruction, was not revealed in the Official Records.

The battles of the Seven Days, Mechanicsville, Gaines Mill, Savage Station, Frayser's Farm, and Malvern Hill ended with the Army of the Potomac entrenched at Harrison's Landing on the James River. The performance of the cavalry, hampered by McClellan's organization dividing his mounted arm among the army corps, was characterized by ineffectual leadership and poor execution of an unclear role. An exasperated Stoneman complained to McClellan at the end of the campaign:

> Commanding officers of scouting parties and brigade commanders complain that men of their commands are taken away by generals to act as orderlies, etc. I have the honor to request that the general commanding give orders that this be stopped in future.[65]

Stoneman was placed on sick leave when the cavalry reached Harrison's Landing, the end of a frustrating campaign. He had at times commanded groups of cavalrymen, but at other times he was ordered to perform administrative duties. His performance was mixed, but he had gained experience in leading large numbers of men in unfamiliar territory, often in severe pain. Stoneman, and more particularly Cooke, had been less than brilliant, but, as Thomas F. Thiele pointed out in his study of cavalry in the Civil War, "Much of the fault found with the Federal Cavalry on the Peninsula should have been found with the organization and limitations McClellan imposed upon it."[66]

Under the protection of Federal gunboats, the Army of the Potomac waited to be evacuated. On August 3, McClellan was ordered to withdraw his army from the Peninsula to Fort Monroe and Aquia Creek to join General John Pope in the defense of Washington.

Stuart Redux

George Stoneman emerged from the Peninsula campaign with a determination to develop and improve the efficiency of Union cavalry, following the humiliation imposed by J.E.B. Stuart. Stoneman was then 41, and the *New York Herald Tribune* described him as follows: "The lithe, severe, gristly, sanguine person whose eyes flashed even in repose."[1] Stoneman was a cautious man, often slow to react, a quality that frustrated his superiors, but was admired by men who served under him. Charles Frances Adams, Jr., of the Massachusetts Cavalry, described Stoneman in a letter to his mother later in the war: "Stoneman we believe in. We believe in his judgment, his courage and determination. We know that he is ready to shoulder responsibility; that he will take good care of us and won't get us into places he can't get us out [of]...."[2]

As Stoneman recuperated from the Peninsula campaign, he courted Mary Oliver Hardisty, a vivacious belle from a prominent Baltimore family. She was a marked contrast to the reserved Stoneman and about half his age. The two were married at the First Presbyterian Church in Baltimore on November 22, 1861, a wedding that was described in newspaper accounts as a brilliant affair.[3]

The groom and groomsmen wore full military uniforms and the bride was dressed "in a full moiré robe with flowing veil, and a wreath of orange blossoms in her hair...." After a short reception at the home of Henry Hardisty, the bride's father, the couple traveled to Washington, where Stoneman resumed his military duties.[4]

The marriage was noted by Washington society, but not always favorably. Elizabeth Blair Lee, who was married to a Union naval officer, Samuel Philips Lee, wrote him every day. In one letter, she referred to Mary Hardisty Stoneman as "a hot Balt. Secsh" or Southern sympathizer.[5]

Stoneman had no time to be concerned with Washington gossip about his new wife. As the Army of the Potomac regrouped after the frustrating and exhausting Peninsula campaign, Stoneman and the Union cavalry were once again about to cross swords with Stuart. Once again, the Federals permitted Stuart to elude capture and gain greater glory at the expense of Union cavalry and infantry.

Stoneman was placed in command of the First Division, III Army Corps on September 10, 1862. Stoneman had missed the battle of Second Bull Run on August 29 when Lee and Jackson defeated their two Federal opponents, Pope and McClellan, and the bloody fighting at Antietam on September 17, brought about by Lee's first invasion of the North. Anxious to return to the struggle, Stoneman established his headquarters at Poolesville, Maryland, and waited for orders while General McClellan decided the next move of the Army of the Potomac.

The two opposing armies seemed to draw back and rest after the climactic struggle at Antietam. General Lee decided he needed more information. He instructed Stuart to mount an expedition into Maryland and Pennsylvania to "gain all information of the position, force, and probable intention of the enemy which you can...."[6] Lee's instructions to Stuart outlined additional objectives of the raid. He was ordered to cross the Potomac above Williamsport, proceed to Chambersburg, Pennsylvania, and destroy the railroad bridge over the Conococheague River. He was to bring as many state and federal officials "as convenient" to be used as hostages and exchanged for Confederate citizens held by federal authorities, and to capture as many horses as possible."[7]

Stuart led a force of 1,800 men, carefully selected from the brigades of Hampton, Fitz Lee and Robertson, across the Potomac on October 9 at McCoy's Ferry near Williamsport and headed north on the turnpike toward Hancock, Maryland. Stuart then marched into Pennsylvania and arrived at Chambersburg late in the evening during a drizzling rain.

Although Confederate officers did invite themselves into private homes for a meal or two during "the day of Rebel Rule in Chambersburg,"[8] they treated their unwilling hosts with the utmost courtesy.

Stuart had on his staff one Captain B.S. White, a former resident of Poolesville, Maryland, who acted as Stuart's principal guide for the hazardous return to Virginia and safety. Stuart resolved to try to recross the Potomac at White's Ferry, considerably below the point where Stuart reasoned Stoneman and his fellow Federals would expect him to return to Virginia. Stuart marched from Chambersburg to Cashtown, where he turned south on the road to Emmittsburg, Maryland. His route now took him through the towns of Woodsborough, Liberty, New London, New Market, Hyattstown, and Barnsville, riding at night on little-used roads.[9]

Stuart's movements had not been unobserved by the Federals. The 12th Illinois Cavalry, stationed close to McCoy's Ferry, had been informed by a citizen that a large group of Confederate cavalry had crossed into Maryland en route to Pennsylvania. Federal outposts at Williamsport and Hagerstown had spread the alarm, but there was little Federal cavalry in the area to oppose them.

It was up to Stoneman and his combined force of cavalry and infantry to trap the Confederates and prevent their crossing the Potomac to safety. Unfortunately for the success of the Federal cause, he failed to do so, and a dubious chapter was added to his record. Stoneman had been advised on October 11 that rebel cavalry, reported to be 2,000 strong, had crossed into Maryland and Pennsylvania and had occupied Chambersburg. McClellan's headquarters advised him that "they may attempt to recross the river opposite Leesburg. The command general directs that you keep your cavalry well out on the approaches

Stoneman and staff. Location and date unknown. Stoneman (seated, right) is handing a dispatch to a courier (from the collection of Andrew J. Potts).

in the direction of Frederick so as to give you time to mass your troops at any point where they attempt to cross."[10]

Stoneman was faced with a formidable problem. He knew Stuart was headed south toward the Potomac and would eventually try to cross into Virginia, but he did not know where. Stoneman had some 30 miles of riverbank from Leesburg to Point of Rocks to cover with about 2,800 men, which he referred to as a "small force." Stoneman acted immediately to comply with his orders. He positioned 600 men at the mouth of the Monocacy to watch the Potomac in the direction of Point of Rocks.[11] Seven hundred men were placed at White's Ford, the 39th Massachusetts was sent to Edward's Ferry, and the 10th Vermont was ordered to guard supplies at the mouth of Seneca Creek. Stoneman kept 250 men at Poolesville, "with a view of moving to any point on the circumference of which Poolesville is the center."[12]

Stuart was aware of Stoneman's force at Poolesville and was determined to avoid it. He boldly marched through the woods towards Poolesville, actually coming as close as two or three miles from Stoneman's headquarters. He then turned off on a road that headed for the mouth of the Monocacy. Here Brigadier General Alfred Pleasonton and about 400 men finally intercepted Stuart with a small force, as the remainder of his command was strung out along the route used in the pursuit of the Confederates. The lead column of

Stuart's men was dressed in captured Federal uniforms so there was some delay in recognition. Taking advantage of this uncertainty, Stuart ordered a charge that forced the outnumbered Federals to hastily retreat, after they fired a volley from their carbines that had little effect. The engagement was important for Stuart, as he occupied a road which had a high bluff that effectively screened his movement towards White's Ford.[13]

All seemed well for the Confederates, but there remained the question of whether White's Ford was defended or not. To their dismay, Stuart's men found Federal infantry occupying a strong position along the Chesapeake and Ohio Canal which ran close to the river at White's Ford. The infantry was entrenched along a high bluff,

Major General Alfred A. Pleasonton, with whom Stoneman was not friendly. Pleasonton would be left behind during the Stoneman Raid at Chancellorsville, but commanded a brigade that remained with General Hooker's Army of the Potomac. His men fought well at Hazel Grove against General "Stonewall" Jackson's infantry (U.S. Army Military History Institute).

well positioned to oppose a crossing of the Potomac by the Confederates. The head of the Confederate column was commanded by Colonel "Rooney" Lee, who realized it would be difficult to dislodge the Federals from their strong position, so he tried a ruse. He sent a note to the Federal commander, Lieutenant Colonel Edwin Biles of the 99th Pennsylvania Infantry, informing him that Stuart and his entire command was approaching the ford and that resistance would be foolhardy. Lee called upon the Federals to surrender or they would be attacked in 15 minutes. The minutes ticked by and then, to the astonishment of the Confederates, the Federals abandoned their position, marching away with flags flying and drums beating.[14] Although Pleasonton harassed their rear guard, the Confederates crossed the river into Virginia, taking 1,200 captured horses and 30 U.S. officials and prominent citizens, who were sent to Richmond as hostages.[15]

It was another Union disaster, and the recriminations began immediately. Stuart had marched from Chambersburg, a distance of 80 miles, despite being encumbered by artillery, hostages, and captured horses, destroying Federal property along the way, and crossed the Potomac under the eyes of Union infantry, without losing a man!

Pleasonton, whose performance has not been faulted by historians as he located Stuart's men and pursued them as he could, wrote in his report that "had White's Ford been occupied by any force of ours, previous to the time of occupation of the enemy, the capture of Stuart's whole force would have been certain and inevitable."[16] Stoneman found this statement "simply ridiculous, as the enemy could have crossed at almost any other point as well as there."¹⁷ As the allegations flew, Stoneman must have felt threatened, as he asked that a court of inquiry be instituted "to inquire into all the circumstances connected with Stuart's escape from Pennsylvania and that the blame, if blame there is, be affixed to the proper persons."¹⁸

Stoneman's defense was that his force was small and his orders to assemble his troops at any point where Stuart would attempt to cross was unreasonable, since he had 30 miles to cover. However, he was advised that White's Ford was a likely spot for Stuart to use, and it is difficult to explain why only 100 men, or at the most 200, were there when Stuart arrived. Biles felt that he could have held his position had he been reinforced. Even briefly delaying Stuart would have permitted reinforcements to move into position. It appears that Stoneman did not expeditiously move the infantry and cavalry he had available to White's Ford, when it became clear that Stuart was headed in that direction.

McClellan stated in his report that Stoneman said he started his reserve from Poolesville at about 9:00 A.M., but Pleasonton reported they did not meet him until 1:30 P.M. The distance from Poolesville is about six miles. It was never explained why Pleasonton or Stoneman, who apparently remained in Poolesville, didn't interfere with Stuart's withdrawal.

McClellan's initial reaction was to put the blame at the feet of George Stoneman. McClellan's chief of staff cabled Pleasonton on October 12 that "General Stoneman has been directed to furnish an immediate report as to the manner in which he carried out his instructions."¹⁹ The next day, Stoneman was ordered to report to General McClellan, who cabled General Halleck on October 12 that Stoneman had not complied with his orders:

> As you will see from the dispatch of Genl. Pleasonton just received ... it does not appear that [Stoneman] complied with this order. He will be called upon for an explanation of this matter. It would seem that Pleasonton's forces although within a short distance of Poolesville, received but little assistance from Stoneman.²⁰

Pleasonton sent his message on October 12, just after his advance guard had met Stuart's men, some of them dressed in captured Union uniforms, near the mouth of the Monocacy. Pleasonton reported that he held the enemy in check for two hours but, due to his lack of infantry support from Stoneman, the rebels escaped. The Confederate McClellan wrote, "The Federal squadron stood only long enough to fire one volley, and then turned and ran back to the main body."²¹ Pleasonton also claimed that he drove Stuart to White's Ford which was bravado, as White's Ford, had been Stuart's intended crossing point all along.

Stuart crossed the Potomac as his men played "Old Joe, get out of the wilderness." Once he was back at headquarters, Stonewall Jackson met him and said that he had heard that "from the time you crossed the Potomac into Maryland until you got back again you didn't sing a song or crack a joke but that as soon as you got back on Virginia soil you began to whistle 'Home, Sweet Home.'"²² Those who rode with Stuart said that he was the only one who was not at times demoralized. When it looked like they might be cut off at the ford, Stuart rode along the line whistling an opera air.²³

McClellan characteristically blamed Stuart's escape on factors beyond his control. He informed Halleck that no more than half of his cavalry's forces were fit for service in the field, many of them used up in the fruitless pursuit of Stuart. "The recent raid of Stuart, who, in spite of all the precautions I could take with the means at my disposal, went entirely around this army, has shown conclusively how greatly the service suffers from our deficiency in the cavalry arm."[24] Halleck replied that the president had read his message and suggested that "if the enemy had more occupation south of the river, his cavalry would not be so likely to make raids north of it."[25]

Although McClellan had now been humiliated twice by Stuart but, in some ways, as Starr points out, Union cavalry had performed creditably during Stuart's raid. Reports on Stuart's strength and movement were accurate and timely, and it could be said that his escape from the trap set for him was just bad luck.[26] Had Stoneman placed most of his forces at White's Ford and Stuart had crossed at the mouth of the Monocacy, he would have been blamed for poor judgment. Stoneman was able to convince McClellan that his decisions had been reasonable, since there was no court of inquiry as Stoneman had requested, and in McClellan's final report, he wrote that the "disposition he made of his troops previous to the arrival of Stuart was a good one."[27] Nonetheless, the incident tarnished the reputations of the Union commanders. Starr offered the view that the reduction of Pleasonton's command from a division to a brigade may have been the result of Stuart's raid.[28]

While the Confederates celebrated, the Federals wrote their reports covering themselves and justifying their role in the Stuart affair. McClellan still had not corrected the basic organizational weakness that hampered his cavalry. Cavalry regiments were scattered throughout the infantry and brigades were assigned administrative duties. Lincoln's dissatisfaction with McClellan in the wake of Stuart's raid was illustrated by a remark he made to a group of associates onboard the *Martha Washington*, returning from a review near Alexandria. Asked about McClellan, Lincoln said: "When I was a boy we used to play a game, three times round and out. Stuart has been around him twice; if he goes around him once more, gentlemen, McClellan will be out."[29] It turned out that twice was enough. On October 28, Lincoln decided that McClellan was the main problem facing the Army of the Potomac, and Ambrose Burnside was appointed Commander-in-Chief. Stoneman's division was assigned to Burnside for special service, and Stoneman was about to be tested once again, in the crucible of Fredericksburg.

Seven

Fredericksburg

While McClellan blamed the success of Stuart's raid on the deficiencies of his cavalry arm, Lincoln chaffed at the continued delay of the Army of the Potomac to come to grips with Robert E. Lee. An exasperated Lincoln wrote McClellan on October 13, 1862, imploring him to attack the enemy's communications with Richmond. "Again, one of the standard maxims of war, as you know, is 'to operate upon the enemy's communications as much as possible without exposing your own.' You seem to act as if this applies *against* you, but can not apply in your *favor*."[1] Pointing out to McClellan that he was closer to Richmond than Lee, Lincoln urged McClellan to beat the enemy to Richmond and to fight him if he made a stand. Lincoln suggested that he move by the cords or inside arcs, positioned as he was just east of the Blue Ridge mountains and the Shenandoah River, while the Confederates were west of his position and thus further from Richmond. Time, the president warned, could not be ignored.[2]

McClellan finally moved in late October and the Army of the Potomac crossed the river at Berlin (now Brunswick), Maryland, entered Virginia and marched to Warrenton. Stoneman, now commanding between 9,000 and 10,000 men, crossed the Potomac at Edwards Ferry near Leesburg, where he established his base. Cavalry pickets were ordered to march to Aldie, Waterford, Purcellville, and as far west as Snicker's Gap, near present-day Bluemont, in Loudoun County.[3] On October 29, Stoneman's division was assigned to Burnside, who was commanding the left wing of the Army of the Potomac, for special service. Burnside appears to have been confused as to exactly what Stoneman's mission was to be but, in any case, Stoneman remained in Leesburg, where he kept his headquarters and searched for the enemy. Several clashes between Stoneman's pickets and Confederate cavalry followed at Mountsville and Aldie, and Stoneman moved to Rectortown by way of Upperville on November 4, primarily to guard the Orange and Alexandria railroad between Piedmont and Salem.[4] War had come to the beautiful and prosperous Loudoun Valley as Stoneman's cavalry foraged for supplies for both men and horses.

While Stoneman's cavalry defended the railway and looked for the Confederates, the main body of the Army of the Potomac took 11 days to cover 35 miles, marching toward

Culpeper Court House. It was clear that McClellan was ignoring Lincoln's advice to hug the Blue Ridge and move his army so that the Federals would be between the Confederates and Washington, as well as Richmond. Moving twice as fast as the Federals, Lee ordered Longstreet to Culpeper, and he arrived there well ahead of McClellan. The Confederates had crossed McClellan's line of advance.[5]

Finally, Lincoln's patience was exhausted. Brigadier General Catharinus P. Buckingham was dispatched by the War Department to ride through a snowstorm to McClellan's headquarters at Warrenton, with orders relieving McClellan of his command. Major General Ambrose E. Burnside was appointed to lead the Army of the Potomac. The change in command boosted Stoneman to Major General, U.S. Volunteers, on November 29, 1862, as he had served in command of the III Corps since the previous October. Morale of the corps had suffered after the death of one of its division commanders, Major General Philip Kearny, who was killed at Chantilly, Virginia, on September 1 after performing brilliantly at Second Bull Run, when he rode accidentally into Confederate lines. Called upon to surrender, he turned and tried to escape but was killed by a volley from the 55th Virginia of A.P. Hill's "Light Division." Kearny and Hill knew each other well, and when Hill saw his friend's body he exclaimed: "Poor Kearny! He deserved a better death than that."[6]

On Sunday, November 9, McClellan received his officers and staff at his tent to bid them farewell. McClellan greeted each officer and served champagne for a toast to the Army of the Potomac.[7] It must have been a difficult moment for George Stoneman, as he parted with his West Point classmate. McClellan had brought him to West Virginia for his successful campaign in 1861, sent him to the Peninsula in command of cavalry, and given him a division to command. Stoneman may have reflected that had he stopped Stuart after his Maryland and Pennsylvania raid, McClellan might not have been in such bad standing with Lincoln.

Burnside moved quickly to carry out Lincoln's directive to take the war to the enemy and threaten Richmond. He decided to take the shortest route and move toward Fredericksburg en route to Richmond. Logistics were a factor. The roads in Virginia were a quagmire due to heavy rains, and supplies were moved by train. An alternative was to transport supplies by the Potomac River from Washington to Fredericksburg, a secure route. There was a short railroad line from Aquia Creek, where supplies could be unloaded, and Fredericksburg. Moreover, the selection of Fredericksburg made sense because the Union army would be between the Confederates and Washington.[8]

The placement of pontoons across the Rappahannock was central to Burnside's plan, as the river was not fordable south of Fredericksburg. A rapid movement across the river from Falmouth was essential, as Lee would certainly react quickly once he perceived the Union objective. To confuse the Confederates, Burnside's cavalry was ordered to feint towards Culpeper to force the Confederates to defend that line while the main army moved towards Fredericksburg. Burnside ordered pontoon bridges to be sent to Falmouth on November 9, and shortly afterwards, the army began the march, Stoneman and his III Corps among them.

There were supply problems. Burnside had suggested to headquarters in Washington that 30 canal boats and barges be loaded with commissary stores and forage, enough supplies to last the army for 30 days. The vital pontoons were to arrive at Falmouth simultaneously with the arrival of the army. When Burnside ordered them, the pontoons were at Berlin, Maryland, where the army had crossed into Virginia at the beginning of the campaign. Incredibly, the order to move them was sent by mail instead of by telegraph. Subsequent delays and difficulties in shipping meant that the pontoons did not arrive at army headquarters at the Lacey House opposite Fredericksburg until November 27. Even after their arrival there were further delays and by December 1, the two Confederate Corps of Longstreet and Jackson were in position along the heights above Fredericksburg.[9]

Major General Edwin Sumner's Grand Division of the Union army had reached Fredericksburg as early as November 17, and Burnside arrived with the balance of the army on November 19. Sumner's march was carried out with unaccustomed speed, for he covered 40 miles in two and a half days, an unheard-of pace for the Army of the Potomac. For once, Lee was caught unprepared, as he did not know the whereabouts of the Union army due to an effective screen by Union cavalry.[10] Although Sumner did not have pontoons available when he arrived at Falmouth, he saw livestock walking across the river. He requested permission to move a portion of his troops across the Rappahannock and dislodge the small Confederate force defending the town and then occupy the high ground. Brigadier General George Bayard, who commanded a brigade of cavalry, advised Burnside on November 16 that the river was "fordable all along towards Falmouth."[11] Major General Joseph Hooker, commander of the Center Grand Division, made a similar request. Despite Bayard's report, Burnside elected not to send part of his army across the river until he could cross with the main body.[12] Although this decision has been criticized, it was not without a rationale. It rained heavily shortly after Burnside decided to delay and the river was soon unfordable. A smaller force could have been trapped on the south side of the river, vulnerable to an attack by Lee's army.

Burnside called a council of war shortly after his arrival on the Rappahannock. The commanders of the grand divisions, Sumner, Franklin, and Hooker, were present, as well as Stoneman and his fellow corps commanders. Major General William F. "Baldy" Smith, commander of the VI Army Corps, later wrote that Burnside announced he had called the council to inform them of his plans, not to put his decisions in front of them for approval.[13] Burnside advised his commanders, all of them professional soldiers long known to him, that he had chosen a place called Skinker's Neck as the point of crossing and that he would offer battle to General Lee. A heated discussion followed. Hooker said that it was preposterous to cross the river in the face of Lee's army. Others did their best to dissuade Burnside from his plan of attack, but he was adamant. He said that he had heard their criticisms and complaints. He reminded them that he had reluctantly assumed the responsibility of command and that he was aware of what he lacked, "but still I have been placed where I am and will do my best. I rely on God for wisdom and strength. Your duty is not to throw cold water but to aid me loyally with your advice and hearty service."[14]

Three or four days after the conference, Burnside invited Smith to take a ride with him. As the two rode near the river opposite the town of Fredericksburg, Burnside told Smith that he had changed his mind. The crossing would take place far closer to Fredericksburg than Skinker's Neck, under cover of Federal artillery. Smith told Burnside that he could cross without great difficulty, "but when your army is across your troubles will begin" and he called Burnside's attention to a range of hills a mile or so from the river. "Oh," Burnside said, "I know where Lee's forces are and I expect to surprise him."[15] He informed Smith that he intended to occupy the hills before Lee could bring anything serious against the Union forces.

Burnside now moved to carry out his plan. He decided that the enemy would be surprised by a crossing at or near Fredericksburg where no obvious preparations were being made, rather than by crossing at Skinker's Neck. He ordered the placement of four or five pontoon bridges across the river, "two at a point near the Lacy House [Chatham] opposite the upper part of the town, one near the steamboat landing at the lower part of town, one about a mile below, and, if there were pontoons sufficient, two at the latter point."[16] The Right Grand Division under Sumner was directed to form near the upper and middle bridges opposite the town, the Center Grand Division under Hooker near and to the rear of General Sumner, and General Franklin's Left Grand Division was ordered to form near the lower bridges below the town.

The engineers began to throw the bridges across the river on the night of December 10. The lower bridges, constructed for General Franklin's command, were completed about 10:30 A.M. with little difficulty. The laying of the upper bridges near the Lacy House was a different story. Confederate General William Barkdale's Mississippians kept up a steady fire from houses near the river and a dense fog prohibited Union artillery from driving the Confederates from their position. Confederate rifle fire stopped construction of the bridges when it was about three-fourths completed. The fog burned off around noon, and Union artillery and infantry finally drove the Mississippians out of the heavily damaged homes. By nightfall, a division and a brigade of Sumner's troops had crossed the river. Franklin's troops had also begun to cross to the south bank farther downstream.

George Stoneman's III Corps was originally scheduled to cross with Sumner's grand division in front of Stafford Heights. Whipple's division, which was part of Stoneman's corps, was to cross the river in support of Sumner, but the town was packed with Sumner's troops and Whipple was ordered to bivouac near one of the three bridges opposite the town. Stoneman now received orders to move with his other two divisions (Birney's and Sickles's) down the river about three and a half miles. Stoneman was also ordered to report to General Franklin and support him as he moved against Lee's right flank.

Burnside planned to fight a holding action against the Confederates occupying the heights west of Fredericksburg while Franklin smashed the Confederate right. Franklin and his two corps commanders, Generals John F. Reynolds and "Baldy" Smith, met on December 12 to form a battle plan. The three had a close relationship, both socially and professionally, and they quickly agreed on what the strategy should be. The 40,000 men of the Left Grand Division should assault the left and right of the old Richmond stage road, which ran north and south a short distance west of the river, assault the ridge behind it and turn Lee's right flank at any cost. About 5:00 P.M., General Burnside arrived to confer with Franklin and his staff and Franklin outlined his plan of attack. He also urged Burnside to order Stoneman's III Corps to cross the bridge and relieve the VI Corps that would then participate in the assault. All the officers present were of the impression that Burnside concurred with Franklin's plan and, after Burnside departed, they expected orders to begin the assault at any moment.[17]

After a long night of waiting, orders finally came on the morning of December 13. Franklin was ordered to "keep your whole command in position for a rapid movement down the old Richmond road ... and you will send out at once a division ... to seize if possible the heights near Captain Hamilton's on this side of the Massaponax, taking care to keep it well supported and its line of retreat open."[18] Another column of General Sumner's division would be ordered up the plank road to seize the heights behind the Confederates. This, it was hoped, would force them to evacuate the entire ridge between the two Union forces. Historians have pointed out that Burnside's orders were not calculated to inspire confidence, as Franklin was advised to "seize if possible" and was admonished to "keep the line of retreat open." The major omission in Burnside's orders, however, concerned Stoneman's III Corps. The VI corps was given the vital task of guarding the bridges across the Rappahannock and keeping the line of retreat open, if necessary. Franklin assumed he would use Stoneman's troops to relieve the VI Corps so that they could participate in the attack, but no authority was forthcoming from Burnside.[19] "Baldy" Smith later surmised that Burnside went to bed after his meeting with Franklin and his staff on the night of December 12 and did not issue his orders until after 5:55 A.M. It was never explained why he failed to use Stoneman's men to relieve the 25,000 men of the VI Corps, thus depriving Franklin of their participation in the attack.

Despite the absence of the VI Corps in the attack, Franklin's troops still represented a formidable force. Major General John F. Reynolds's I Corps was assigned to lead the advance, led by Meade's division. Gibbon's division supported Meade on the right. Meade was able to begin his advance within 45 minutes after receiving his orders, a remarkable feat in itself. The Federal advance was hidden from Confederate eyes by a dense fog until about 10:00 A.M. When it lifted, a military pageant of breathtaking proportions was observed by the waiting Confederates. Franklin's Left Grand Division moved across the plain with flags flying and bayonets flashing, advancing toward Stonewall Jackson's veteran Second Corps.[20] Meade's troops crossed the Richmond Stage Road, passed through a ravine, and headed for a point of woods called Prospect Hill. Confederate artillery fire from batteries located at Hamilton's Crossing and from Pelham's guns on the Union right slowed the advance and inflicted heavy casualties. Gibbon's division also advanced on Meade's right.

Stoneman received orders about 11:30 A.M. to send a division to support General Reynolds and to report in person to General Franklin. The First Division under General David B. Birney was sent across about 12 noon. Meade continued his advance, but Confederate batteries, plus a strong counter-attack, eventually drove Meade's men back in a disorderly retreat. Every attempt to rally them failed, and Stoneman, who had left Franklin's headquarters and moved to the front, reported that "they sullenly and persistently moved to the rear...."[21] At this point, Birney saved the situation. His First Division, followed by Sickles' Second Division, also of Stoneman's Corps, attacked the Confederate right flank and drove the counter-attacking Confederates back into the woods with a loss of about 500 men.[22] Stoneman's troops had saved the whole left wing of the army from disaster, but it was costly. The First Division lost, Stoneman later reported, "upward of 1,000 of as brave men as ever pulled a trigger."[23]

Stoneman, second from right, wearing the uniform of a brigadier general, with, from left, Captain Edwin V. Sumner, Jr., First U.S. cavalry, cited for gallantry at the Battle of Todd's Tavern, Virginia; he was the son of General Edwin V. Sumner; Lieutenant Jonathan Alexander, Stoneman's aide; and Doctor McMillan, wearing a medical sword attached to his belt (from the collection of Andrew J. Potts).

Birney's role in the battle was not without controversy. Meade claimed after the battle that he sent aides to Birney requesting him to bring his men forward. Twice, Meade complained, Birney refused to comply with his requests, saying that he was under the command of General Reynolds. Meade, using his authority as a recently commissioned Major General, finally ordered Birney to move his men forward. By the time Birney complied, the situation was desperate. Birney, testifying before the Joint Committee on the Conduct of the War, denied that he had received two requests from Meade before acting. Neither Stoneman nor Birney referred to Meade's charge in their official reports. On the contrary, Stoneman complimented Birney "upon the handsome manner in which he handled his division...."[24]

Reynolds's corps regrouped at the railway line by 2:00 P.M., supported by Stoneman's two divisions. Additional attempts to dislodge Stonewall Jackson's veterans proved unsuccessful and the entire Union line reformed at the Richmond Road where the morning attack originated.

While Franklin was attempting to destroy Lee's right flank, the attack by the Right Grand Division opposite the center of Fredericksburg was forming for the assault. By December 13, the town was a shambles, due to the Federal artillery barrage that had preceded the infantry advance across the pontoon bridges. Most of the civilians had fled and the streets were packed with General Sumner's troops. Despite the efforts of Provost Marshals, homes were looted. Piles of furniture and household belongings were stacked by the bridges near the river.

The town was blanketed by fog when General Burnside ordered Sumner to assault the Confederate positions on Marye's Heights, which was located a short distance west of the town. The terrain heavily favored the defenders. The Union soldiers had to traverse an open field which was bisected by a ditch that had to be crossed. The entire field was covered by Confederate infantry and artillery. Major General Couch, a classmate of Stoneman's at West Point and commander of the II Corps, was ordered to seize the heights near the rear of the town. French's and Hancock's divisions were divided into three brigade lines and the assault began. The Union soldiers rapidly moved out of town on two parallel streets toward the entrenched enemy on Marye's Heights. They crossed the canal with some difficulty and were deployed under a bank at the foot of the plain they were about to cross. The planks across the canal had been removed and the men had to cross on stringers, single file.

As they charged, the Federals were ripped by Confederate artillery and withering infantry fire. Longstreet's Confederates lay hidden behind a stone wall that ran along the base of Marye's Heights. Georgian troops, under the command of General T.R.R. Cobb, fired into the massed bluecoats. Four times the brave men attacked and four times they were driven back to a swale or hollow which offered some protection. Though the Union infantry fought with incredible bravery, no man reached the stone wall where the Georgians stood in ranks four men deep.

When the attack began, General Couch climbed to the steeple of the courthouse, which rose above the smoke and haze, to get a better look at the attack. As he witnessed the slaughter of his men, he turned to General Howard and said "Oh, great God! see how our men, our poor fellows are falling!"[25] Couch saw the futility of continued attacks against the wall, so he ordered Howard's division to move to the right and flank the Confederates. However, Hancock and French had sent urgent requests for reinforcements and Howard was recalled. Whipple's Third Division, which formed part of Stoneman's corps, was ordered to relieve Howard and continue the attack to the right of the stone wall, but it was a futile effort and succeeded only in adding another 1,000 men to the list of Union casualties.[26]

As night fell on the thousands of wounded men, the bitter cold caused suffering and death. The battle was over, although Burnside was determined to continue the assault on the following morning, an attack that he would personally lead. General Sumner convinced Burnside not to continue the attack, telling him that none of his staff approved of it and further action would prove disastrous to the army. Burnside reluctantly accepted his defeat.

The Army of the Potomac, minus 1,281 killed and with over 9,000 wounded, retreated across the Rappahannock. George Stoneman was promoted to brevet colonel in the regular army for "gallant and meritorious service," but Fredericksburg was an exercise in frustration for him and the army. He did what was asked of him, acting primarily in a supporting role, although his divisions under Birney and Sickles saw active combat in the attack by the Left Grand Division. In fact, Stoneman's troops saved the day when Meade's and Gibbon's troops retreated in confusion and disorder under pressure from Stonewall Jackson's counter-attack. Little credit has been given to Stoneman for his role in preventing an even greater Union disaster. Whipple's Third Division also fought well when they supported Howard's right flank during the assault against the stone wall, although Stoneman had little to do with that action as Whipple had been detached from his command.

Stoneman mourned the loss of "many noble-hearted brothers in arms" and wrote, in his report, that the survivors of Fredericksburg were not "discouraged or dispirited by the failure of our efforts to conquer a brave and powerful foe...."[27]

Eight

The Bursting Shell

General Alfred Pleasonton put his finger on the problem just before the Battle of Fredericksburg. There were defects in the Union cavalry organization. Each of Burnside's "Grand Divisions" had two infantry corps and a cavalry component. The subordinate role of cavalry had plagued Union cavalrymen since the beginning of the war. Before the Union defeat at Fredericksburg, Pleasonton, who commanded two brigades of cavalry attached to the Right Grand Division, stated his views on the organization of Federal cavalry.

"The cavalry is a distinct arm of the service," Pleasonton wrote, "having specific duties to perform, that can only be properly discharged under an organization conformable to those duties."[1] Pleasonton proposed a corps organization under an independent commander who should report to the commanding general. The rebel cavalry, Pleasonton observed, owe their success to an independent cavalry which permits freedom and responsibility.[2]

The costly battle of Fredericksburg led to the appointment of Major General "Fighting Joe" Hooker as commanding general of the Army of the Potomac. Hooker proved to be a controversial choice, in view of his conspiracies against Burnside and later his leadership at the Battle of Chancellorsville. There is no denying, however, that the army, under his command, 100,000 strong, stood up to tough fighting at Chancellorsville.

Some of Hooker's actions in the months of April and May 1863 benefited the entire army. Rations and medical care were improved, additional clothing provided, a rational system of furloughs adopted. Burnside's grand divisions were abolished. It was Hooker's reorganization of the cavalry, however, that endeared him to Stoneman and his fellow cavalry officers. His General Orders No. 6 of February 5, 1863, specified the following: "The cavalry of the army shall be consolidated under one corps under the command of Brigadier General Stoneman, who will make the necessary arrangements for detached duty."[3]

Stoneman assumed command of the newly established corps three days later. As of February 10, Stoneman had 11,110 officers and men "present for duty."[4] Stoneman organized the corps into three divisions. Pleasonton commanded seven regiments in the First Division, which also had an independent squadron. General William W. Averell commanded seven regiments of the Second Division and General David McM. Gregg had six regiments and an independent company in the Third. Ironically, General John Buford, who was considered to be the ablest of the Union cavalry commanders, ended up commanding a brigade, a smaller unit than a division. Historians have speculated why Buford was not given a division command and it was assumed that he was the victim of political intrigues and the resentment of less qualified men.[5]

Stoneman had organized his corps with the best Union cavalry officers available in the eastern theater of the war. Averell, although he would be criticized by Hooker for his performance at Kelly's Ford, was an experienced officer. Known as "Swell" by his colleagues, he had fought at First Bull Run and he was a brigade commander in the Peninsula campaign. Stoneman's brigade commanders would be leaders in the development of Union cavalry. Colonel Judson Kilpatrick, known as "Little Kil" or "Kil-Cavalry" because of the way he used up men as well as horses, was the most controversial of Stoneman's choices. Commanding the First Brigade, he was known for his courage, sometimes considered reckless, and for his political intrigues, but he did the most damage to Confederate installations and facilities in the ensuing Stoneman Raid.[6] Colonel Percy Wyndham commanded the Second Brigade. An aggressive soldier of fortune, he had fought with the English, French, Austrian, and Sardinian armies and was knighted by King Victor Emmanuel for his service under Garibaldi. He was known for his temper and gaudy uniforms.[7]

Major General David McM. Gregg was the commander of the third division during the Stoneman Raid at Chancellorsville. He later fought with distinction at Brandy Station, Middleburg, Upperville, and Gettysburg (U.S. Army Military History Institute).

Captain Wesley Merritt was a rising star in the ranks of Union cavalry. He had served as Stoneman's aide in the spring of 1863, as well as ordnance and mustering officer. Merritt was promoted by Alfred Pleasonton from captain to brigadier general at age 27 in June 1863 for his outstanding service.

Morale of the Union cavalry, as well as that of the infantry, had suffered in the harsh winter of 1863. The men lived in log huts and firewood became scarce as the winter progressed. Hooker improved rations and the men enjoyed bread, beef, pork, and vegetables.

Better mail service improved morale as men received packages from home. The improved logistics under Hooker meant that additional clothing was available to protect the men in winter weather. Stoneman, determined to whip the cavalry into shape for the coming spring campaign, kept the men busy with constant drills and training. Hooker tightened discipline and established boards of examination for officers. He dismissed old and incompetent officers and replaced them with younger, more aggressive men.[8]

The first test of Union cavalry after the reorganization took place at Kelly's Ford on March 17, 1863, the first cavalry battle which was fought exclusively by cavalry units without the support of infantry. Averell was ordered to take a force of 3,000 cavalry and six pieces of artillery and "attack and rout or destroy" Confederate cavalry under the command of General Fitzhugh Lee. Averell and his command reached Kelly's Ford early on the morning of March 17, but Fitz Lee's scouts had learned of the movement and felled trees to block the ford. Sixty sharpshooters took up positions on the south bank of the Rappahannock. Numerous attempts to cross the ford were beaten back, but Averell's troopers finally crossed and engaged five Virginia regiments. The numbers involved heavily favored the Federals, but the 800 Virginians challenged Averell's 2,100 troopers. The Federals drove the Virginians back until they came within range of Lee's artillery. At this point, Averell withdrew, reasoning that he didn't want to attack entrenched positions, a decision that did not endear him to his new commanding officer, "Fighting Joe" Hooker.

The next and more decisive test of Federal cavalry was to be handed to George Stoneman in mid–April 1863. President Lincoln visited the Army of the Potomac in early April and witnessed the grand review of Stoneman's cavalry corps on the plains of Falmouth, Virginia. Hooker decided that it was time to offer battle to Robert E. Lee and presented his plan to the president following the review. A key part of his plan was to send Stoneman and his dragoons, with light artillery, across the Rappahannock and turn the Confederate position toward the Union right flank, while severing Lee's communications and supply lines with Richmond. While Stoneman was creating havoc in the Confederate rear, the main force of the Army of the Potomac would force the Confederates to retreat or fall back toward Culpeper and Gordonsville.[9]

Hooker and Stoneman knew each other well. They had served in the old army together, first in California in 1849, where they shared a house in Sonoma along with Major Phil Kearny. Hooker relieved a young lieutenant named William T. Sherman, who had temporarily held the position of adjutant general.[10] Both Hooker and Stoneman participated in the Peninsula Campaign in May 1862, Hooker as a division commander in the III Corps and Stoneman as Chief of Cavalry of the Army of the Potomac. They served together again at Fredericksburg in December, where Hooker commanded the Center Grand Division, which included Stoneman's III Corps of infantry. Despite their long association, the acrimony following the coming Battle of Chancellorsville would destroy whatever comradeship that existed between these two veteran officers.

Stoneman knew Hooker well enough to put his finger on Hooker's tragic flaw. "[Hooker] could play the best game of poker I ever saw until it came to the point where he should go a thousand better and then he would flunk. He was the most brilliant of generals up to a certain point, but when his limitation was reached he was utterly helpless," Stoneman told journalist Alex K. McClure shortly before Chancellorsville.[11]

Hooker advised President Lincoln that the cavalry would cross the river above the Rappahannock Bridge and "would probably have a fight" in the vicinity of Culpeper, but "not one that should cause much delay or embarrassment." Once the cavalry had reached the enemy's rear, Hooker would cross the river with the main Federal force. Lincoln concurred with Hooker's plan.[12]

Stoneman received his orders on April 12, 1863, directing him to move at 7:00 A.M. on April 13 with all of his available force, turn the enemy's left, and place his command between Lee and Richmond. Stoneman's movement would isolate Lee from his supplies, check his retreat, "and inflict on him every possible injury which will tend to his discomfiture and defeat."[13]

Stoneman in winter quarters (U.S. Army Military History Institute).

Hooker suggested to Stoneman that he ascend the Rappahannock by different routes, keeping well out of view of the enemy, throwing out small parties to mask his movement. Stoneman was urged to "have the word given out" that he was in pursuit of Brigadier General W.E. "Grumble" Jones's Confederate guerrillas, who had been operating extensively near Winchester.

His orders suggested that he cross the Rappahannock at "some point west of the Orange and Alexandria railroad," but that would be determined by the existing situation. Stoneman was advised that he was likely to come across Fitzhugh Lee's cavalry brigade of about 2,000 men but he was expected to "disperse and destroy" them in view of his clear numerical advantage.[14]

Stoneman was further instructed to destroy the enemy's small provost guard of infantry at Gordonsville, and to proceed to the Aquia and Richmond Railroad in the vicinity of Saxton's Junction. Along this route, he was ordered to destroy railroad bridges, trains, cars, provisions and communications. Hooker reasoned that this threat to Lee's communications, and to Richmond itself, would force Lee to abandon Fredericksburg and retreat southward. The Army of the Potomac would follow and attack when an opportunity presented itself.

Hooker evidently felt it was necessary to motivate Stoneman with a call for action. He advised him to harass the enemy day and night. "If you cannot cut off from his columns larger slices, the general desires that you will not fail to take small ones. Let your watchword be fight and let all your orders be fight, fight, fight, bearing in mind that time is as valuable to the general as the rebel carcasses."[15]

Hooker's orders stressed that the primary objective of the raid was to cut the enemy's connections from Fredericksburg to Richmond. Everything else was to be subservient to that objective, although several subordinate operations were suggested. For example, he was urged to detach a force to Charlottesville, which was reported to be lightly defended, and destroy supplies along the Aquia Railroad in the direction of Richmond.

Stoneman was admonished to "bear in mind that celerity, audacity, and resolution are everything in war and especially is it the case with the command you have and the enterprise upon which you are about to embark."[16]

On the morning of April 13, Stoneman led his troopers out of their encampment at Falmouth. This was the moment he and his men had been waiting for. The largest cavalry force that had ever been assembled in the war was riding to attack the enemy as an entire corps in an independent operation. Each trooper carried an overcoat, a shelter tent, and a rubber poncho. Saddle bags contained a curry-comb and brush, extra ammunition, a knife, fork, and spoon. A carbine was slung from the left shoulder and hung on the right side, a holster and revolver hung on the right hip, a saber hung on the left side. Superfluous articles were discarded after a few days in the field until they moved in what was called "light marching order."[17]

Stoneman issued detailed orders to his division commanders as they departed camp. General Averell was instructed to cross the Rappahannock at Beverly Ford, to be followed by General Buford's division, which was to cross in the vicinity of the Rappahannock railroad bridge. After both divisions had crossed, Averell was ordered to push on to Culpeper Court House. Gregg was ordered to cross the river as soon after Averell as possible and keep close on his rear. Averell was advised that he might encounter Fitzhugh Lee's brigade at Culpeper Court House. If they did, Stoneman ordered that the Confederate brigade be attacked with the utmost vigor.

Stoneman had covered some 20 miles from his headquarters to Morrisville on the first day out but, cautious and methodical as usual, used up a day of fair weather when attempts by the Federal troopers to cross were opposed by small units of the 9th and 13th Virginia cavalry. Buford was engaged near Beverly Ford and Averell was delayed near Kelly's Ford. By the evening of the 14th, Stoneman's cavalry was still on the north bank of the Rappahannock.

Then it began to rain. The ensuing downpour caused the river to rise precipitously. An officer on Stoneman's staff, Colonel Charles S. Wainwright, wrote in his diary that the river had risen seven feet at Rappahannock Station where Stoneman was waiting to get across. Wainwright noted that Stoneman's plan of march "is by this time fully known to Lee.... Even the privates seemed well informed of it, so that we get our late news through

Eight. The Bursting Shell

Major General William W. Averell led the Second Division at Kelly's Ford on March 17, 1863. Although he withdrew after a sharp encounter with Confederate cavalry, Kelly's Ford demonstrated the increasing competence of Federal cavalry. The recall of his division during the Stoneman Raid deprived Stoneman of over a third of his force (U.S. Army Military History Institute).

Major General John Buford, promoted to that rank shortly before his death of typhoid fever. Buford commanded the Reserve Brigade on the Stoneman Raid at Chancellorsville and died in Stoneman's home in Washington, D.C., on December 16, 1863. Many called Buford the best cavalryman in the Union Army (U.S. Army Military History Institute).

rebel deserters as we do direct." Rebel pickets were calling across the river asking "What is the matter with your cavalry that it does not get across?"[18]

Hooker assumed that Stoneman would cross the river on April 15 and so informed Lincoln that he would do so before daylight. Hooker was more than a little irritated when Stoneman reported that he was unable to cross due to flooding. Hooker was also vexed by Stoneman's orders to his staff that seemed to indicate that the entire corps of 10,000 men would move against Fitz Lee's 2,000 at Culpeper Court House. Hooker became impatient and was embarrassed by his misleading message to Lincoln. He advised Stoneman to leave his artillery if necessary and "proceed with the execution of your orders without it.... This army is awaiting your movement."[19]

Lincoln also began to express his frustration. On April 15, he sent a message to Hooker, saying that he was uneasy at the continuing delay. "The rain and the mud were, of course, to be calculated upon. General S. is not moving rapidly enough to make the expedition come to anything."[20] Lincoln calculated that Stoneman had traveled only 25 miles in three days of good weather and still had 60 miles and another river to cross, under enemy fire. Lincoln feared that the raid was already a failure.

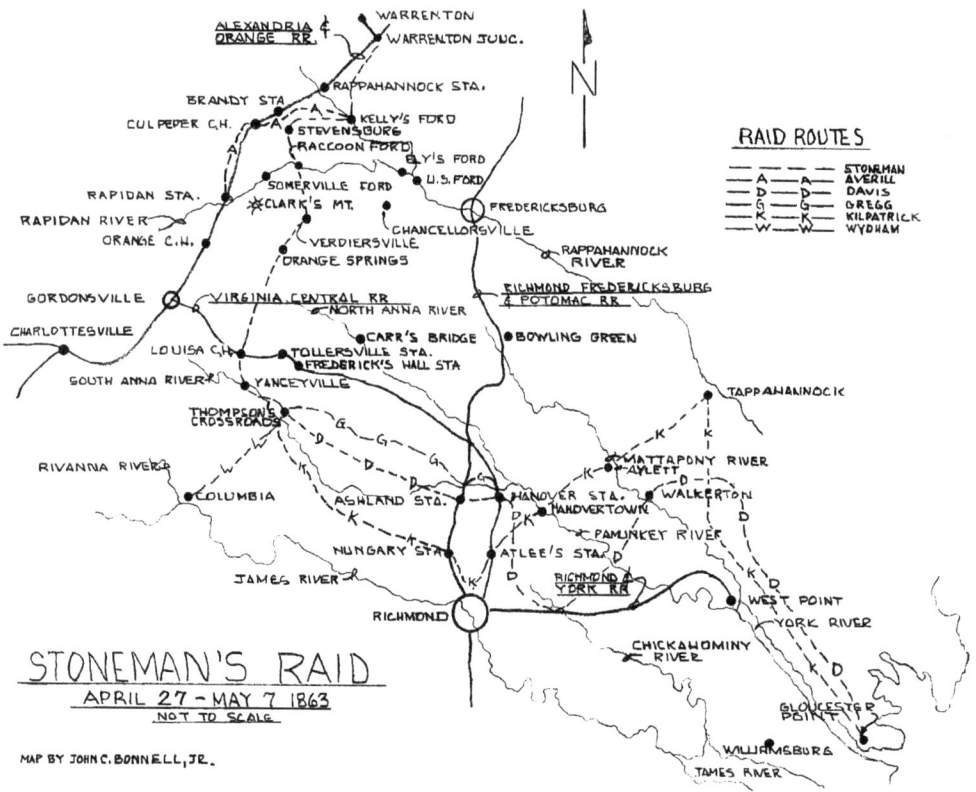

The rain continued and Stoneman's cavalry remained on the north bank of the Rappahannock. Stoneman reported to headquarters that no command had higher hopes or was more confident of success, but the elements seem to have conspired against him. The incessant rain could prevent "the accomplishment of a brilliant cavalry operation."[21]

While Stoneman fretted, Hooker decided to change his grand strategy. The element of surprise was lost. He dropped the idea that Stoneman would force Lee to abandon Fredericksburg. Hooker instructed Stoneman to cross the Rappahanock and Rapidan rivers and subdivide his command. Detachments would dash to the right and left, inflict as much damage as possible, and bewilder the enemy as to the intention of the main body. On April 28, two weeks after the original date Stoneman was supposed to cross the Rappahannock, Stoneman was ordered to move against Louisa Court House while the main body attacked the Orange and Alexandria Railroad, the object of his original instructions. Hooker also recommended that the columns unite on the Pamunkey River, close to the anticipated enemy line of retreat.

Late on the evening of the 28th, five days' rations were issued to the men and three days' forage for the horses. All regiments were ordered to be in readiness to move at a moment's notice. Tents were struck, wagons loaded, and horses saddled, but no orders came to move. At midnight the rain came again and became worse as the day dawned. Finally, on the morning of the 29th, the cavalry marched to Kelly's Ford on the Rappahannock and executed a hazardous crossing through the swift and rising waters.[22]

Eight. The Bursting Shell

Robert E. Lee read the reports of his scouts on the Union cavalry with apprehension. He was advised that Stoneman's destination was the Shenandoah Valley, but Lee was not deceived. He wired Jefferson Davis and asked for troops to be sent to Gordonsville, which was clearly threatened by Stoneman. He asked Davis to send him Longstreet's two divisions under the command of Generals Pickett and Hood, who were south of the James River gathering provisions and keeping an eye on Federal forces at Newport News and North Carolina. Lee wasn't sure what Stoneman was up to, but the prospect of an entire corps of Federal cavalry in his rear was alarming. He recognized the threat to his communications with Richmond and moved to take steps to protect them.

Under the watchful eye of Confederate scouts, Stoneman was finally able to move his entire command, including artillery, across the swollen Rappahannock. Once across, he stopped to spread his maps and meet with his division and brigade commanders. Stoneman faced a dilemma. On April 22, Hooker ordered him to scatter his command after crossing the two rivers and cause as much damage as possible in a wide area. His modified orders of April 28 directed him to send part of his force across Raccoon Ford to Louisa Court House to mask the movement of his main force, which would make a forced march to the Richmond, Fredericksburg, and Potomac Railroad and destroy it. Stoneman had to decide whether he should follow his orders of the 22nd and scatter his command or follow his modified orders of the 28th, which gave him more specific objectives. Stoneman chose to subdivide his command according to his orders of April 22, thus violating military dogma of always obeying the last order given.

Stoneman had been advised in his original orders that he faced two small brigades of poorly mounted Confederate cavalry "numbering between 4,000 and 5,000 sabers, in the vicinity of Culpeper."[23] Stoneman now made his second dubious decision of the campaign. He dispatched General William Averell's entire division, more than a third of his force, to march by way of Brandy Station and Culpeper to strike at the Confederates. It was not clear whether Averell should rejoin Stoneman's main column after he had engaged Rooney Lee's cavalry or unite with Stoneman later at the Panunkey.

Shortly after leaving Stoneman, Averell, en route to Brandy Station, ran into Brigadier General Rooney Lee's advance regiment, the 13th Virginia commanded by Colonel John R. Chambless, Jr. Although he was outnumbered, Chambliss occupied Averell's troopers until nightfall when it was too dark to tell friend from foe. Averell then learned that Major General J.E.B. Stuart was at Brandy Station with his entire force of four brigades and fifteen pieces of artillery. Unwilling to risk an encounter with Stuart, Averell marched to Culpeper Court House where he destroyed Confederate food supplies, after distributing some to poor people, and perused captured Confederate mail.

Stuart, as well as Lee, was concerned about the possibility of Stoneman's cavalry marching unopposed through the interior of Virginia and threatening communication links with Richmond. Stuart was located at Brandy Station, as Averell had surmised, but Lee was concerned that Federal troops would position themselves between his left flank and Stuart's cavalry. Although uneasy about Stoneman, Lee decided to order Stuart to cross the Rapidan and continue to Ely's Ford to oppose Hooker's main body of infantry as best he could.

Lee was keeping a wary eye on Stoneman's main column that was headed toward Gordonsville. The Confederate commander sent a dispatch for help to Richmond on April 29 asking that all available troops be sent forward as rapidly as possible by rail or otherwise. Since he had moved Stuart to oppose Hooker, Lee had only Rooney Lee's two regiments to counter Stoneman's thrust.

Stoneman was still having trouble focusing on his main objective, the destruction of Lee's communications and supplies. On April 30, he ordered Averell to continue with his sideshow against "Rooney" Lee, who had dismounted his troopers and placed his artillery on the north bank of the river at Rapidan Station. Acting on orders from Stoneman, Averell reached the opposite bank of the river and spent the day trying to dislodge the Confederates. Averell attempted to burn the bridge as if to keep the enemy from reaching him rather than attacking the small Confederate force. Lee finally saved him the trouble by torching the bridge himself and then slipped away to contest Stoneman, who was reportedly headed for Richmond.

Hooker was furious when he learned that Averell was ineffectually floundering about at Rapidan Station. Hooker's aide-de-camp sent an angry message to Averell, asking what he was doing at Rapidan Station and ordering him to proceed to United States Ford and report in person. Averell responded by citing Stoneman's orders instructing him to march to Rapidan Station and engage Rooney Lee, but Hooker was not satisfied. Averell had been in his bad graces since the engagement at Kelly's Ford, and Hooker was enraged by his dilatory tactics at the Rapidan. Averell was summarily relieved and replaced by Brigadier General Alfred Pleasonton.

Stoneman's troopers finally began to carry out their mission on May 1. Stoneman sent Gregg's division ahead to Louisa Court House, located on the Virginia Central Railroad, while the corps headquarters and Buford's brigade followed in the same general direction and camped on the south side of the North Anna River. Gregg's division arrived at Louisa Court House at 3:00 A.M. on May 2. Colonel Kilpatrick charged into the town, but there was no opposition. A pioneer corps began to destroy a five-mile section of the railway, tear down a water tank, and burn commissary stores. The post office and other public buildings were destroyed. While this was going on, a squadron of the 1st Maine was sent towards Gordonsville to determine the whereabouts of Confederate cavalry. Confederate Rooney Lee had, in fact, reached Gordonsville about 11:00 A.M. and learned that a large body of Union cavalry had reached Trevilian Station and Louisa Court House. Lee dispatched the 9th Virginia to reconnoiter, and they promptly ran into advance units of the 1st Maine. The ensuing firefight made Lee aware of the presence of Stoneman and most of his corps at Louisa Court House, and Stoneman learned that Lee was at Gordonsville with infantry, cavalry, and artillery.[24]

In the meantime, Stoneman was able to place an operator in the telegraph office at Louisa Court House who received Confederate messages for over an hour. Stoneman learned of Hooker's movements south of the Rappahannock through rebel intelligence, but when it was discovered that Yankees were on the line, the wire was cut after some pungent remarks were delivered.[25]

George Stoneman, possibly suffering from a recurrence of hemorrhoids that some feel

Eight. The Bursting Shell

may have influenced his judgment, now made a number of critical decisions regarding his orders. His original orders called for him to go along the line of the Virginia Central Railroad to Hanover Junction where the Virginia Central met the Richmond, Fredericksburg, and Potomac Railroad, the nerve center of Lee's communications. Stoneman was further directed to establish defensive positions at Hanover Junction and harass Lee on his probable line of retreat. Stoneman sent Captain Richard S.C. Lord with the 1st Cavalry to destroy the track and buildings of the Virginia Central Railway as far east as Frederickshall, about twelve miles away. The main column proceeded from Louisa Court House to Yanceyville, where they crossed the South Anna River. Captain Wesley Merritt was left to destroy bridges which crossed the river, while Stoneman continued to Thompson's Crossroads. Rooney Lee, lacking the resources to engage Stoneman, retired to Gordonsville which he was determined to defend.[26]

Stoneman was now ready to carry out his mission. He explained to his regimental commanders that they had dropped into that region of the country like a bursting shell and he intended to "burst it in every direction, expecting each piece or fragment would do as much harm and create nearly as much terror as would result from sending the whole shell, and thus magnify our small force into overwhelming numbers."[27] This was the apex of Stoneman's career. After years of service, often in a subordinate role, he was in position and had the resources to make a significant contribution to his cause and career.

He made a crucial decision to divide his force and send them off in different directions. The colorful Colonel Percy Wyndham led the 1st New Jersey, 400 men in all, to march to the James River at Columbia with the mission to destroy the aqueduct over the Rivanna River. Then he was to proceed in the direction of Richmond, doing as much damage as possible. Wyndham and the 1st New Jersey had a score to settle with the Confederates. They had been routed and Wyndham captured by Turner Ashby's cavalry troopers at Harrisonburg, Virginia, during Stonewall Jackson's Shenandoah Valley

Colonel (Sir) Percy Wyndham, colorful soldier of fortune, commanded the 1st New Jersey and part of the 1st Maryland Cavalry that attacked the town of Columbia, Virginia, during the Stoneman Raid at Chancellorsville (U.S. Army Military History Institute).

campaign in 1862. Colonel Judson Kilpatrick, with the 2nd New York, known as the "Harris Light," also with about 400 men, was to attack the railroad bridges over the Chickahominy, destroying them and the telegraph, and also operate in the direction of Richmond. Another force, under Lieutenant Colonel Hasbrouck Davis, with about 300 men of the 12th Illinois Cavalry, was to penetrate to the Richmond, Fredericksburg, and Potomac and Virginia Central railroads in the vicinity of Ashland and to destroy communications. An additional party, under Brigadier General David Gregg, was ordered to follow the South Anna River and destroy all the road bridges as they went. The 5th U.S. Cavalry, under Captain Thomas Drummond, was to follow this movement to ensure that the destruction was complete. Captain Merritt, with the 1st Maryland, was to constitute a flying party, sent out to destroy whatever bridges he could. Finally, Buford's regular brigade and the 6th Lancers remained in camp as a provost guard.[28]

All of the raiding parties were off by 3:00 A.M. with instructions to accomplish their objectives by 3:00 P.M. the same day. None of the raiding parties, six in all, were ordered to attack Hanover Junction where Hooker expected the main attack to be made. For reasons known only to him, Stoneman decided that the outskirts of Richmond were his primary target. Stoneman may have had freeing of prisoners at Richmond's infamous Libby Prison in mind. Later in the war, Stoneman was to lead a raid to free Union captives at Georgia's notorious Andersonville prison, which led to his capture at Sunshine Church near Macon. Perhaps a lightning strike to capture Confederate leaders, even Jefferson Davis, may have seemed to be a possibility. In any case, a concentrated attack at Lee's main supply and communications center at Hanover Junction would have been a more telling blow than the extensive but temporary damage Stoneman's raiders inflicted on the Confederates.

Captain Lord and Colonel Wyndham returned to camp on May 3 and reported on the damage done. Lord had destroyed Carr's bridges over the North Anna and disabled fifteen miles of the Virginia Central Railroad. Wyndham cut the James River Canal at Columbia, burned five bridges and destroyed a large quantity of supplies. He did not have the proper equipment to destroy the stone aqueduct across the Rivanna River, and he abandoned that objective when he learned that Rooney Lee was pursuing him with cavalry and artillery. Wyndam did not attempt to reach the Appomattox River or to proceed to Richmond as Stoneman had ordered. He retreated to Thompson's Crossroads to join the main column instead.

The raid on Columbia caused considerable damage and had an enormous impact on the citizens there. Samuel H. Merrill, of the 1st Maine, described the reaction of the townspeople. "Nothing could exceed the surprise and consternation of the people as the Yankee troops entered town. A report of their coming had been laughed at. A man who rode ten miles to give warning was hooted at as a fool or a madman...." The idea of the Yanks near Columbia was considered to be impossible. An eyewitness reported that the citizens were at the point of mobbing the messenger as the Yankee troops dashed into town. One lady ran out and asked the troops not to murder the women and children. She was assured that the intent of the Yankees was to destroy government property. No citizen was molested or insulted in any way and the troopers left quietly after carrying out most of their mission.[29]

"Rooney" Lee, with about 800 horsemen of the famed 9th Virginia Cavalry, was hot on the trail of Wyndam and his raiders. The 9th had earned a reputation for hard fighting in most of the cavalry operations in the eastern theater. Many of the men were from Stafford, Westmoreland, and Spotsylvania counties and were eager to punish the marauding Federals. Unaware that Wyndham was headed back to corps headquarters at Thompson's Crossroads, Lee headed north on the Cartersville [Columbia] Road spoiling for a fight. He would administer the only punishment Confederate forces managed to inflict on Stoneman's command.[30]

Stoneman was concerned about the possibility of an attack from Confederate cavalry believed to be in the area. He sent the 5th U.S. Cavalry with about 80 men to Shannon's Crossroads, about six miles to the rear of Stoneman's headquarters. The 9th Virginia charged the Federal raiders with piercing rebel yells and drove them back. The Federals counterattacked and fierce hand-to-hand fighting followed. The 5th Cavalry, badly outnumbered, retreated toward Yanceyville, but Lee, learning that Stoneman was close by at Thompson's Crossroads, lacked the strength to engage the main Federal body and headed for safety at Gordonsville.[31]

Major General Wesley Merritt was a captain at the time of Chancellorsville and led a "Flying Party" of the 1st Maryland, destroying bridges along the South Anna River. He was also the Ordnance and Mustering Officer of the newly formed cavalry corps (U.S. Army Military History Institute).

Although Federal accounts stress the correct behavior of the troopers, not only in Columbia but in other sections as well, private citizens writing after the war painted a different picture. Stoneman's men, established in camps at Yanceyville, Frederickshall, Thompson's Crossroads, and Louisa Court House, killed mules and horses, confiscated corn and wheat, and pillaged mills along the rivers. A letter, written from Louisa County, vividly describes what happened:

> This party's [Stoneman] were at Thompson's Four Corners, as they called it in their account of the fear, and it seems we were a little far off for them to haul corn from here, for the short time they stayed. If they had stayed a few days longer, they would have used everything in the world we had. Persons living on that side of the river lost everything; all the corn, bacon, fowls, flour, hogs, etc. I have neither time nor paper to tell you of all that our kind friends lost.... They destroyed a good deal of Mr. Payne's and Cousin Mary Kean's than anywhere else. They destroyed a good deal at Mr. Payne's; took all his bacon, and everything out of his mill. They ransacked sister Anne's house; every drawer and repository of trinkets or valuables; stole Mr. Woodworth's clothes.... They must have given the clothes to the negroes, for these grim sons of Mars could not have wanted them for their own use.[32]

Other accounts refer to women pouring wine out to prevent the Federal raiders from worse behavior. Planters, it was alleged, were stripped and left nude in the woods, apparently out of pure meanness. Losing livestock meant that farmers did not have work stock left to plant corn for harvest.[33]

While Wyndham was carrying out his orders in Columbia, Kilpatrick made a forced march to Hungary Station. Some 15 miles short of his objective, he made camp and remained hidden during the day and early into the night. At daybreak on the morning of May 4, Kilpatrick reached Hungary on the Richmond, Fredericksburg & Potomac Railroad, where he destroyed the depot and wrecked the railroad for several miles. The New Yorkers then drove rebel pickets down the Brook turnpike, charged a battery, and forced them to retreat within two miles of Richmond. The New Yorkers captured the aide-de-camp of General John H. Winder, provost marshal of Richmond, and 11 of his men, whom they promptly paroled. One of Kilpatrick's men described the situation: "There we were, only a remnant of a regiment, many miles from any support, with no way to retreat, as we had burned all the bridges and ferries in our rear, nearer to the Confederate capital than ever any Union troops were before."[34] The Union troopers continued to advance until they saw the church steeples of Richmond and reported that they were "knocking on the doors of her rebellious heart." The resourceful and colorful Kilpatrick must have been tempted to go even farther, but they encountered Confederate cavalry and infantry, supported by artillery, and elected to withdraw, burning the Meadow Bridge across the Chickahoniny on the Mechanicsville Pike.

Stoneman had given Kilpatrick the option of heading toward Williamsburg and Yorktown if circumstances dictated. Kilpatrick decided to head for Gloucester Point opposite Yorktown on the peninsula that was in Union hands. Destroying bridges, ferries, wagons, and food supplies as they went, the New Yorkers reached Gloucester Point, where Kilpatrick reported that he found "safety and comfort under our brave old flag within our lines...." This raid around the entire rebel army, a march of nearly 200 miles, had been made in less than four days, with the loss of one officer and 37 men, having captured and paroled upward of three hundred men.[35]

General Judson Kilpatrick, as a colonel, commanded the First Brigade during the Stoneman Raid at Chancellorsville and marched to within two miles of Richmond. Kilpatrick's men did the most damage to Confederate installations and ended up in Yorktown, behind Union lines (U.S. Army Military History Institute).

Kilpatrick wasn't the only one who decided to head for Gloucester Point. Colonel Hasbrouck Davis, leading the 12th Illinois, made the same decision. Davis had begun his march by destroying buildings, track, and supplies at Ashland where he astonished the inhabitants of this small village by his presence. While he was at work destroying as much as possible, a train approached and was captured. It proved to be an ambulance train, filled with 250 sick and wounded officers and men. It was here that Stoneman's men first learned of the Union disaster at Chancellorsville. Davis continued his march to Hanover Station where telegraph wires were cut and depot buildings and storehouses burned, along with 100 wagons and 1,000 sacks of flour and corn. Davis got to within seven miles of Richmond before he headed for Williamsburg after inflicting more damage at Turnstall's Station.[36]

Stoneman's raid soon had the Confederate communications system humming. James A. Seddon, the Confederate Secretary of War, informed Lee that "twenty-seven regiments have been making raids from Louisa Court House to Columbia; in Goochland, to Ashland, Hungary Station, Hanover Court House; the line of the central railroad to the Chickahominy."[37] Seddon advised that, while the Yankees were menacing Richmond, the Confederates could protect the bridges across the Annas and defend the city but "we want to punish the marauders."

Generals Lee and Jackson had won their decisive victory over Hooker at Chancellorsville on May 3, and Hooker was retreating to the Rappahannock. Stoneman's cavalry was now the only remaining threat to the Confederate capital. Confederate headquarters pressed General James Longstreet to get Hood's and Pickett's divisions to the vicinity of Richmond. Longstreet rapidly assembled Hood's division at Ivor, a town about 40 miles southeast of Petersburg, and advised Richmond that everything possible was being done to rush troops to defend the capital.

Lee had requested Longstreet's two divisions before Hooker crossed the Rappahannock to initiate the battle of Chancellorsville. Apparently Longstreet was sensitive to the impression that he was dilatory with his movement to reinforce Lee, even though events were to prove that he was not needed. Nonetheless, the Confederate War Department ordered Longstreet to "move without delay your command to this place [Richmond] to effect a junction with General Lee."[38] Longstreet advised that it would take several days to reach Lee but he would move as soon as possible. Lee was confident enough by May 7 to advise Longstreet that he was no longer needed. After informing Longstreet that the emergency had passed, Lee advised that "the only immediate service that your troops could render would be to protect our communications from the enemy's cavalry, and in assisting in punishing them for the damage they have done us."[39] Lee's message of May 7 to Longstreet was calculated to reassure his sensitive "warhorse" that he wasn't at fault. In reality, Lee showed his exasperation at the lack of reinforcements in a message to the Confederate Secretary of War on the previous day. He advised Richmond that Hooker had not recrossed the Rappahannock after his defeat the previous Sunday but had fortified a position in front of United States Ford. "I have received none of the troops ordered from south of the James River.... I had hoped Longstreet would have been here by this time.... I hope every effort will be made to restore the railroads; *else we shall have to abandon this country*" (italics mine).[40]

The offensive-minded Lee, following his victory at Chancellorsville, had hoped to strike at Hooker and further damage his army. Nevertheless, he had barely 40,000 effectives as opposed to Hooker's 140,000, a three-to-one manpower advantage for the Union. Because of Stoneman's raid, Longstreet's two divisions, perhaps totaling 12,000 men in each, did not join Lee, thus permitting the Army of the Potomac to withdraw in order. The diversion of Longstreet to resist Stoneman is clear in the light of Longstreet's message to the Confederate Secretary of War on May 7. He advised that President Jefferson Davis had urged him to move his command and join Lee, but Longstreet was convinced that his responsibility was to protect Richmond and restore Lee's communications to the south, which had been damaged by Stoneman. "There are some indications, too, that the enemy may bring one or other two other columns against this city [Richmond] with the hope of getting possession with a sudden dash. I think that it is important that these things should be considered and that we should have our forces on hand as to meet any such contingency."[41]

Stoneman's raid had caused consternation in Richmond. Citizens drilled in capital square and a Richmond newspaper reported that the city was in a high state of excitement. "The raid was bold and caused perhaps more than its due share of alarm in this community. The Yankees will crow over it as much as they can in order to diminish the force of the terrible blow General Lee has given them."[42]

While rumors of Yankee depredations swept Richmond, the last units of Stoneman's "bursting shell," consisting of the 1st Maine and 10th New York commanded by Brigadier General D. Gregg, returned to Yanceyville following action at the South Anna Bridge. There, he met Stoneman, along with Colonel Wyndham and Captains Merritt and Drummond. Stoneman's command was now unified, except for Colonels Kilpatrick and Davis, who were safe at Gloucester Point.

After penetrating enemy country by surprise, Stoneman was now faced with the task of getting back to the Army of the Potomac. He knew that Confederate cavalry under Rooney Lee and Wade Hampton were to the west of his position. He believed they thought the Yankee raiders would now head west toward Charlottesville to destroy bridges across the Rivanna and depots in that area. Stoneman ruled out any further activity in the direction of Richmond. The countryside was thoroughly alerted by then and movement in that direction would have been rash indeed. Further destruction of Confederate equipment, communications and supplies around Charlottesville was a possibility, but the presence of enemy cavalry, the jaded conditions of their horses and the absence of Kilpatrick and Davis argued against further raiding. Moreover, Stoneman was still suffering from his chronic hemorrhoids, a condition that had no doubt worsened after several days in the saddle.

Stoneman was picking up vague rumors of the Union disaster at Chancellorsville. Since the cavalry raid was to be in concert with a successful infantry assault against Lee and was never intended to be an independent operation, there was no point in further activity if the rumors of a Union debacle were true.

To deceive the Confederates, Stoneman dispatched a detachment of 646 men under Buford on May 4 to oppose any enemy force that might be in the direction of Gordonsville and to lead Lee and Hampton to believe that the Yankee raiders were headed in that direction. Buford was ordered to rejoin Stoneman at Orange Springs the following day. The main body started the long trip back to the Army of the Potomac with the 1st Maine acting as an advance guard. On May 5, the lead units started out in a steady rain. The 1st Maine historian describes the march through "swamps, thickets, woods, and cow-paths" avoiding traveled highways. A whippoorwill sang a doleful note and guerrillas broke the silence of the night with an occasional shot. Pickets were stationed at crossroads to prevent a flank attack. It was learned the following day that the column passed within two miles of General Lee's baggage train and within three miles of General Stuart's cavalry.[43]

With the exception of isolated guerilla activity, and an occasional attempt by Confederate scouts to lead unsuspecting troopers off the road, Stoneman's withdrawal was unopposed. However, on May 6, after halting for breakfast and rest, he resumed the march with great caution. Stoneman still had not received any intelligence from Hooker, but he learned from freed slaves he encountered that the rumors of Hooker's defeat were true. There was, of course, no option but to continue the withdrawal. True to his cautious nature, he stopped every few miles and patrolled his front and flanks. He met Buford at Orange Springs as planned, and after watering and feeding the horses, the column pushed on to the plank road leading from Fredericksburg to Orange Court House and on to Raccoon Ford which, to their great joy, they found passable.[44]

The men had been in the saddle for two nights and were wet, cold, tired, and hungry, and they still had to cross the Rappahannock at Kelly's Ford. After resting and cooking whatever they had, the men marched to the swollen river, arriving about 9:00 P.M. on May 7. The entire command succeeded in swimming across the 20 yards of the river except for one man and six horses that drowned. Stoneman's exhausted troopers reached headquarters of the Army of the Potomac on May 10.[45]

Lieutenant Colonel Austin, Stoneman's commissary officer, was ordered to ride ahead to Falmouth to give an informal report on the Stoneman raid to Hooker's headquarters. After all the suffering Stoneman's troopers had endured, it must have been a bitter moment for Austin when he was received coolly by Hooker's chief of staff, General Daniel Butterfield. Butterfield remarked: "From your account, I don't see but that you are ready to start on another expedition right away." Austin, nettled by this reaction, replied testily: "Perhaps, sir, your long experience with infantry has unfitted you to form a fair estimate of the works of cavalry," or words to that effect.[46]

The Confederates were confused by Stoneman's maneuvers and the dash to Gloucester Point by Kilpatrick and Davis. Longstreet bemoaned the fact that nothing had been done to punish the Yankee raiders. He advised Confederate Secretary of War Seddon that "the enemy's main cavalry force [was] returning to the Rappahannock by the same or nearly the same route that he came. I fear no effort has been made by our forces to obstruct his routes."[47] Lee apparently underestimated the ability of Stoneman to extricate himself from territory deep within enemy lines. Freed slaves or "contrabands" had provided Stoneman with excellent guidance and intelligence. In fact, they assisted the Union raiders throughout their mission by supplying mules and horses, as well as information. As late as May 11, Lee ordered J.E.B. Stuart to guard bridges over the North Anna and "scatter Stoneman." By this time, Stoneman was safely back in Union lines.

Although Hooker was dissatisfied with the results of the raid, Lincoln's initial reaction seemed favorable. On May 8, he informed Hooker that he had just interviewed an exchanged Union prisoner who had been in Richmond. "He says there wasn't a sound pair of legs in Richmond and that our men, had they known it, could have safely gone in and burned everything and brought in Jeff Davis."[48]

Lee saw Stoneman's raid as a harbinger of the future. He informed Jeff Davis that they could expect to be constantly subject to aggressive expeditions of Yankee cavalry. "Their cavalry force is very large, and no doubt organized for the very purpose to which it has been recently applied." Lee predicted further expeditions that would "augment their boldness" as the Union troopers become more familiar with the territory.[49]

Hooker, whose view of Stoneman became increasingly negative in the wake of his own loss of nerve at Chancellorsville, complained that he had to have "a wooden man" as a cavalry commander due to Stoneman's seniority. In a newspaper interview after the war, Hooker complained that the War Department tied his hands at Chancellorsville and would not even let him appoint his own aide de camp. He also complained that he had to put Stoneman in command and "neither he nor Averell were any account. I sent them to cut off Lee's communications and the devils went so far around to avoid an enemy that they never accomplished anything they were sent for." Hooker went on to say that if John Buford had been given the command, "things would have been different."[50]

A cryptic comment also appears in the unit history of the 9th Regiment, New York Volunteer Cavalry. An officer named Greeley, commenting on Hooker's orders to Stoneman calling on him to take the initiative "in the forward command of this grand army," remarked that "it is hard to repress a suspicion that irony lurks in such language when addressed to an officer like George Stoneman."[51] Colonel Hampton S. Thomas, of the 1st Pennsylvania Cavalry, also participated in Stoneman's Raid. In his reminiscences, Thomas wrote that after crossing the Rappahannock and Rapidan Rivers, they pushed boldly into the enemy's country but came back faster than they went. "As a stupid failure, 'Stoneman's Raid' was a complete success. Our only accomplishments were the burning of a few canal boats on the Upper James River [at Columbia] some bridges, hen-roosts, and tobacco houses." Thomas went on to write that he and his fellow officers had a quiet laugh "when remembering conversations about our new corps commander who promised to show Hooker a few dead cavalrymen. His career was happily soon cut short, and he was succeeded by General Pleasonton...."[52]

This view was not by any means shared by all of the participants in the raid. The troopers who took part judged it in terms of its moral impact on Union cavalry. The historian of Wyndham's regiment, the 1st New Jersey wrote,: "For the first time, the cavalry found themselves made useful ... and treated as something better than watchmen for the army.... It gave our troopers self-respect, and obliged the enemy to respect them...." The raid, it was recorded, inaugurated the "cavalry combats" of Brandy Station, Upperville, Gettysburg, Shepherdstown and Sulphur Springs.[53] His colleague in the 1st Maine concurred. The raid "passed into history as the first great achievement of the Union cavalry of the Army of the Potomac ... it was ever after a matter of pride with the boys that they were on 'Stoneman's Raid.'"[54]

Eight. The Bursting Shell

Despite the enthusiasm of the participants and initial favorable reaction by Lincoln and the War Department, the magnitude of the Union disaster at Chancellorsville caused bad blood in the Army of the Potomac. Hooker needed scapegoats, and as Starr pointed out, Stoneman was an obvious choice. On May 10, Hooker reported to Secretary of War Stanton that railroad communication between Fredericksburg and Richmond had been interrupted for only one day and important bridges were left untouched. "With the exception of Kilpatrick's operations, the raid does not appear to have amounted to much. My instructions appear to have been entirely disregarded by Stoneman."[55]

The Joint Committee on the Conduct of the War did not hold hearings on Chancellorsville until February 25, 1864, but once started, they lasted for fourteen months. The committee was under the control of Radical Republicans. There was a powerful group in Washington promoting Secretary of the Treasury Salmon B. Chase for the presidency. Chase had adopted Hooker as the military commander who could win the war and, apparently, had no political ambitions. The committee had supported Hooker since Fredericksburg and had strongly urged Lincoln to appoint Hooker as Commander of the Army of the Potomac in January of 1863.[56]

Hooker, in his testimony before the committee, left no doubt where he felt the blame should be placed. He testified that "no officer ever made a greater mistake in construing his orders, and no one accomplished less in doing so. Had Stoneman thrown his cavalry in the enemy's rear and on his communications, the effect could readily be estimated. But instead, that important arm of the army became crippled to an extent that seriously embarrassed me in subsequent operations."[57]

Many historical accounts of the Battle of Chancellorsville have not only minimized the effect of Stoneman's Raid but have maintained that the absence of Union cavalry was an important factor in the Union defeat. Longacre wrote that "the most significant effect of Stoneman's Raid was that it deprived Hooker's army of a major portion of its cavalry support at a critical time. Confederate cavalry under Fitzhugh Lee were then free to roam around the Virginia wilderness and thus spot the exposed Federal flank and tip the balance in favor of the Confederates."[58] Douglas Southall Freeman wrote that Hooker's plan to send almost all of his cavalry against Lee's communications was his "initial blunder." Freeman quoted Stonewall Jackson, who, when asked by an attendant while riding in an ambulance to Guinea Station after his wounding at Chancellorsville, said that Hooker's sending away his cavalry "enabled me to turn him, without his being aware of it, and to take him by his rear. Had he kept his cavalry with him, his plan would have been a very good one."[59]

Jackson had no way of knowing that his flanking march had indeed been spotted and it was only through the incompetence of Hooker's staff that reports on Jackson's movement from junior officers were ignored. The supposed importance of the absence of Federal cavalry at Chancellorsville has long been noted but this assumption is difficult to accept. Stephen Z. Starr said it best when he wrote that, first of all, the terrain, except for a few widely scattered clearings, was impassable for cavalry; second, Jackson's flanking march had been observed; and finally, Pleasonton's cavalry brigade was present.

Many in the Federal cavalry saw immediately that Hooker was looking for scapegoats.

Charles Francis Adams, Jr., grandson of President John Quincy Adams, who served with the 1st Massachusetts Cavalry, wrote his mother on May 12, 1863 as follows:

> But the troubles of the cavalry are by no means over. Hooker, it is said, angrily casting about for someone to blame for his repulse, has, of all men, hit upon Stoneman. Why was not Stoneman earlier? Why did not he take Richmond? and they do say Hooker would deprive him of his command if he dared.[60]

Hooker's curt order to Stoneman for a full accounting, accompanied, no doubt, by rumors reporting his unhappiness with the cavalry corps, convinced Stoneman that he should apply for sick leave. Stoneman continued to suffer from hemorrhoids, a common complaint of cavalry, but in Stoneman's case they appeared to be debilitating. On May 22, Brigadier General Alfred Pleasonton assumed command of the cavalry corps and Stoneman went on a well-deserved rest and to ponder his future.

Nine

"We were whipped..."

Although controversy surrounded Stoneman's Raid at Chancellorsville, the cavalry corps had survived its first independent operation. Major, if temporary damage was inflicted on the enemy and Stoneman's raiders panicked the government and residents of the Confederate capital. The Union troopers had gained more confidence in themselves, and Pleasonton inherited eight brigades of cavalry under three capable brigadier generals: John Buford, David Gregg, and Judson Kilpatrick.

The raid had drained the cavalry corps of horse flesh. Over half of the cavalry's horses were abandoned or shot. Alfred Pleasonton lost no time in reporting the deplorable state of the cavalry corps to his commanding officer, Joseph Hooker. Referring to the "unsatisfactory condition in which I find this corps," Pleasonton stuck the knife in Stoneman with the comment that he would "bring it to a state of efficiency at the earliest possible moment, but the responsibility of its present state ... does not belong to me."[1]

Hooker wrote historian Samuel B. Bates after the war and blamed Stoneman as much as the XI Corps commander, Major General Oliver Howard, for the defeat at Chancellorsville. "Stoneman had married just before a Rebel wife and at the same time was terribly afflicted with piles, and between the two had become completely emasculated, and I might as well had a wet shirt in command of my cavalry...."[2]

Proof that the Union cavalry corps was not in the deplorable state that Pleasonton and Hooker sought to imply was evident shortly after the Stoneman Raid. Two weeks after Pleasonton's self-serving report to Hooker, John Buford splashed across the Rappahannock at Beverly's Ford with his First Division, accompanied by a 1,500-man brigade of infantry, approximately 5,500 troops altogether. David Gregg's two divisions, the Second and Third, also supported by infantry and horse artillery, crossed at Kelly's Ford. Another Union column, under Colonel Alfred Duffié, would march to Stevensburg and join Buford and Gregg at Culpeper. Pleasonton was carrying out orders from Hooker to destroy the Confederate cavalry under J.E.B. Stuart that Hooker believed to be concentrated at Culpeper.

The cavalry battle at Brandy Station, a decisive step in the development of Federal cavalry, took place on June 9. It was a day of surprises and mortal combat between Stuart's veteran cavalrymen and the surging bluecoats. Buford, expecting to cross the Rappahannock River without opposition and then converge at Brandy Station with Gregg, ran into opposition from the 6th Virginia almost immediately upon crossing Beverly's Ford. The aggressive Federals drove the Confederates back to a hastily constructed defensive line at St. James Church.[3]

The Confederates' position extended from a private home known as the Gee House, where Wade Hampton's brigade was headquartered, to the brick St. James Church where Brigadier General E. "Grumble" Jones's brigade prepared to make its stand. It was here that the 6th U.S. and the 6th Pennsylvania Cavalry, the latter formed by Colonel Richard H. Rush and which once carried lances,[4] made a particularly gallant charge against the Confederate gun line. The performance of the 6th Pennsylvania, Rush's Lancers, was admired even by their foes.[5]

J.E.B. Stuart was at St. James Church in the opening stages of the battle when he received the shocking news that Federal cavalry was approaching his rear at Fleetwood Hill. This was Gregg's Third division, led by two other Stoneman veterans, Kilpatrick and Wyndham, who had crossed Kelly's Ford and now threatened Stuart's entire position. Abandoning their lines at St. James Church, the 12th Virginia, followed by the 35th and 6th Virginia, raced toward the southern end of Fleetwood Hill to meet the Federal threat.[6]

Fortunately for Stuart, the Confederates had a six-pound howitzer on the hill that served to slow down the Union advance led by the 1st New Jersey, as Wyndham thought there might be more artillery in the treeline. The lead Confederate regiment, the 12th Virginia, charged without forming up and was repulsed, but Stuart, who had reached the action, threw in the brigades of Wade Hampton and Grumble Jones. In the classic cavalry battle that ensued, charges were followed by counter-charges and confusion and dust made recognition difficult. The confused fighting forced the Federals back across the railroad tracks, where they were finally joined by Duffie, who arrived too late to be a factor. After fourteen hours of combat, Pleasonton finally ordered a withdrawal across the Rappahannock.

Casualties were high on both sides. The Confederates suffered 485 killed and wounded, the Federals 866, Buford losing 500 of that number. But the Federals fought well and fought the Confederates stirrup to stirrup. Federal cavalry had indeed come of age.

Further proof of Federal improvement of the cavalry arm was evident in a series of sharp engagements following Brandy Station. Hooker knew that the Army of Northern Virginia was on the move, but where was Lee headed? Confederate President Jefferson Davis had approved Lee's plan to invade Maryland and Pennsylvania to follow up the great victory at Chancellorsville and seize the initiative from the enemy. Lieutenant General Richard Ewell's Second Corps left Culpeper on June 10, crossed the Blue Ridge mountains, and moved toward Winchester by way of Front Royal. On June 13, Ewell captured Major General Robert H. Milroy's command at Winchester, while Longstreet's First Corps moved along the eastern face of the Blue Ridge, which he was to cross via Ashby's and Snicker's gaps. Until he crossed into the Shenandoah Valley, Longstreet's right was to be screened by Stuart's cavalry.[7]

Hooker ordered Pleasonton to place the main body of his command in the vicinity of Aldie, and push out reconnaissances toward Winchester, Berryville, and Harper's Ferry. He was told "the commanding officer relies upon you and your cavalry force to get us information of where the enemy is, his force, and his movements.... Drive in his pickets and get us information."[8]

Judson Kilpatrick, now a brigadier general and perhaps the most successful participant in the Stoneman Raid, led the first of several savage encounters between Stuart's legions and the increasingly confident bluecoats. Kilpatrick led the advance of Gregg's division into the small village of Aldie in Loudoun County on June 17. He encountered Fitzhugh Lee's brigade, commanded by Colonel Thomas Munford. The Yankees pushed the Virginians through town along the Little River Turnpike, but were driven back by Colonel Thomas Rosser's 5th Virginia. The cavalry battle see-sawed back and forth until the Confederates were outflanked and forced to withdraw. There were several wild encounters along the Snickersville Pike, one of the two parallel roads leading out of Aldie but in the end, honors were about even.[9]

Pleasonton had further confrontations with J.E.B. Stuart's cavalry division as the Federals tried to penetrate the Confederates cavalry screen. Duffié's 1st Rhode Island surprised Stuart and his staff while they were resting and entertaining young ladies in the village of Middleburg on June 17. The Confederates fled just in time as the Yankees trotted into town, not knowing what prize had just eluded them. Duffié made the unwise decision to remain in Middleburg, as it was likely that the Confederates would return in force. They did and Duffié's regiment was badly cut up when the Confederates attacked from the west and east.[10]

Duffié survived the slaughter but was out of touch with Pleasonton, who ordered Colonel John Gregg's brigade to Middleburg on June 18. Three regiments cleaned the Confederates out of Middleburg, forcing Stuart to abandon his position and retreat to Fort Defiance north of town. Once again, Federal cavalry, supported by infantry, were more than a match for the Confederates.

The final act of these encounters was the Battle of Upperville on Sunday, June 21. Stuart's entire force was now in the Loudoun Valley. Pleasonton moved against him, again supported by infantry, and drove the Confederates four miles through Upperville and beyond to the safety of Ashby's Gap. Stuart reported a "leisurely retreat," but he left wounded officers behind, an indication that the Confederates were in haste. Confederate accounts acknowledge the bravery and skill of the Federals. "They were certainly the bravest and boldest Yankees that ever fought us on any field," wrote Sergeant George M. Neese of Stuart's staff.[11]

Stoneman could only read about these major campaigns at Brandy Station and Upperville. After he was relieved of his command, he was on sick leave in Washington, recovering from his arduous raid and his hemorrhoid condition which continued to plague him. He sent a surgeon's certificate to the Adjutant General of the Army on June 10, 1863, which stated that Stoneman was "suffering from hemorrhoids, for the cure of which he submitted to an unsuccessful operation whilst serving in Texas, and that since he has suffered from frequent and copious [loss] of blood, he is 'not fit for duty' for three months." Stoneman advised the War Department that he would "report for duty as soon as I am able to ride on horseback."[12]

While recuperating, he took advantage of the Washington social scene and even attended the wedding of Kate Chase, the daughter of the Secretary of the Treasury, Salmon B. Chase to Rhode Island governor William Sprague. The wedding was also attended by President Lincoln.

As Stoneman was convalescing, the steady engagement of Union cavalry was taking its toll on men and horses. The War Department decided that it was time to centralize and streamline the cavalry service. On July 28, a cavalry bureau was created. All purchases of equipment and horses were to be made by the Quartermaster's Department under the direction of the Chief of the Cavalry Bureau. Depots were to be established "for the reception, organization, and discipline of cavalry recruits and new regiments, and for the collection, care and training of cavalry horses."[13] In a long general order issued on July 29, 1863, the instructions were issued to the cavalry service. Horses were divided into four classes, depending on their condition. All supplies and equipment purchases were to be approved by the Chief of the Cavalry Bureau in Washington.

In terms of rank and experience, Stoneman was the logical choice for the new position, but that view was not unanimous. Secretary of War Edwin Stanton, who had accepted Hooker's version of the ill-fated Chancellorsville campaign, had deep reservations about Stoneman. Despite Stanton's misgivings, Stoneman's appointment as Chief of the Cavalry Bureau was announced in the General Order which established the bureau itself.

Stoneman's appointment was a classic "kick upstairs," and it fit Stoneman's administrative talents. He moved quickly to centralize. Offices of the new bureau were established at 374 H Street in Washington, and plans were made to construct a dismounted camp where new regiments were to be equipped, trained, and mounted.[14] A large facility was established near Washington to house from ten to twelve thousand horses for training and drilling of horses and men. The location, soon to be named Camp Stoneman, was on the Potomac at Giesboro Point, close to land and water transportation. It had a good water supply and was close enough to Washington that Stoneman could closely supervise the operation.

By October, Stoneman was able to submit a long report on the progress of his bureau to headquarters of the Army of the Potomac. He noted how quickly Camp Stoneman had been established with the able assistance of Lt. Colonel C.G. Sawtelle, who had been his quartermaster on the Chancellorsville raid. In addition to Camp Stoneman in Washington, stables and barracks at St. Louis, suitable to house 10,000 to 12,000 men and horses, had been turned over to the bureau.

The principal problem Stoneman faced was the supply of horses. The exhausting campaigns of Chancellorsville and Gettysburg, as well as the encounters with J.E.B. Stuart in Northern Virginia, had worn down horses and men to an alarming degree. Stoneman reported that over 35,000 horses had been provided since the inception of the bureau, but they were not trained for combat as they were in European armies before they were sent to the field. Both horses and riders were often sent into battle insufficiently trained to withstand the confusion and the din of battle.[15]

By late 1863, Stoneman wearied of the administrative battles in Washington and longed to get back into the field. His reputation had suffered in the wake of the Chancellorsville campaign and he was anxious to redeem himself. His chance came when General John

General Stoneman and his wife, Mary Oliver Hardisty Stoneman. Photograph was taken in Baltimore, Mrs. Stoneman's hometown, in February 1864, probably while Stoneman was on leave from his assignment in Washington (courtesy of George B. Stoneman, M.D.).

Schofield, a fellow native New Yorker and a friend and ally of Stoneman's, was given command of the Department of the Ohio in January 1864. Stoneman was given command of XXIII Army Corps, but in a confusing series of staff changes, Schofield took Stoneman's place on April 4, while also keeping his command of the Department of the Ohio. Stoneman was assigned to the command of a special cavalry force, but on the following day, he was placed in command of the cavalry of the entire department and ordered to prepare them as quickly as possible for service in the field.[16]

Stoneman was delighted with his new assignment. Before departing Washington, he advised J. Couts, a close friend in California, that he was finally going back to a field command:

> I am now on my way to the Army in Tennessee. Having thank god [sic] got out of the Cavry [sic] Bureau and into the field again.
> We are all in hopes that the coming summer will finish up the bulk of the hard fighting but I do not expect the thing to terminate for several years to come — certainly I think not for the next fourteen months.[17]

He also asked Couts to send him, "by return steamer, a model California saddle such as one we used to get fifteen years ago. I want a complete *muchillos* and all neatly stamped." In addition to a saddle for his own use, he wanted to examine the possibility of using the California saddle for the entire cavalry service. His friend Couts gave specific instructions to the supplier:

> [I] want it made of *good even leather* and well stamped — the muchillos particularly all even. If convenient, stamp the piece of each on some part of it. The stirrup leather hide and doubled, with good buckle.... Want this well done, cheap, and *immediately*.[18]

Stoneman had a formidable task on his hands. The Army of the Ohio cavalry was in terrible shape and had to be re-mounted, equipped, and reorganized. He hoped to have 6,000 troopers ready for duty that spring, but Schofield stepped up the timetable and in early April ordered Stoneman to join the main army with all that he had. Stoneman mustered 2,000 men, leaving behind 2,300 at Lexington who were mounted, but only partially armed. An additional 1,700 had neither mounts nor arms.

Stoneman's cavalry was intended to be an integral part of General William Tecumseh Sherman's campaign to capture Atlanta. Sherman had relieved Grant of command of the Military Division of the Mississippi as Grant headed east to assume command of all the armies of the United States. Sherman accompanied Grant as far as Cincinnati to discuss details of the coming campaign.[19] Grant was determined to plan Union offensives so that the Confederates could not move men back and forth to counter uncoordinated Union attacks. Grant's drive on Richmond was to be paralleled by Sherman's march on Atlanta, and Sherman lost no time preparing for a thrust into the heart of the Confederacy. On March 10, Sherman met at Chattanooga with his generals: McPherson, who commanded the Army of Tennessee, Thomas, commanding the Army of the Cumberland, and Schofield. The plans for the upcoming campaign were covered.

The main concern was over supplies. Nashville, the chief depot, was in enemy territory and the routes of supply from Louisville to Nashville, by rail and by the Cumberland

River, had to be guarded "every foot of the way." Bridges, trestles, and culverts had to be protected from southern sympathizers and Confederate cavalry. As the army advanced into Georgia, the railway would have to be repaired and used, and, of course, guarded. Sherman fixed May 1 as the date when everything was to be in readiness.

As General Schofield returned to Knoxville to prepare his troops, Stoneman issued marching orders to the cavalry to move to Georgia. Stoneman ordered the use of packmules to move forage for the horses and supplies for the men, a new experience for the Army of the Ohio, and it was the first bone of contention between Stoneman and his troopers, many of whom were from Kentucky. Stoneman favored the use of mules based on his pre-war experience, but they were accepted only grudgingly. Stoneman issued a number of orders designed to maintain discipline among the free-spirited Kentuckians. A commissioned officer was to march in the rear of each company and no one was to leave the ranks except for reasons of dire necessity. Each regiment was to have a rear guard; no stragglers were to enter a private dwelling-house. (This was designed to prevent visits back home.) Provost guards were established for each brigade. Even falling out to procure water was prohibited. Men were to fill their canteens before marching.[20] The historian of the 1st Kentucky described Stoneman as follows:

> Perhaps the stern iron will of the great raider was thought best to bend the dashing, frolicsome mountaineer cavalry of this department into rigid discipline.... We had often read of Stoneman who had gained an extensive reputation in his raids around Richmond, Virginia and had an enthusiastic admiration for his daring feats. We had pictured in our minds romantic ideas of the person of Stoneman, as being free from the imperfections of those in high rank with whom we had been familiar with grand form and courtly airs, as belonged to the knight-errants in the days of chivalry.[21]

The "stern iron will" of Stoneman soon clashed with the free spirits of the Kentucky cavalry as the regiments marched toward their destination of Dalton, Georgia. The men wanted to pick up fresh horses, see wives and girlfriends, and leave pay with their families. When they reached Danville, Kentucky, the troopers broke ranks, even marching through Stoneman's bodyguard, driving him into a fury. By the time the command reached Kingston, Tennessee, only two officers and 71 men answered roll call out of a roster of 800 men. Stoneman placed most of the officers under arrest.

Once in Dalton, Stoneman reported further difficulties to General Sherman. His subordinate officers were incompetent, and he had to post every regiment himself. Stoneman wrote Schofield and warned him that he must use the horses sparingly. They had been ridden nearly 20 miles a day for 23 days and had been without hay or grass. The horses, Stoneman reported, were "pretty nearly played out."[22]

Stoneman's difficulties with the 1st Kentucky abated somewhat when the Kentuckians relieved Brigadier General Edward M. McCook on the left of the main army on May 12. They were soon attacked by Wheeler's cavalry and both the 1st and 11th Kentucky were heavily engaged near Dalton; Stoneman himself was pressed so closely that he lost his hat while evading the enemy. Stoneman released the officers from detention for the action and Colonel Silas Adams led in a charge against the enemy, causing them to retreat in disorder. The charge brought about reconciliation, and even Stoneman's hat was retrieved.

Stoneman dropped all charges against the officers and the Kentuckians forgave him for "all his infirmities of temper" and looked upon their commander with pride.[23]

The Atlanta campaign was under way, but the cavalry played a minor role in the beginning. Sherman used his cavalry in a traditional way: scouting, protecting the flank of the infantry, and by ordering movements calculated to mislead the enemy. Sherman was notorious for his mistrust of the cavalry arm, and the wooded and hilly terrain in Georgia supported his conviction that cavalry was little more than a support for the main army.

What little Sherman saw of the cavalry did not impress him. In mid-June he wrote Grant a "not purely official" letter in which he expressed himself much more frankly than he did in official dispatches concerning Stoneman and Brigadier General Kenner Dudley Garrard, commander of the Second Cavalry Division. "Our cavalry is dwindling away," Sherman complained. "We cannot get full forage and have to graze, so that the cavalry is unable to attempt anything. Garrard is over-cautious, and I think Stoneman is lazy.... Each has had a fine chance of cutting in but were easily checked by the appearance of the enemy."[24]

Stoneman was ordered by Sherman to Campbellton and Sandtown, eight miles downstream on the Chattahoochee River, to mislead the Confederates as to where the main army would cross. Stoneman was to do more than demonstrate. He was ordered to attack the Atlanta and West Point Railroad after crossing the river. He reached Moore's Bridge, Georgia, on July 13, which the Confederates tried unsuccessfully to burn. When Stoneman, commanding the 11th Kentucky, tried to cross the following day they were opposed by four pieces of artillery and infantry. Stoneman elected not to attempt to cross and ordered that the bridge be burned instead, reporting that to proceed further "would incur risks inadequate to the results." Stoneman pointed out that it was impossible to proceed without discovery, as women as well as men acted as scouts and messengers. Fearing capture, Stoneman advised Sherman that he was retreating to Sweet Water town. This is not what Sherman wanted to hear, and Stoneman remained in disfavor.[25]

Sherman was remarkably forgiving of his senior officers, despite his dissatisfaction with their performances thus far in the campaign. Sherman referred to Stoneman in his memoirs as "a cavalry officer of high repute." When he consolidated his cavalry into two divisions, he entrusted Stoneman with one of them, while the other was commanded by General Edward McCook. Stoneman was now at Decatur, Georgia, with three brigades: the First with 700 men of the 5th and 6th Indiana commanded by Colonel James Biddle, the Second under Colonel Silas Adams, which consisted of 550 men of the 1st and 11th Kentucky, and the Third, under Colonel Horace Capron, which included 800 men of the 14th Illinois, 8th Michigan, and a section of the 1st Ohio. The 24th Indiana battery with two 3-inch regulation guns and fifty-four men was also attached to the division. McCook commanded about 3,500 troopers, while Stoneman had 2,050 men of his own division and commanded an additional 4,000 troopers under Brigadier General Kenner Garrard. It was a formidable cavalry force.[26]

Sherman now developed his plan of battle to capture Atlanta. He intended to move the Army of the Tennessee to the right "rapidly and boldly" while the cavalry was to divide into two commands and march by the right and the left of the army to intercept the Macon

Stoneman (standing hatless) and foreign observers. Falmouth, Virginia, 1863 (courtesy National Archives, 90–CM–47).

road above Jonesboro and break up the Macon and Western Railroad there. The movement was to begin on July 27.

Stoneman and his fellow officers met with Sherman to plan the cavalry campaign. Kenner Garrard's division was to remain behind Stoneman and prevent Major General Joseph Wheeler's Confederate cavalry from attacking Sherman's rear or intercepting Stoneman. Stoneman was ordered to move to the left around Atlanta to McDonough and reach the Macon road near Lovejoy station, a supply center for the Confederate forces at Atlanta. McCook's division was to march to the right around Fayetteville and meet Stoneman at Lovejoy station south of Atlanta, where they would destroy the railroad as effectively as possible. Given the size of the Union cavalry, Sherman and his generals were convinced that they could whip anything Wheeler could put up against them. Sherman wrote later that he and his officers agreed that there was "not a doubt of perfect success."[27]

Just before the operation was to commence, Stoneman made a daring proposal to Sherman. After destroying Wheeler's cavalry, he proposed that he proceed to Macon and Andersonville and liberate Union prisoners confined at those two points. There were 1,500 Union officers imprisoned at Macon "barely fed and harshly treated," according to Sherman, and 23,000 enlisted men at Andersonville where conditions were appalling. "There was something most captivating in the idea and the execution was within the bounds of probability of success," Sherman later wrote, but he made it clear that such a dramatic step should take place only after the defeat of Wheeler and the destruction of the railroad at Lovejoy.[28] Nonetheless, Sherman was captivated by the proposal. In fact, he seemed to lead Stoneman on:

> I see many difficulties but as you say even a chance of success will warrant the effort and I consent to it.... If you can bring back to the army any or all of those prisoners of war, it will be an achievement that will entitle you, and the men of your command, to the love and admiration of the whole country.[29]

With the advantage of hindsight, the prospect for the success of Stoneman's proposal seems slight. How could Stoneman's force of 2,200 troopers defeat Wheeler and then march sixty miles south through hostile territory and bring out thousands of sick and emaciated prisoners back to Union lines? There was great emotion in the North over the conditions at Andersonville, where men were dying by the day. Emotion rather than a realistic analysis seems to have influenced both Sherman and Stoneman and convinced them that the raid had a good chance of success. Sherman expressed his feelings in a letter to General Henry Halleck: "Nothing but natural and intense desire to accomplish an end so inviting would have drawn me to commit a military mistake at such a crisis, as that of dividing and risking my cavalry to the success of my campaign." Later he wrote a letter to the Sanitary Commission, again expressing his feelings: "I don't think I ever set my heart so strongly on any one thing as I did in attempting to rescue those prisoners."[30]

Many of Stoneman's officers did not share his enthusiasm for the raid. When he briefed his brigade commanders and other senior officers on the mission he informed them he had "discretionary orders" permitting him to march to Macon and Andersonville if he thought it "proper and expedient" after destroying the railroad between the Confederate army and their supplies. "He did not explain what he would do with this vast army of sick and helpless soldiers," Colonel Thomas H. Butler, of the 5th Indiana Cavalry, said to a reunion of the regiment after the war, "but intimated he might strike for the South Atlantic coast." Butler reported that he advised his brigade commander, Colonel Biddle, that he should advise his wife "that he was going on a raid and she would not hear from him for some time and in all probability he would serve the rest of his term in some rebel prison pen." When asked to explain his remark, Butler said he had no confidence in Stoneman's ability to command a raiding party. "I will state here that this was the opinion of almost every officer in the command."[31]

Stoneman moved out at 4:00 A.M. on July 27 and met Garrard at Decatur, where there was confusion in the darkness as the two divisions met. In fact a vedette from Garrard's command fired on Stoneman's advance guard. Fortunately, no one was hit.[32] Garrard's orders called for him to march to Flat Rock (sometimes called Flat Shoals or Flat Creek) to protect the rear of the main army eight miles southwest of Decatur, and prevent Wheeler from pursuing Stoneman.

Wheeler, Lieutenant General John Bell Hood's Chief of Cavalry and a native Georgian, was a restless, energetic man, known to be fearless. He was anxious to defend his native soil from the Yankee intruders. His men were in the trenches near Atlanta having relieved General William J. Hardee's infantry. Such an assignment, Wheeler believed, was an insult to his cavalry. Wheeler saw an opportunity to ride into battle when he learned of Garrard's approach to Flat Rock. After convincing Hood that he must blunt this threat, Wheeler marched quickly down the Flat Shoals Road with three brigades under Brigadier General Alfred Iverson. Sharp fighting followed on the following day as Garrard's troopers, armed with Spencers, defended themselves against the numerically superior Confederates. The Federals were surrounded, but finally extricated themselves after twelve hours of hard fighting.

Garrard's stiff resistance held Wheeler up for a day and gave Stoneman a day's lead on pursuing rebel cavalry. Garrard later reported that Stoneman abandoned him and his division and left it to its fate, apparently forgetting that protecting Stoneman and the rear of the main army from Wheeler's cavalry was his assignment.[33]

While Garrard fought off Wheeler, Stoneman's division headed east through the towns of Lithonia and Conyers along side the Georgia Railroad, and crossed the Yellow River before resting a few miles from Covington. When the 1st Kentucky rode into Covington on their way further south, one of Stoneman's officers observed that "The ladies were better dressed than any I had ever seen in Georgia" and "were very polite." Whiskey and brandy were also found and "a number got drunk and noisy and the ranks got into confusion which caused the officers much trouble." The Federal troopers demanded food and stole belongings from the inhabitants, harassed Confederate wounded in the local hospital, and generally behaved badly. Stoneman came on the scene and "commenced cursing and ordering." Stoneman always insisted that the men ride in columns of four and he turned the air blue when he saw the confusion in the ranks.[34]

Stoneman's command marched toward Monticello. After reaching Monticello, Confederate soldier Sam R. Watkins, with the Maury Grays of the 1st Tennessee Regiment, described how his regiment was sent by rail to Jonesboro where they engaged what Watkins described as "Stoneman's men." A regiment of rebel infantry and a brigade of cavalry had formed a line of battle on the Federals' rear, while the 1st Tennessee attacked them in front. Stoneman's men rode right through and over the line of infantry and headed towards Macon, tearing up railroad track as they went. It became a race between cavalry and infantry:

> We went to work like beavers, and in a few hours the railroad track had been repaired so we could pass. Every few miles we would find the track torn up, but we would get out of the cars, fix up the track, and light out again. We were charging a brigade of cavalry with a train of cars, as it were. They would try to stop our progress by tearing up the track, but we were crowding them a little too strong. At last they thought it was time to stop that foolishness, and then commenced a race between cavalry and cars for Macon, Georgia.[35]

Stoneman's troopers had traveled toward Macon on two parallel roads toward Monticello and on to Clinton, less than 30 miles from Macon. Stoneman was still thinking of a possible rendezvous with McCook as he sent Colonel Adams and the 1st Kentucky westward from Monticello to scout along the Ocmulgee River. Adams was to rejoin Stoneman at Monticello after determining whether or not there were any bridges along that section of the Ocmulgee. Stoneman had been advised that there were three bridges that could be used to reach Lovejoy station. When Adams returned, he gave Stoneman the alarming news that there were no bridges along this section of the river, only ferries that would be too time-consuming and dangerous to use. Stoneman now decided that there was no alternative but to proceed to Macon and carry out his plan to liberate Union prisoners there and destroy the Savannah and Macon railroad in the process. "This change of plan, if we call it by no harsher term, was the beginning of the end," Butler later observed.[36] Stoneman again divided his column and sent Adams to scout along the Ocmulgee while he headed for Clinton with the remainder of his command. They would reunite at Clinton that evening.[37]

After Stoneman had destroyed two cars full of livestock for the Confederate army and torn up a good deal of railroad track, he pushed on to his objective. The 14th Illinois struck the Macon and Milledgeville Railroad near Gordon. Small bridges were burned, three trains of cars and three engines were destroyed, and 22 boxcars loaded with supplies were destroyed.[38] The two columns joined together about one and a half miles from Macon when they learned that the Confederates had from four to six thousand State Militia and regular troops in the city. Stoneman's skirmishers reached the outskirts of the city on July 30 but the raiders were too late. Stoneman soon learned that the Federal prisoners had been moved from Camp Ogelthorpe on July 27. Lt. Richard Huffman, of the 1st Kentucky, lamented their delays:

> Oh, slowness. If we had only hurried a little, we could have released nearly 1,500 of our officers confined in prison at Macon and have so materially injured the Atlanta and Macon Railroad as to have caused the enemy to evacuate Atlanta. We were twelve hours behind time. They had only 500 men in Macon twelve hours before, guarding the Union prisoners, and we could have defeated them easily.[39]

Confederate Major General Howell Cobb commanded the Georgia reserves at Macon. An additional 2,500 troops under Brigadier General John H. Winder guarded prisoners at Andersonville. Cobb had been warned that a Yankee raiding party was moving toward Covington in considerable force, destination unknown.[40] Another message from Hood on July 27 advised Cobb that the destination of Stoneman's raiding party was still unknown and that he should be prepared.[41]

While Stoneman's command was preparing to engage Confederate militia across the river from Macon, the other Union cavalry thrust, commanded by General McCook, was carrying out his orders. He crossed the north bank of the Chattahoochee River on July 27 with perhaps no more than 1,300 men,[42] crossed the south bank at Riverton on the 28th, and worked his way down to Lovejoy Station, destroying two and a half miles of railroad track near Palmetto. The raiders also damaged sections of the Macon and Western Railway near Lovejoy Station. McCook reported after the raid that he obeyed his order from Sherman "implicitly, and accomplished all that it contemplated or directed."[43] In reality, the damage was promptly repaired by the Confederates.[44]

McCook reached McDonough on the 28th, where he was to meet Stoneman, but Stoneman was riding hard for Macon, considerably to the south. McCook didn't wait very long, as he heard that Wheeler's Confederates were in the area. These units must have been Brigadier General William H. "Red" Jackson's two brigades who were positioned between

Nine. "We were whipped..."

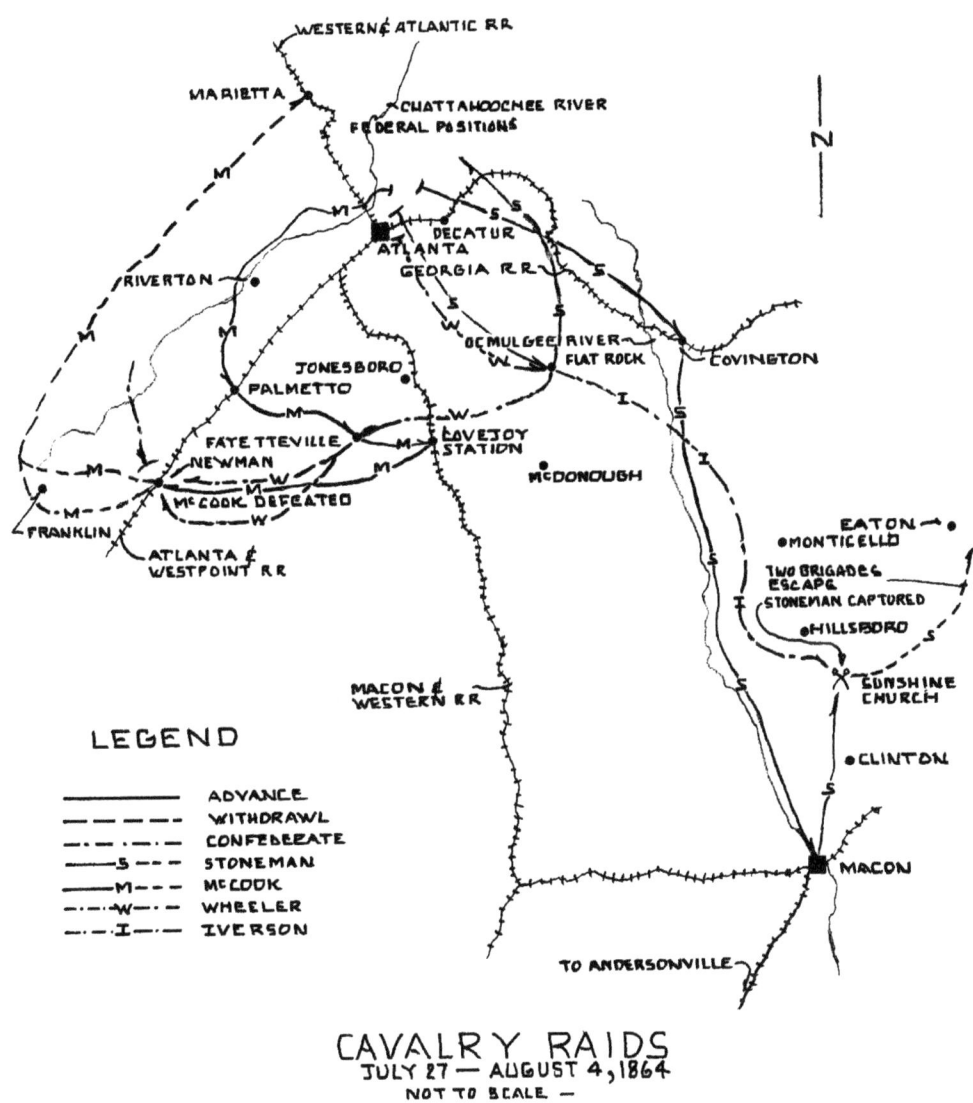

CAVALRY RAIDS
JULY 27 – AUGUST 4, 1864
NOT TO SCALE –

McCook and the town of McDonough, just 13 miles from Lovejoy. McCook headed for the Chattahoochee River and safety, marching in the direction of Newnan. Wheeler's cavalry, under Jackson, intercepted McCook and harassed his rear, inflicting heavy casualties. McCook continued toward Newnan where Wheeler again caught up with him. To his surprise, Confederate cavalry under General Philip Roddey occupied the town. By pure chance, Roddey had come up from north Alabama and was in Newnan just as McCook expected to find refuge there. Surrounded by Wheeler, Jackson, and Roddey, McCook fought his way out, losing 500 men in the process.[45]

While McCook struggled back to Federal lines, Stoneman faced a combined force of the 5th Georgia Reserves and Georgia State Militia at Macon. The governor of Georgia, Joseph F. Brown, appealed to every man in the city of Macon who had a gun to report for duty.[46] Stoneman reached the outskirts of Macon on July 30 and engaged the assortment of reserves and militia, who tenaciously fought the veteran Federals with their backs to the Oculmulgee. Shells from Stoneman's horse artillery, some fifteen rounds in all, landed in the city, most exploding harmlessly.[47]

Stoneman believed that Fort Hawkins, an old log fort built to guard against Indian raids, was the key to the defense of the city. Biddle's Indiana brigade was ordered to attack the fort to dislodge two artillery batteries placed there, but the Federal invaders were repulsed. The attacks made along the Clinton road by troopers of the 1st Kentucky who were nearing the end of their enlistments were desultory. The Kentuckians had freely engaged in drinking and plundering along the route of the raid. After eight hours of inconclusive skirmishing, Stoneman ordered his troops to withdraw.[48]

Stoneman knew that Wheeler's cavalry would soon be on him, so there was nothing to do but make their way out. He couldn't cross the Ocmulgee River in front of Macon because of the Confederate resistance and the wagon bridge to the city had been washed out.

According to Colonel Robert W. Smith, one of his field officers, he considered trying to escape through southern Georgia and Alabama, perhaps to Pensacola, but that was over 300 miles away. He sent Adams south along the east bank of the Ocumulgee with that plan in mind, but after the head of the column, encumbered by a pack train, advanced some two miles, they encountered 1,000 to 1,500 Confederate cavalry. Stoneman feared that the Confederates would intercept him at the ford where he had planned to cross the river, so he ordered Adams to return from the Ocumulgee.

Stoneman's officers were understandably anxious to know how the command was to return to Federal lines. Acting Chief of Staff Major Myles Keogh, who had a long association with Stoneman going back to the Chancellorsville raid, encouraged Butler to approach Stoneman and ascertain his plans.[49] Butler asked Stoneman which way he intended to march back to Sherman's lines. Stoneman replied that he had not fully decided. "I then asked the privilege of making a suggestion which was granted," Butler later reported. Butler suggested that they return on the Milledgeville road leaving the Macon (Clinton) road and rapidly march to safety, destroying bridges across some of the streams to frustrate their pursuers. Butler reasoned that the main force of the enemy would certainly be on the Macon road which had been used by the Federals on the way south. Stoneman told Butler he accepted the suggestion as a good one.[50]

Although Stoneman had agreed with his officers to take the Milledgeville road to safety, he changed his mind when he was advised that Confederate cavalry blocked his way. Instead, he headed north toward Hillsboro, which he believed was lightly defended and would give him the choice among three roads which he could take from that point at daybreak. The Confederates under Brigadier General Alfred Iverson's command blocked that road as well, and Stoneman was stopped some eight miles south of the village of Hillsboro at Sunshine Church.[51]

Stoneman still had the option of moving to his right and escaping from Iverson's main body. Butler found Stoneman, hoping to persuade him "to take the command out of that place…. On reporting to the general, I found him very much excited, walking to and fro and swinging his arms violently." Stoneman told Butler that he was glad he was present as

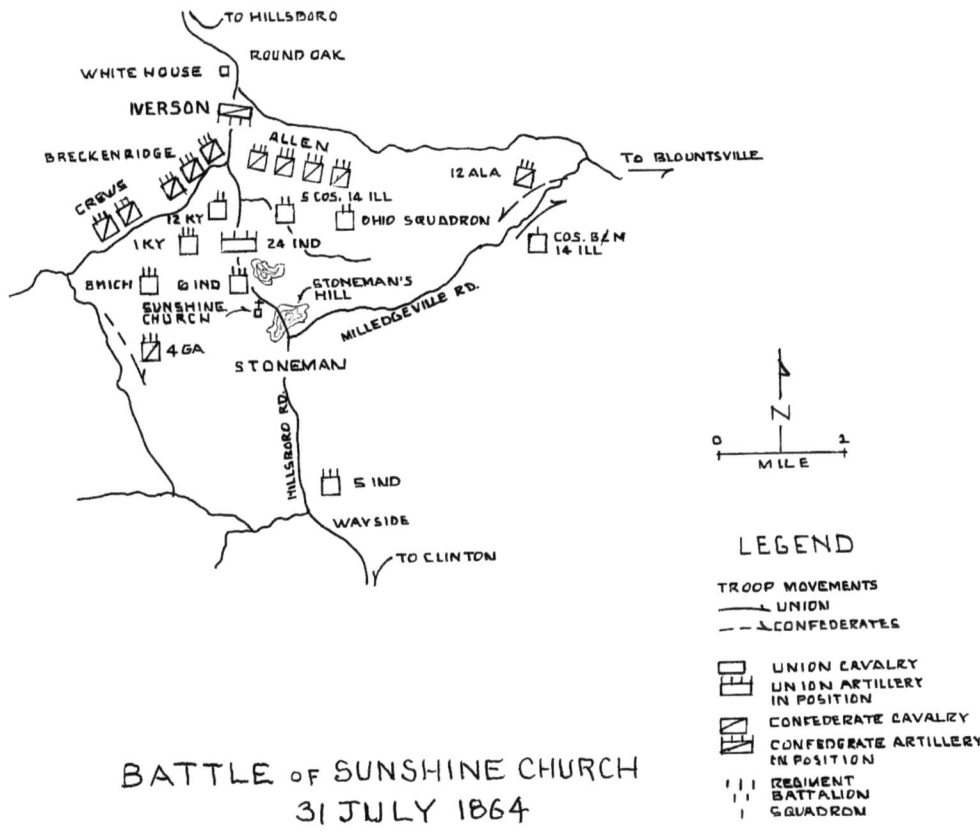

BATTLE OF SUNSHINE CHURCH
31 JULY 1864

he wanted a regiment that he could depend on. "If I had a dozen regiments like the 5th Indiana Cavalry I could whip all the cavalry in the Confederacy. Why that brigade [Adam's] broke before there were two hundred shots fired, and I couldn't rally twenty-five men around me." Butler felt the compliment fell quite flat under the circumstances.[52]

Despite efforts by Stoneman's officers to avoid a standing fight, always a dangerous position for cavalry to take, Stoneman announced that he intended "to fight it out right here." Desperate efforts were made to crack the Confederate lines and break free. Casualties among officers and men were heavy. Stoneman himself advanced with the skirmishers but ammunition was running low and the men were "fatigued almost beyond endurance."[53] They had been in the saddle for four days with little to eat, always moving quickly. The situation was critical.

The strength of the Confederate defenses, barricades reinforced with logs and rails, made it necessary for the Union troopers to fight dismounted. A quarter of the men were needed to guard the horses in the rear. The Confederates also had several batteries on the field while Stoneman's men had one third of a battery, consisting of two guns. When the pursuing Confederates from Macon showed up, the raiders were outnumbered six to one.[54]

Lt. Richard Huffman put the blame for the perilous situation at the top. From the junior officer's point of view, Stoneman should have placed a small force to skirmish with the enemy while the main body escaped by moving to the right. Huffman concurred with

Butler's account, censuring Stoneman for ignoring the advice of his staff and ordering an assault on the superior force of Confederates who had formed along the Covington road in a V shape. Stoneman had been under fire all day on July 31 and Huffman later recorded that he "appeared almost mad."[55] Stoneman himself admitted that he was exhausted and in severe pain and debilitated by his hemorrhoid condition. His horse, Beauregard, had been shot out from under him and he was scarcely able to mount the worn-down one that replaced it, he reported later.[56]

Stoneman called a council with his officers to decide what to do. The first alternative agreed upon was to fight their way out through the right rear, but just as Stoneman issued that order, the Confederates opened up with batteries on the right and left flanks, followed by an infantry charge. If the troopers of the 1st Kentucky are to be believed, Stoneman decided to surrender his entire command at this point. Again, Lt. Huffman reported:

> We now learned that Gen. Stoneman had determined on surrendering. I have seen excitement in our regiment, but when our men, whose time was nearly out, learned that they were about to be made prisoners, the excitement was uncontrollable. Already many of the men of their own accord had taken out on foot to make their way through the enemy's line.[57]

Colonel Silas Adams, of the 1st Kentucky, went to Stoneman and "vehemently protested" the surrender of his brigade, pointing out that the enlistments were about to expire and "that it was unjust ... to consign his men to captivity to waste their lives in the horrid prisons of the south."[58] Many of the men of one battalion of the 11th Kentucky had once served in the Confederate army and their treatment would have been severe indeed if they had been captured. In the words of the historian of the 14th Illinois, "All chose death on the field rather than Andersonville," which he called "Andersonhell."

The Kentuckians later recorded that the following exchange took place between Stoneman and Colonel Adams:

> If you attempt to get out, your command will be cut all to pieces and killed. Adams rejoined: I will take the responsibility. Stoneman then said: If you attempt it, you must take the responsibility on your shoulders.[59]

Other versions of Stoneman's decision differ from that of the 1st Kentucky. Lt. Colonel R.W. Smith, who was also with Stoneman, reported that he met Adams just after his conversation with Stoneman. Adams said that he had permission from Stoneman to "cut out if he could" and that the general was about to surrender "but that he desired all to get out who could, and he would remain in person and engage the enemy as long as possible, so as to give those making their escape as much start as possible."[60] Major Haviland Tomkins, of the 14th Illinois, reported that Stoneman said "he would not refuse any from going"[61] but that he saw no other means then surrender to protect the lives of the men. "The general was much broken down at the thought of a surrender; he seemed to have little regard for his own personal safety, if he could only save his command."[62] According to Tomkins, Stoneman said he could delay pursuit of the Confederates by five hours.

Major Duvall English, of the 11th Kentucky, an aide on Stoneman's staff, carried the white flag through the dispirited Federals. Colonel Butler refused to let it past, at first, and returned to Stoneman for permission to "cut our way out" but he was again refused. After a consultation with his officers, and taking note of the fact they were almost surrounded, he let the white flag pass.[63]

The terms of surrender were accepted and Stoneman handed over his sword to Colonel Charles C. Crews, one of Iverson's brigade commanders, although Stoneman had asked to surrender to Iverson. Weakened by days of hard riding and loss of blood, and humiliated by his surrender, the old soldier collapsed on a log and wept.[64] "My capture was mainly due to my almost complete prostration from excessive loss of blood, weakening me to such an extent as to render further bodily effort almost impossible," Stoneman later reported.[65]

Trooper C.M. White, of the 5th Indiana Cavalry, described how the men were ordered to dismount and throw down their arms and "marched from the hill as prisoners of war." White reported that the "thickets" were searched to flush out Federal cavalrymen who were hiding under leaves and dirt but most were captured. While the Confederates stripped the men of possessions, White wrote later that "for the most part, our captors treated us as 'comrades out of luck' and compared to the Home Guards to whom we were soon transferred, they were gentlemen."[66]

White and his comrades were held overnight in a makeshift pen "used to carroll [sic] mules in and also [as] a hog pen as it was covered with corn cobs." The prisoners were marched into Macon, passing where they had fought three days before, eating raw corn as they passed fields along the way. White wrote after the war that they stopped in front of a fine residence "whose inmates had at the time of the attack on Macon carried cakes and wine to the boys on our skirmish line, and professed great friendship for us, but now the old lady of the house came down to her gateway and reviled us fearfully."[67]

In a masterful feat of leadership, Adams led his men over hills and across ditches, avoiding rebel pickets, and headed toward the town of Edonton. Colonel Capron also escaped with most of the 14th Illinois, the 8th Michigan, and the 1st Ohio squadron. Part of the 6th Indiana escaped as well. Somewhere between 1,200 and 1,300 men eluded capture. The men fought with desperation, slashing through Confederate cavalry and infantry. Capron's brigade had joined Adams on July 31 around Edonton but, as the exhausted troopers headed for the Chattahoochee River and safety, Capron took a different road and rested for the night. A large party of freedmen were following their liberators. Confederate cavalry, told by local farmers that Union cavalry were in the vicinity, caught up with the group, charged through the freedmen, causing confusion, and set on the exhausted and sleeping Yankees, many of whom had no arms or ammunition. A stampede took place as the men panicked and rushed toward nearby woods. Many of Capron's men were killed, captured, and wounded, pursued through the woods for several days by citizens, soldiers, and even bloodhounds. Less than one-half of the regiment reached Union lines.[68] Adams and his men, on a different road, crossed the river and made their way to Marietta.

It was a disaster for Stoneman and his command. Forced to surrender were 600 men in all, and an additional 400 were lost in the days after the battle. Close to half of Stoneman's command was killed or captured.

Stoneman gave his version of events in a report to Sherman sent under a flag of truce several days after his capture. Suffering from humiliation and physically spent, Stoneman was brief, due to his circumstances, but he took the opportunity to place the blame on others. Stoneman reported that after he had discovered that a large force of Confederate cavalry "was close upon my rear and the only course for me to pursue to get out was to turn about and if possible whip this force. This I think we might have done had my command fought as it ought to and as I hoped it would have done." Stoneman concluded that "we were whipped, and this principally on account of the bad conduct of the Kentucky brigade in the attack during the morning and in fact throughout the day." Stoneman ended his report with a bitter comment. "I feel better satisfied with myself to be a prisoner of war, as much as I hate it, then to be amongst those who owe their escape to consideration of self-preservation."[69]

This was a charge the 1st Kentucky felt compelled to answer. The brigade historian wrote it would be charitable to "pass it by as the ebullition of a distempered brain" but he pointed out that the 1st and 11th Kentucky cavalry had too many experiences in combat not to know that it was futile to continue charging an impregnable front while simultaneously under attack on the flank. His account went on to refer to Stoneman's "ungovernable temper" and his reluctance to bestow compliments on subordinates. Hence, he could not give Colonel Adams, who escaped with his men, the honors he deserved.[70]

Colonel Butler of the 5th Indiana also joined in the bitter recriminations of Stoneman after the war:

> No harsh language, nor even the punishment of responsible parties, could bring back the dead comrades of the Fifth Indiana Cavalry, who were sacrificed to save General Stoneman from a military disgrace.[71]

McCook put as fine a face on his participation as possible, referring to his achievement of extricating himself as "a great success" but laid the blame, with considerable justification, at the feet of George Stoneman. The raid, he reported, was a brilliant success, but "had the forces of General Stoneman been able to unite with mine near McDonough ... I think we might have successfully carried our arms ... and accomplished more magnificent results than any raid in the history of the war."[72]

To General Sherman, the demolition of half of his cavalry strength confirmed his worst fears about the effectiveness of his mounted arm. In his official report, he sardonically observed that "On the whole, the cavalry raid is not deemed a success."[73] In his *Memoirs*, Sherman was more critical of Stoneman and the cavalry arm in general:

> Stoneman had not obeyed his orders to attack the railroad *first* before going to Macon and Andersonville but had crossed the Ocmulgee River high up near Covington and had gone down the river on the east bank.... Stoneman shelled the town [Macon] across the river but could not cross over by the bridge, and returned to Clinton, where he found his retreat obstructed, as he supposed, by a superior force. There he became bewildered, and sacrificed himself for the safety of his command.[74]

Most historical accounts accept Sherman's judgment of the Macon raid and blame Stoneman for disobeying orders and "riding for glory" in a vain and unrealistic effort to liberate Union prisoners of war. However, there were other failures that contributed to the debacle, some of them Sherman's. He vastly underestimated the strength of Wheeler's cavalry, and the Federals faced over 10,000 Confederate cavalrymen, although perhaps a third of that number were poorly armed and equipped. Garrard separated from Stoneman's command, depriving him of 4,000 troopers, and left him with 2,100 to 2,200 men to fend off Wheeler and the Confederates at Macon. Finally, faulty intelligence led Stoneman to believe there were three bridges across the Ocmulgee, north of Macon, so he believed he could link up with McCook. These bridges did not exist. If he crossed the river, he would have had to do so at Macon, far too late to join up with McCook, and which proved impractical in any case.

Stoneman never publicly defended himself from criticism after the raid, except for the short report he wrote from captivity. Even his health problems did not surface until after the war when he disclosed that he was exhausted and in severe pain at the time of his capture.

The failure of his cavalry convinced Sherman that only the main army could cut the railroad below Atlanta and eventually cut off the "Gate City of the South." To that end, he moved to "recompose" his cavalry into what he deemed essential for offense and defense. Judson Kilpatrick was assigned the right rear of Schofield's flank which was exposed, Garrard was kept on the army's left, replacing Stoneman, and McCook's division was in reserve, close to Marietta.

Stoneman, along with two of his fellow prisoners of war, injected themselves in the issue of prisoner-of-war exchanges which had been stopped because the Confederates refused to exchange Negro prisoners. In a joint letter to President Lincoln, Stoneman, who was the senior officer among the three, showed that he was not particularly sensitive to the principle supported by Lincoln, that captured black soldiers would not be consigned to slavery or even death. Confederate authorities, anxious to reinstate prisoner exchanges, permitted letters like Stoneman's to be carried to Washington by couriers. Stoneman pointed out that there were 35,000 Union enlisted men confined at Andersonville, on a field of thirty acres. Of that number, 20,000 had no shelter at all. A prisoner must live or die on three-fourths of a pound of bread or meal and one-eighth of a pound of meat of a quality that, in the North is "consigned to the soap-maker." Stoneman and his fellow petitioners had been told that the only obstacle in the way of exchanges was the status of enlisted Negroes. Stoneman wrote that Negro prisoners were seldom imprisoned, "they are distributed among the citizens or employed among government works. Under these circumstances, they receive enough to eat and are worked no harder than accustomed to; they are neither starved nor killed." Stoneman admitted that they were consigned to slavery "but their slavery is freedom and happiness compared with the cruel existence imposed among our gallant men."[75] Stoneman clearly believed that a different status could be applied to black soldiers.

The pressure on Lincoln was enormous, but he was unwilling to concede the principle that there could be no difference in the question of Union prisoners. The Lincoln administration informed the Confederates that they would renew exchanges when "all" classes of prisoners were involved.

George Stoneman was to suffer the humiliation of captivity but only for a brief time. He was moved to Charleston but later sent back in Georgia late in September at the town of Rough and Ready, exchanged for Confederate General D.C. Govan. He emerged from prison, the highest ranking officer ever captured by the Confederates, determined to settle accounts and salvage his reputation as a soldier.

Ten

Payment of a Debt

John Schofield came to the rescue once again. After the abortive Macon raid and his imprisonment, Stoneman was exchanged and returned to Knoxville. Schofield appointed him second-in-command of the Department of the Ohio, much to the disgust of Secretary of War Stanton, who expressed his misgivings to Grant. "If you approve of his doing so, I am content, although I think him one of the most worthless officers in the service, and who has failed in everything entrusted to him." Grant replied that he was not in favor of using officers who had failed but he deferred to Schofield's judgment. He should be allowed to use his officers in his own way. "I would simply suggest the transmission of the dispatch to General Schofield, and leave it discretionary with him to employ General Stoneman, or relieve him from duty, as he deems best."[1] Clearly, Stoneman's standing was at a low ebb late in the winter of 1864, but Schofield's order was to stand.

Stoneman was determined to redeem himself with a bold strike through the gaps in the Alleghenies. They could be a back door into the heart of the Confederacy, and Stoneman had a plan.[2] His objective was Saltville in southwest Virginia, a major resource of the Confederacy and vital to the preservation of food intended for Lee's army. Stoneman wanted to use the cavalry commanded by General Stephen Gano Burbridge. The cavalry commander in Kentucky was ready to operate against the enemy with his 4,000 men, adequately armed with carbines and rifles. The 2nd Ohio Heavy Artillery was also to be used with about 1,000 men, as well as the 1st U.S. Colored Artillery. Other units included the 34th Kentucky, the 4th Tennessee, the 3rd North Carolina, and the 10th Michigan. All told, Stoneman had 9,000 to 10,000 troopers available.

Stoneman had a more ambitious raid in mind, as well. He proposed to move quickly to Bristol and cut off the enemy from Saltville. If the 3,000 to 6,000 Confederates in the area could be neutralized, North Carolina could open up to the Federals and perhaps South Carolina, as well. Salisbury, North Carolina, the site of a large Confederate prison and a military supply center, was the ultimate objective. Stoneman urged Schofield to approve his plan. "I owe the Confederacy a debt I am anxious to liquidate, and this appears to be a propitious occasion," he wrote.[3]

Schofield approved the first part of Stoneman's plan to "push the enemy as far back as practicable and destroy the salt-works and railroad" but deferred his approval on extending the raid into North Carolina "until affairs here take a definite shape."[4]

The salt works were important to the Confederate cause. There were only five productive sources of salt in the South when the war broke out. Two were in Kentucky and one was in what was later West Virginia along the Kanawha River. All three fell under Union control early in the war. Louisiana was another source of supply but this, too, was lost after the fall of Vicksburg. Only Alabama and Saltville, Virginia, provided salt for the Confederacy by 1863, and since Alabama served the Gulf Coast, only Saltville supplied the remainder of the Confederacy, especially Lee's Army of Northern Virginia. Each Confederate state had its own furnace at Saltville, and it was not unusual to see hundreds of wagons lined up to receive their share. Production reached 3,000 bushels a day by 1862. Payment was made in wood, needed to keep the kilns going, and in Confederate dollars.[5] Of interest is the fact that a partner in the firm managing the salt works was William Alexander Stuart, younger brother of J.E.B. Stuart, the flamboyant Confederate cavalryman.

Without salt, the Confederacy had no means of preserving food for either military or civilian use, especially beef, so protecting the salt works was a matter of great necessity. Two additional militarily significant objectives made Southwest Virginia a tempting target for Stoneman. The Wytheville Union Lead Mine Company, located at Austinville, Virginia, provided lead for Confederate bullets, despite its name. An additional target was the Virginia and Tennessee Railroad, an important rail system for the Confederates.

Stoneman's plan was not the first Federal attempt to destroy Saltville, and the Confederates had allocated substantial forces to protect this vital resource. In July of 1863, Major General Ambrose Burnside captured East Tennessee and then threatened Southwest Virginia and the salt works, but he was held off by Confederate forces. In a more determined attack in September 1864, General Stephen Burbridge led veterans of the 12th Ohio, the 11th Michigan, and 100 men of the 1st Kentucky in a raid that proved to be one of the most punishing expeditions suffered by Union cavalry. The Kentuckians thought that their enlistments had expired, but they were pressed into service and led across the Laurel Mountain into Virginia in a violent thunderstorm. Crossing the mountain in pitch blackness on a narrow path, the men dismounted and led their horses into the valley beyond and engaged Giltner's Brigade under Colonel Edward Trimble. After sharp fighting, the Confederates fell back to Laurel Gap, which is described as "a veritable Gibraltar," only five miles from Saltville. The Federals pressed forward and could have taken the town, as it was defended by untrained militia, but Burbridge camped in front of the gap as darkness fell and gave the Confederates time to organize a defense of the town.[6]

On October 2, Burbridge advanced and engaged troops under Brigadier General Alfred "Mudwall" Jackson, so named when he was compared to the other Jackson. The Confederates enjoyed an advantage of natural defenses created by the hills and bluffs surrounding Saltville. After heavy fighting, the Confederates, using long-range Enfield rifles, inflicted heavy casualties on the advancing Federals and Burbridge, leaving his dead and wounded on the battlefield, ordered a withdrawal. "Come right up and draw your salt," the Confederates taunted, as the bluecoats, out of ammunition, retreated after suffering 350 casualties.[7]

The presence of the 5th United States Colored with Burbridge, many of whom were dismounted, may have led to one of the war's worst atrocities against black troops. Subjected to ridicule from their fellow Union soldiers as they marched, the black unit took part in the assault against Saltville and their casualties were high, 114 men and four officers killed out of four hundred men engaged. A Confederate courier named Mosgrove reported that troops from Tennessee shot every wounded black soldier they could find, including the only slightly wounded who were standing in groups. Confederate General John Breckinridge ordered the massacre to stop, but the killing continued after he left the scene. A Union surgeon, William Gardner, left behind to care for the wounded, reported that armed men entered the field hospital on the nearby Emory and Henry college campus and killed five wounded enlisted men of the 5th U.S. Colored and later returned to kill two more, including a white lieutenant, Elza C. Smith, of the 13th Kentucky.[8]

The extent of the "Saltville Massacre" is still a subject of historical dispute. William Marvel, writing in the *Blue and Gray Magazine*, argues that the murder of five black soldiers reported by Union surgeon Gardner, may have been the extent of the "massacre."[9] The 118 reported black casualties would not account for the hundreds allegedly killed by Tennessee troops. Marvel checked the carded medical records for the 5th U.S. Colored Cavalry at the National Archives, which confirmed the 118-casualty figure in the official records. Of the 118 total, only thirty-one are listed as missing. These missing soldiers are the only candidates to account for the hundreds of black soldiers allegedly massacred. Other accounts point out that the Tennesseans, and possibly troops from Kentucky and Texas as well, enraged by the sight of armed blacks on Southern soil, shot wounded blacks at will on the battlefield after the Federal withdrawal.

The attitude of the Confederates was expressed in an account of the battle which quotes "Mudwall" Jackson talking to his subordinate, Colonel Preston, before the engagement:

> "Kernel," said he, "my men tell me the Yanks have got a lot of nigger soldiers along. Do you think your reserves will fight niggers?"
> "Fight 'em?" said the old Colonel, bristling up; "by — —, sir, *they'll eat 'em up!* No! not eat 'em up! That's too much! By — —, sir, we'll cut 'em up!"[10]

Mosgrove, who wrote, "It was bang, bang all over the field, negroes dropping everywhere," was the main source of the massacre report, although William C. Davis, writing in the *Civil War Times Illustrated*, is convinced there was a massacre of appalling dimensions. He quotes wounded Federals, as well, who witnessed the cold-blooded executions of black troops. Only one man was tried for the Saltville atrocities after the war. Champ Ferguson, a Confederate guerilla, was sentenced and later hanged, on October 20, 1865, only for the murder of Lieutenant Smith, not for the killing of black troops.[11]

The behavior of Confederate troops at Saltville may well have been a factor in Stoneman's determination to destroy this important Confederate resource. He ordered Burbridge to find every available man he could from Lexington, Kentucky, to Cumberland Gap and gave him authority to impress horses wherever he could find them. Burbridge was to force-march to the Cumberland Gap on the Virginia border and await further instructions.

Stoneman moved from the Ohio Department's headquarters at Louisville to Knoxville, where he marched quickly to organize his troops. The Federals in East Tennessee, under Brigadier General Alvan Cullem Gillem, were demoralized after suffering a rout at Bull's Gap a month before. Stoneman moved to correct the "personal animosities" that had developed among the units concerned. Burbridge was to join forces with Gillem's men and meet Stoneman at a hamlet called Bean Station on December 11. Stoneman had kept his plans secret, even from his officers. The Confederates did not learn of his movements until several days after his departure.[12]

General Gillem's men drew the first blood of the expedition. Confederate General Basil Duke had assembled the remnants of Brigadier General John Hunt Morgan's old command under Morgan's brother, Colonel Richard Morgan, since Duke was absent on leave. Gillem captured Morgan and his entire wagon train in a sharp fight.[13]

Stoneman now moved to execute his plan to destroy the salt works and also the lead mines near Wytheville, Virginia, for good measure. Gillem, reinforced by the 11th Michigan and the 11th Kentucky, pursued the Confederates, under Brigadier General John C. Vaughn, northward until they were in striking distance of the salt works. Stoneman now had a choice. He could descend on the salt works, which were probably heavily defended, or bypass them for the time being, proceeding with the main force to Wytheville. There he could destroy Vaughn, damage the railroads as far as possible, as well as the lead works on the New River, and "take the salt works at our leisure." Stoneman decided on the latter course.[14] It proved to be a wise decision, as General Breckenridge had 3,000 infantry, several hundred cavalry, and a battery of field artillery at Saltville, in addition to the heavy guns of the fortifications and the regular garrison. Had Stoneman attempted to storm the salt works, he would have confronted that force in fortified positions with Vaughn's cavalry on his flank. Burbridge's disaster two months before would have been repeated.[15] Gillem sent a brigade toward the salt works as a feint and moved to Marion where he pursued Vaughn and virtually eliminated the effectiveness of his command, although 200 Confederates escaped over the mountains, leaving behind their artillery train and 198 prisoners of war.

Stoneman was waging total war. He ordered Colonel Buckley's brigade to march to the lead mines "to make a complete destruction of everything that was destructible," while Gillem destroyed stores, supplies, and buildings in Wytheville. Confederate General Vaughn advised the community at the lead mines that he was unable to defend them and that they should leave. When Buckley's brigade arrived at the mines, they discovered that the boat which might ferry them across was on the south side of the river. According to local accounts, they offered 500 dollars to anyone who would bring it over. No one responded, so 25 troopers swam their horses across the river. They sank the boats and were prepared to destroy all property at the mines, but the superintendent raised a white flag. Nonetheless, a furnace was destroyed and the raiders threw oil on buildings and set them on fire. The ore-washing equipment and smelting plant were partially destroyed and other reports indicate that the crushing machine, bellows, shot utensils, furnaces, grist, and saw mills were burned.[16] The property and supplies at Wytheville destroyed by the raiders, according to Stoneman's report, included 25,000 rounds of small-arms ammunition, pack-saddles, medical supplies, several hundred wagons and ambulances, ten pieces of field artillery, two locomotives, and several railroad cars. More importantly, railroad bridges were destroyed as far as Marion.[17]

Stoneman was ready to finish off the salt works as he moved south towards Marion. Breckinridge, seeing that his forces were being cut to pieces by Federal cavalry, left his strong defensive positions at the salt works and moved east to confront the Federals, just as Stoneman hoped he would. On December 18, the Confederates put up a "spirited resistance" near Marion, according to Stoneman, while Confederate accounts called the engagement "a substantial victory for the Confederates who held their position against largely superior forces."[18] The battle was fought on foot, but the Federals' Spencer carbines made the difference in the see-saw battle, although the Confederates were holding the better ground. At one point, Confederate cavalry got in the Union rear and attacked them from the direction of Wytheville. However, the 12th Ohio Cavalry beat off the enemy. If anyone doubted Stoneman's personal bravery, he proved them wrong in this battle as he formed the lines and fought alongside his men. Finally, Stoneman sent Gillem around the Confederate left, which effectively cut them off from the salt works, were now largely undefended. Breckenridge, in danger of being surrounded, broke off the engagement and escaped over a mountain road to North Carolina.[19]

Stoneman now set upon the salt works and the town of Saltville where the workers lived. The town was burned to the ground and the entire day and night of December 21 "was devoted to the destruction and demolition of the buildings, kettles, masonry, machinery, pumps, wells, stores, material, and supplies of all kinds." On the following day, Stoneman reported that the ruins of the salt works were a desolate sight.[20]

Although there were differences in Confederate and Union accounts concerning the extent of the damage, the destruction at Saltville was a major blow to the Confederacy. Salt had been in short supply in Lee's Army of Northern Virginia and now it was almost nonexistent. What little meat there was available for Lee's hungry men now could not be preserved.[21]

With the destruction of Saltville now complete and the Confederates routed, the Federals returned to Kentucky. It was one of the most difficult marches of the war. Continuous rain flooded the rivers, and roads were nearly impassable. Mountain passes were covered with ice and snow. A captain of the 12th Ohio described the suffering of the men and horses in much more graphic detail than the official reports. He recounted how the men dismounted and led their animals, worn out by famine and exhaustion. Horses fell by the wayside and were left to perish while the riders pushed through the storm on foot. Shoes and boots began to fail and some of the men were barefoot. Many suffered frostbite on hands and feet so severe that amputation was the result. Recrossing the Cumberland Mountains proved to be fatal to hundreds of horses and caused great suffering to Stoneman's victorious, but miserable, troopers. The raid into Virginia finally ended with victory and redemption for Stoneman, but his men suffered greatly as they marched in the dead of winter across the Clinch River and through Pound Gap into Kentucky.[22]

Major General George Thomas, Commander of the Department of the Cumberland and Stoneman's immediate superior, congratulated him on his "complete and splendid success" and informed him of other Union victories. Hood was defeated at Nashville and

Sherman was marching through Georgia to Savannah, but Stoneman had carried out only half of the plan he had proposed to General Schofield back in November. North Carolina and perhaps South Carolina were vulnerable and Stoneman was anxious to carry out the next stage of his atonement.

Stoneman did not realize until after the Saltville success how close he had come to being removed from his command. Upon his return to Knoxville, Schofield advised Stoneman that he had been ordered by General Grant and Stanton to relieve him from command on the ground of his failure in Georgia. The order was revoked because of Schofield's strenuous protest and willingness to take responsibility for retaining Stoneman in command. Schofield congratulated Stoneman "upon your complete success and vindication of your reputation as a general."[23] The flurry of dispatches concerning Stoneman began when Stanton, in a message to Schofield, directed that Stoneman be relieved and that he report to Cincinnati for further orders. Schofield disregarded this order, pointing out to Stanton that Stoneman's appointment as second-in-command of the Department of the Ohio had been approved by Sherman. He wryly suggested that if Grant had an officer "in which he had more confidence he should send him"[24] That was the end of the matter.

It was Grant who finally got matters moving in January. His dispatch to Thomas on January 31 included the following:

> Stoneman might penetrate South Carolina well down toward Columbia, destroying the railroad and military resources of the country, thus visiting a portion of the state which will not be reached by Sherman's forces. He also might be able to return to East Tennessee by way of Salisbury, N.C., thus releasing some of our prisoners in rebel hands. Of the probability of doing this, General Stoneman will have to be the judge.[25]

Grant suggested that 3,000 cavalry could do the job, including two regiments of Kentucky cavalry "which Stoneman had in his very successful raid into Southwestern Virginia."[26] Three Federal cavalry raids were in preparation, and competing with one another for men and supplies, especially horses. Major General James H. Wilson was ordered to march to Tuscaloosa and Selma, Alabama. Major General Edward R.S. Canby was to head for Mobile, and Stoneman was to move toward the Carolinas.

Stoneman learned of his orders from a member of Grant's staff who was carrying the orders to Thomas. Stoneman was ecstatic over the prospect of carrying out this raid, which was so similar to the operation he had proposed the previous November. He immediately advised Thomas what his requirements were. If Thomas could provide 2,000 good cavalry, 2,000 horses, and 600 Spencers, assembled in either Chattanooga or Nashville, Stoneman could make up the rest of the required force from troopers in East Tennessee. Stoneman used Grant's orders to dramatize the urgency. "General Grant says 'Let there be no delay.' Please get me off as soon as possible."[27]

Stoneman fired off a dispatch to General Gillem in Nashville—"I have just received orders from General Grant directing a movement in which your fine body of Cossacks is to play a very important part"[28]—and advised him to get his men ready as soon as possible.

Despite Stoneman's enthusiasm, there were delays. Major W.P. Chamblis, of Wilson's staff, told Thomas that "perhaps" he could equip Stoneman in ten to fifteen days, but it took close to six weeks for Stoneman to get the supplies he needed and assemble his men.

Many of Stoneman's units came from East Tennessee, which had long been a region of divided loyalties. The division was under the immediate command of General Alvin C. Gillem, who was from Tennessee and was known as a "home Yankee," a Southerner fighting for the Union. Many of his men were in the same category. Events were to prove that these were the raiders who exacted revenge on Southern supporters in North Carolina and Tennessee in the form of pillaging, looting and burning.[29] Gillem's division included Colonel William J. Palmer's First Brigade, which consisted of the 12th Ohio, 10th Michigan, and the 15th Pennsylvania. General Simeon B. Brown commanded the Second Brigade, the 11th Kentucky, 12th Kentucky, and the 11th Michigan. The Tennessee units, under Colonel John K. Miller, included the 8th, 9th, and 13th Tennessee.[30]

Grant became increasingly impatient as delays to the expedition mounted. Dispatches flowed to Thomas's headquarters prodding him to get Stoneman moving. Grant finally decided to change Stoneman's orders in view of his late start. Sherman was now in South Carolina, so there was no point in Stoneman raiding there. Grant was now pressing Lee's Army of Northern Virginia at Petersburg, and Stoneman could be used to block Lee's anticipated line of retreat from Richmond southwestward to Lynchburg. Stoneman was ordered to repeat his raid of the previous December, destroying the railroad as far toward Lynchburg as possible. In tandem with Stoneman, General Sheridan was departing Winchester for Lynchburg and that would aid Stoneman. Grant continued to lament the delay. "If it had been possible to get Stoneman off in time, he would have made a diversion in favor of Sherman.... It is too late now to do any good except to destroy the stock."[31]

Stoneman felt compelled to explain the delay. "You cannot be more anxious to have me get off than I am to go," he informed Grant. He described the difficulties in getting troops, equipment, and horses together from all over Kentucky. Horses, worn out or lost in the Saltville raid, had to be replaced. Grant never forgave Thomas or Stoneman for what he considered an unpardonably late start.

Stoneman finally got away on March 20, 1865, leading a division of some 6,000 men toward the Virginia line, assembling at Mossy Creek, Tennessee. Colonel John K. Miller's Third Brigade moved toward Carter's Station, close to Bristol and the Virginia line, while Colonel William J. Palmer's First Brigade and Brevet Brigadier General Simon B. Brown's Seventh Brigade crossed the Watauga River and headed for the mountains. This movement was designed to convince the Confederates that the raid was headed for Virginia. The bluecoats were all veterans, well mounted and equipped, and they traveled as lightly as possible. Only one wagon, ten ambulances, and four guns with their caissons accompanied the expedition. Stoneman had abandoned his usual practice of including cumbersome pack mules. Rations for only five days were carried by the men. After that, they would live off the land, a requirement that was feasible, since the countryside had not been pillaged by previous military intrusions.[32]

Stoneman's nine regiments of cavalry marched into Morristown, Tennessee, on March 23, receiving a hearty welcome from loyal citizens. A member of the 15th Pennsylvania noted, "These people came from all the surrounding country to see us and while perched on their rail fences greeted us with smiles and many a ludicrous expression."[33] It was here that the men received four horseshoes, a sure indication of a hard campaign ahead.

Stoneman's command marched toward the Appalachian Mountains and the Tennessee-North Carolina border and, after a difficult night march, stormed into Boone, North Carolina, the county seat of Watauga County, on March 28. According to Union accounts, Rebel Home Guards bravely, if foolishly, tried to stop the raiders. Stoneman gave this opposition short shrift in his report. "We arrived here in the A.M., captured the place, killing 9, capturing 62 home guards and 40 horses. We are getting along very well."[34]

Confederate accounts give a different picture. Cornelia Phillips Spencer, a Southern apologist who lived in Chapel Hill, North Carolina, during the Civil War, described Stoneman's entrance into Boone. "The village was taken completely by surprise. No one was aware of the approach of the enemy till the advance guard dashed up the main street, making no demand for surrender but firing right and left at every moving thing they saw...." Spencer wrote that she wasn't sure what Stoneman's policy was, but noted that "there were subordinate officers in his command who were only too happy in the opportunity to retort upon a defenseless and unresisting population."[35] One observer reported that the home guards were not prepared to fight, but someone fired accidentally at Stoneman's advance guard and this led to a fight in which three home guards were killed, not nine as Stoneman claimed. One innocent farmer, whom Spencer identified as Jacob Council, was killed because a negro [sic] working beside him called him "an infernal rebel." Such incidents were a harbinger of the internecine warfare that was to come.[36] In town, General Gillem

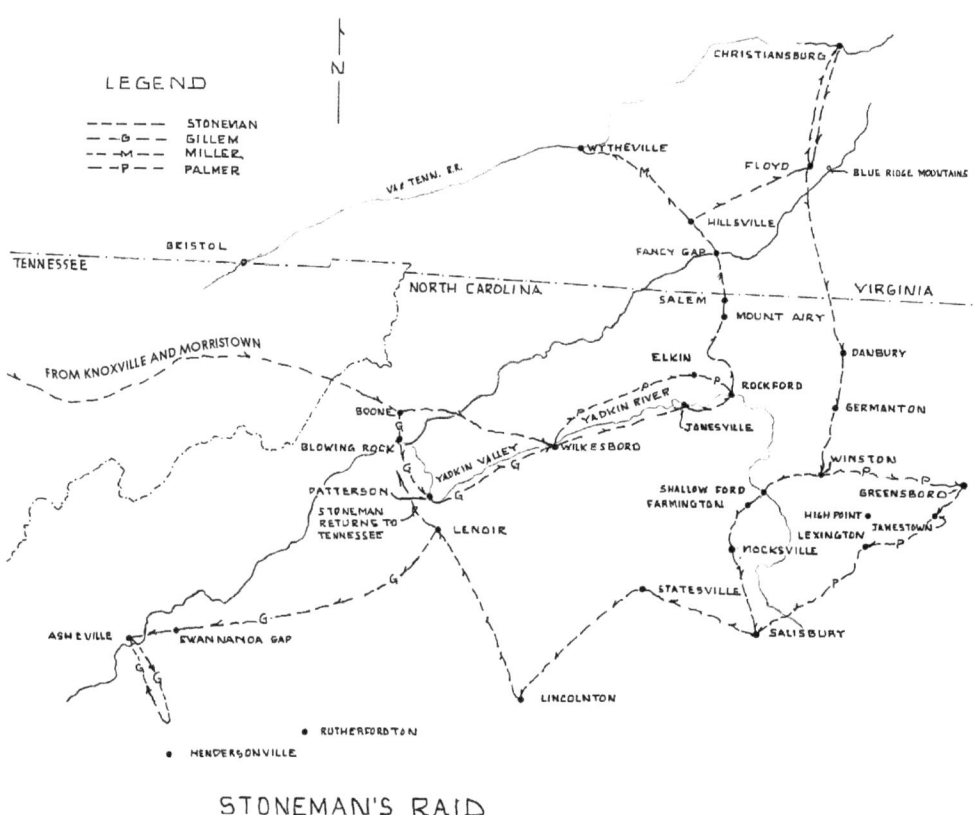

STONEMAN'S RAID
MARCH 22 – APRIL 24, 1865
NOT TO SCALE

ordered the jail burned and all county records destroyed, acts that seem senseless and for which Gillem was strongly censured by Stoneman, but this was mild compared to what happened to Boone later. Colonel George W. Kirk, commanding the 2nd North Carolina, occupied the town after Stoneman had departed. Kirk was ordered to prevent disbanded Confederate soldiers, who were traversing the area, from plundering as they moved south, and also to barricade roads and protect Stoneman's rear from Confederate cavalry. Kirk had recruited deserters, bushwhackers, and Union sympathizers from the mountains of North Carolina in his ranks, and they extracted a terrible vengeance on Confederate civilians, so much so that General Palmer, of the 15th Pennsylvania, recommended that Kirk be recalled later in the campaign, to "prevent his men from pillaging and committing excesses...."[37] The contrast between Stoneman and his subordinate Kirk was striking. Stoneman had treated Boone's inhabitants fairly while Kirk's men ransacked homes, stole food, and generally abused the population.[38]

Stoneman divided his command at Boone, taking Palmer's brigade to Wilkesboro, while Gillem moved toward the same destination by the Flat Gap road through Patterson. The raiders were now in the fertile Yadkin Valley, where there was an ample supply of food for both men and horses. Gillem showed his "home Yankee" tendencies by putting a large mill at Patterson to the torch despite assurances to the owner, Mr. Patterson, that it would be spared.[39] Local diarists noted that Stoneman regretted the destruction of the mill, as it supplied much of East Tennessee. Gillem's policy of destroying civilian property brought him into conflict with Stoneman more than once, but Gillem was determined to punish the rebels and did so when he could get away with it.[40]

The divided force was reunited at Wilkesboro where the 12th Ohio, followed closely by the 10th Michigan and 15th Pennsylvania, drove the Confederates from the town "like an avalanche."[41] Although the Confederates abandoned horses and supplies, forage for the raiders' horses was, once again, a problem. Gillem found it necessary to move most of his command to the north side of the Yadkin River to find forage, but heavy rain made further crossings impossible. Palmer was able to cross on March 30, but the Second Brigade, with Stoneman and Gillem, was prevented from crossing due to the swollen river. The command was separated once again.[42]

Stoneman was not happy with this division of his command deep in enemy territory. His troopers were in awe of him and he intimidated those around him, especially when he was in a towering rage. Howard A. Buzby of the 15th Pennsylvania, who had been left behind on the south side of the river to show where the command had crossed, left a colorful account of Stoneman's reaction to the day's events. "Swearing does not look well in print, nor sound well in talking, so what he said you will not know," Buzby later recounted when Stoneman found out most of his command had crossed one and a half hours before. Stoneman ordered one of his staff on a fine, big horse to cross, but as the horse began to flounder, "Stoneman swore at him to come out, that he would drown the horse ... some cavalry officers would as soon lose a man as a horse." Buzby continued with his narrative:

> I thought both man and horse would be drowned, but after some trouble they got out. I also thought Gillem's last day had come. In fact, I thought everybody around Stoneman would be killed. He fairly roared like a lion, and in his roaring would say "Palmer on one side of the

river with those Pennsylvania boys and me on this side. Gillem, I am going to see what you have." So, we drew back from the road and Gillem's troops passed in review before us.⁴³

Stoneman had decided to review Gillem's troops, many of whom were drunk on corn whiskey. Stoneman blamed his officers and showed his temper as a long train of captured wagons passed by in review. Buzby described the scene:

> Of all the reviews that were ever seen this one beats them all. The very heavens had opened their floodgates, and the water was coming down in sheets, which accounted for the appearance of the troops on the outside, and several whiskey stills, which had been struck back of the Ridge, accounted for their appearance on all sides. The number of the 'wounded' was startling and a good many were 'dead,' for corn whiskey is fearful stuff....
> All the carriages and omnibuses along the route had been confiscated. There was a carriage of the George Washington kind, filled with soldiers, their big boots sticking out in all directions.... If memory serves me right, this caravan of carriages and buses reached a mile or more.... General Stoneman was a powerfully built man, standing six feet four, with a face that showed the marks of long and hard service in the field. He would stop the parade occasionally and make a general reduction of Captains and Lieutenants. But when the 'wounded' came along in the carriages he said something like this: By-if-I-I'll — you-can it-where in-this-beats-they ought-to be-be killed — if I don't —.⁴⁴

Stoneman had a great fear of finding himself with a command divided by a river, subject to piecemeal attacks by the Confederates. He did not send any of his units across the Rappahannock at Chancellorsville when the river began to rise, and it stopped him at Macon as well. In this case, he was angered by his predicament and the condition of his troops. Even when his headquarters wagon arrived with his tent, he refused to be pacified by his staff. Only when Palmer signaled from across the river that all was well and no enemy was in sight did he begin to relax. By morning, Stoneman was composed and the "wounded" were refreshed after a good night's sleep.⁴⁵

Stoneman crossed the Yadkin and pushed his column of over 6000 men north toward Virginia by way of the town of Mount Airy. Resting for only half an hour, he swept eastward through Jacksonville (now Floyd, Virginia),⁴⁶ and then north again to Christiansburg, an important rail center on the Virginia and Tennessee railroad.⁴⁷ The 10th Michigan was sent east to destroy bridges over the Roanoke River while the 11th Michigan marched west to burn a large bridge over the New River. Brigadier General Luther S. Trowbridge, of the U.S. Volunteers, noted that the railroad crossed the Roanoke River about 20 miles east of Christiansburg six times and the 10th Michigan burned six "beautiful bridges, five of them covered, a destruction that could have been avoided could the events of the next ten days be foreseen." Trowbridge obtained a Lynchburg paper which gave an account of the evacuation of the Confederate capital. He sent the paper "by the fleetest horse to be found in the regiment to General Stoneman at Christiansburg, and was thus fortunate in giving him the first information that he had of the fall of Richmond."⁴⁸

Wytheville was once again to suffer from the bluecoats, as Colonel Miller with 500 men was sent by Stoneman to destroy supplies there and railroad bridges. Two regiments of Tennessee cavalry tore up train track and pushed within four miles of Lynchburg.⁴⁹

The citizens of Christiansburg were astonished to see thousands of Yankee raiders ride into their town. The telegraph office was captured and the raiders forced the telegraph operator at gunpoint to ask the operator at Lynchburg for news about Confederate forces. "I believe I am talking to the Yankees now," the Lynchburg operator finally determined and terminated the conversation. Before he did so, the Federals learned of the evacuation of Richmond.[50]

The Federal troopers and brigade commanders wondered exactly what Stoneman was up to as he zigzagged his way from Knoxville to Christiansburg, since Stoneman had kept them all in the dark. But the strategy became clear as the men grasped that, as they were destroying the railroads, they were cutting the last avenue of escape for Robert E. Lee. The soldiers realized the end of the Confederacy was near. They would be present at the death.[51]

Stoneman's raiders had indeed eliminated Lee's options by crippling the supply line past Lynchburg. Any hope of joining General Joseph E. Johnston's Army of Tennessee, confronting Sherman in North Carolina, was now dashed. Phil Sheridan had all but eliminated Early's army at Waynesboro and could be counted on to rapidly threaten Lee's westward lines of supply. Now Stoneman had cut the Virginia and Tennessee Railroad, and the noose around Lee tightened.

Lee's collapse at Petersburg and the evacuation of Richmond led to the drama of Confederate President Jefferson Davis's flight to North Carolina and Georgia. On April 2, Davis attended church at St. Paul's in Richmond, where he was given a note from Lee informing him that Grant had breached his lines. Richmond must now be abandoned. Davis's wife Varina and her four children had left the month before and traveled to Charlotte. Now, Davis and his cabinet, with what was left of the Confederate treasury, left the ruined and looted capital on a special train.

Davis and his party traveled to Danville, Virginia, crossing the Roanoke River, and moved slowly on to Clover Station, 40 miles from the North Carolina line, where he was loudly cheered. The remnants of the Confederate government were on that train, treasury, post office, and Bureau of War. Davis still believed that Lee could join Johnston in North Carolina and even supervised the construction of fortifications along the Dan and Roanoke rivers. On April 10, Davis received word that Lee had surrendered his army to Grant at Appomattox on the day before.

It was determined that the Confederate party must leave Danville immediately as Yankee cavalry under Stoneman were in the area. The train departed Danville in a driving rainstorm. Capturing this party was the dream of every cavalryman in Stoneman's command, and for Stoneman himself. They all knew the war was almost over, and to capture Davis would be the crowning achievement for Stoneman and would have erased past failures forever.

Glory eluded Stoneman's grasp by four hours. Union raiders burned the Dan River bridge shortly after Davis had crossed. When he was informed that he had almost been captured, Davis responded with a smirk that "A miss is as good as a mile."[52] The bluecoats were probably from Palmer's brigade, who had been ordered by Stoneman to destroy the bridges between Danville and Greensboro.

North Carolinians, who had breathed a sigh of relief when Stoneman and his columns headed north to Virginia, now learned that their ordeal was not over. Stoneman wheeled south from Christiansburg and led his troopers back to North Carolina to carry out the second part of his campaign. Palmer was ordered to send the 10th Michigan to Martinsville (Henry Court House) where they found 500 Confederate cavalry (some accounts say 250) commanded by the brother of Stoneman's nemesis, Joe Wheeler. After a brief skirmish, the Confederates were driven from the town and took refuge in a deep depression where they were excellent targets for the 10th with their Spencers. The balance of the brigade, the 15th Pennsylvania, came up the following day.[53] Life at this point was not bad for the Federal raiders. "If we are working hard, we are living well," reported an officer of the 15th Pennsylvania. Food was plentiful — chicken, hams, eggs, and biscuits — and there was plenty of forage for the horses. There was some plundering as well:

> Started at 2 in the morning, passing through a fine section of country, the home of aristocratic Virginia tobacco planters. The houses and yards are beautiful. Tobacco is plentiful that all are smoking very fair cigars. We captured some fine horses, for although all the stock has been run off in the woods, the Negroes tell us where they are concealed, and if we have time we go and get them.[54]

Stoneman reunited his command at Danbury, North Carolina, and quickly moved further south to Germanton. While there, Stoneman directed that several hundred freed slaves, who had attached themselves to the command and were hindering his movements, be sent to East Tennessee under guard for their protection. The men were enlisted in Colonel Bartlett's 119th United States Colored Troops.[55]

Stoneman was now ready to descend on Salisbury, a major military depot. Military hospitals were there, as well as an ordnance plant and, most important for Stoneman, a large Confederate prison where ten thousand men had been crammed into a six-acre compound. He sent Palmer off to Salem with orders to "destroy the large factories engaged in making clothing for the rebel army and thence send our parties to destroy the railroad between Greensboro and Danville."[56] At Winston and Salem, Palmer's men received a cordial welcome, after a delegation formally surrendered. The towns were inhabited by Moravians from Bethlehem, Pennsylvania. Captain Weand, in his account, described how the inhabitants wept and took off their hats as the "old flag" was carried through the town. "It was a charming place and they were good Union people but we had no time just then to do more than acknowledge it."[57]

Palmer's men marched on toward Greensboro, where they missed another opportunity to snare the fugitive Confederate president and his cabinet. Davis had arrived in Greensboro later on April 11, and his reception there was far less friendly than it had been at Danville. Greensboro was full of Union sympathizers, and only the president was offered accommodations in town, sharing a room with his nephew John T. Wood. Wood's landlord, fearing reprisals from Stoneman's raiders known to be in the area, kept asking Davis when he was leaving.[58]

His arrival at Greensboro was another near miss for the Confederate president. The Davis train passed over the Reedy Fork bridge one hour before the raiders burned it. The 15th Pennsylvania arrived on the outskirts of Greensboro and burned another bridge over South Buffalo Creek while the Davis train was on a siding two miles away "expecting to be captured," Captain Weand remarked.[59] As the Federals moved on to join Stoneman at Salisbury, no one realized that Davis had been within their grasp.

Davis held a council with General Pierre Gustave Beauregard and later with General Joseph Johnston, both of whom advised Davis that the situation was hopeless for the Confederacy. On April 12, Johnston asked Davis for authority to discuss a truce with Sherman, but this was rejected out of hand. Davis refused to acknowledge the fact that his cause was irredeemably lost. Lee's men lay down their arms and surrendered on April 9. Wilson, after destroying much of Selma, was headed for Montgomery. Canby was entering Mobile and Sherman was on the outskirts of Raleigh. The most immediate danger was from Palmer's men who were close to Greensboro. Davis finally agreed to leave on Good Friday, April 14.

While Palmer was the focus of the Confederate's immediate attention, Stoneman was marching to Salisbury with the remaining two brigades of his division and accompanying artillery. Salisbury was a prize, a town of stately houses and a center of industry. It was also a major military depot where trainloads of war materials had been sent in anticipation that Lee would eventually arrive there by way of Burkeville, Virginia. The presence of a military prison in the town was an emotional issue for Stoneman. He had failed in his raid to free prisoners at Macon and Andersonville, suffering the humiliation of captivity himself. Salisbury was no less notorious than Andersonville. In 1862, the 1,427 prisoners imprisoned there were manageable. Citizens of Salisbury remember prisoners singing and baseball games being played on prison grounds. When the exchange of prisoners stopped due to the Union decision to reduce the ranks of Confederate soldiers, and the refusal of the Confederates to exchange black prisoners, the number of prisoners at Salisbury jumped to 10,000. Prisoners were held under inhuman conditions and reports of the "dead house," where corpses of prisoners were placed before a most primitive burial in ditches, spurred Stoneman and his men on.

There was a very high death rate of prisoners at Salisbury during the last five months of the war. The deaths at Andersonville had been well publicized, but they were equally high at Salisbury. One out of every three prisoners incarcerated at Salisbury died between October 1864 and February 1865. The shortage of food was the main cause, as this led to a general debilitation of the prisoners, making them susceptible to disease. Louis A. Brown, in his definitive work on the Salisbury prison, calculates that approximately 4,000 Union prisoners died in the prison. Confederate reports put the death rate at 28 percent for Union prisoners, and this does not include citizens and Confederates who were also confined there.[60]

The defense of Salisbury was left to Brigadier General William M. Gardner, who had 3,000 men[61] under the immediate command of Colonel John C. Pemberton, who, as a lieutenant general, had surrendered Vicksburg in 1863. His luck was no better at Salisbury. Stoneman ordered a general charge against the Confederate line which was placed along the Mocksville Road along Grant's Creek, just north of Salisbury. One of the Confederate batteries was manned by "galvanized yanks," prisoners at Andersonville who joined the Confederates. Most of the men were Irish who had been recruited "off the boat" to fight in the Union Army and then, after capture, were persuaded to join the Confederates to get something to eat. As these troops were charged by Stoneman's men, they fired over the heads of the advancing Federals and then cheered for their "old flag."[62]

The Confederates collapsed, and Stoneman bagged fourteen pieces of artillery and 1,364 prisoners, including 53 officers. The survivors scattered and ran into nearby woods. The rich prize of Salisbury was now open to the determined and grim Federal cavalrymen.

Salisbury yielded a prodigious amount of industrial supplies, military equipment, and weapons to the raiders. Four large cotton factories, 7,000 bales of cotton, magazines with 10,000 stands of small arms, 70,000 pounds of powder, 35,000 bushels of corn, 50,000 bushels of wheat, food, uniforms, army blankets, and medical supplies were destroyed.

As anxious as Stoneman was to inflict as much damage as possible on the enemy, he issued strict orders that private property was to be protected. The destruction of military stores continued for two days, April 12 and 13, but food and other supplies were placed in the streets on Stoneman's orders for "poor whites" and Negroes who could take whatever they wanted.

It was a dreadful scene of destruction for the citizens of Salisbury and the fires could be seen for miles around, but Stoneman, to the relief and gratitude of the people, maintained the discipline of his men and, for the most part, private property was respected.[63]

There were some exceptions. Since able-bodied men were away or in hiding, women had to walk to Stoneman's headquarters to ask for guards. Some homes were plundered and women were harassed. The 11th Kentucky burned a train that was carrying the widow of Confederate General Leonidas Polk and her two daughters. The contents of their trunks were burned, with the exception of the general's sword, which the Yankees kept.[64]

Captain Weand of the 15th Pennsylvania wrote: "A great fire in the town that night lighted up the heavens, while the bursting of the shells sounded like a heavy battle. Salisbury had been a hated place and was paying dearly for its inequities."[65]

Destruction of the Confederate prison gave the Union troops a special satisfaction, although they found the prison empty of Union soldiers except a few who were too sick to move. On February 16, 1865, commanders at Confederate prisons were informed that a general exchange of prisoners was to take place. The Salisbury Commandant, General Bradley Johnson, was ordered to send all able-bodied prisoners of war to Wilmington, North Carolina. The sick and injured were sent by train to Richmond. On February 22, 2,823 prisoners marched out of Salisbury on their way to freedom, shouting and singing. They reached Greensboro on February 25 and then traveled to Raleigh by rail. The emaciated men finally reached Union lines near Wilmington on March 2.[66]

The 12th Ohio was given the privilege of destroying the buildings. One of the officers, W.M. Bushong of Co. C, described the scene:

> That part of the work at Salisbury in which the soldiers took most delight, was the burning of the infamous prison pen in which so many thousands of our comrades had starved and frozen to death. There were the burroughs and holes which these wretched men had dug in the ground for a miserable shelter.
> There were the walls from which the brutal sentinels had fired on the starving defenseless men, and there were broad areas of thickly planted head boards, beneath which 12,126 soldiers of the republic, dead from starvation and exposure, were laid to their last sleep.[67]

Bushong reported that a few survivors were found, but all who could walk had been removed by Confederate authorities. The prison made a great impression on Stoneman and his men, but control was maintained. "That they did not at once sweep the town from the face of the earth was because they were soldiers actuated by a higher motive than even a just revenge," Bushong observed.

The raiders stayed in Salisbury until 3:00 P.M. on April 13. The moderate treatment of civilians, who expected the worst after hearing reports of the depredations of Sherman's men as they marched through Georgia, was greatly appreciated. One Salisbury citizen wrote: "Salisbury people will always hold Stoneman in grateful remembrance for the strict control exercised over his troops. Again and again he stated that no private property should be plundered — and his officers seconded him — whether willingly or not."[68]

There are a number of theories that try to explain Stoneman's lenient policy toward the citizens of Salisbury. Rowan County Historian James S. Brawley has written that Stoneman provided guards to families who requested them "to protect their homes from ravages by camp followers and licentious soldiers."[69] Local tradition has it that Stoneman was lenient toward private property because of the intervention of Nathaniel Boyden "who had gone to school with Stoneman in their native state of Massachusetts."[70] This explanation is erroneous since Stoneman, a native of New York State, never went to school in Massachusetts. Another theory is that the mayor of the town, Mr. W.C. Coughenour, a Major Windsor and Boyden "asked their fellow Mason, Stoneman, to spare the court house and other important buildings in the city."[71] There is nothing in the historical record to indicate that Stoneman was a Mason.

Another intriguing example of local lore recounts that a prominent merchant, T.J. Meroney, treated Stoneman and his staff to "a courteous and ample meal" at his home on the edge of town on the morning of April 13. Meroney followed Stoneman into the city, where he saw a fire headed for the court house, which was located a block from his tobacco warehouse. If the court house burned, the warehouse would follow. An item in the city archives records the following:

> In great crises all personal barriers fall, and on this day in 1865, our peace loving local citizen hastened to the northern general, forgetful of party and past. With deep earnestness he explained to the conqueror that when his warehouse went up in flames, everything he possessed was gone.
> It has always been said that good resides in the worst of us and whether Stoneman actually sympathized with Mr. Meroney, or whether he was still feeling the good effects of the unsurpassable southern cooking he had just enjoyed in the Meroney household, he heard the plea. While not actually commanding the small blaze to be put out, Stoneman gave no further order to continue burning the court house.... So, to Thomas Jefferson Meroney and to General Stoneman we owe a never-ending debt of gratitude for leaving the community building untouched in all its serene beauty.[72]

The work was done. On April 13, Stoneman left Salisbury and headed west to return to Tennessee. The presses of the local Salisbury paper, the *Carolina Watchman*, had been destroyed by the raiders, but the paper resumed printing, and a year later remembered the Stoneman raid:

> These days twelve months ago were the scenes of the greatest calamity that ever befell our city. Our hills and valleys for the first time in the memory of the oldest citizens, resounded the echoes of hostile canon and death dealing shells.

> At day break on the morning of the twelfth our citizens were aroused from their quiet slumber by the loud detonations of artillery.... The foemen were slowly but surely advancing. All was excitement, all was terror. Terror stricken women and weeping children were running from house to house, or secreting themselves in cellars.
>
> The conflict was short, the small companies of invalid soldiers hastily gathered from the hospitals and thrown out with a battalion of artillery were unequal to the five thousand trained and armed troopers led by Stoneman. They were soon pressed back, our city given up to plunder and destruction.... Stoneman had arrived–his prisoners had quartered in the old Garrison, and the work of destruction commenced. Thousands upon thousands of dollars worth of Commissary and Quartermaster's stores, shipped here from Raleigh, were indiscriminately thrown to whoever would take them–whites, negroes, prostitutes, until all were satisfied.... The destruction of the property was immense....
>
> These days will long be remembered by our citizens as the saddest and most distressing in our history.[73]

The raiders reached Statesville on the evening of April 13, preceded by an advance guard who rode into town firing their weapons. Pickets were established in town and the main body arrived about midnight. Stoneman arrived in a carriage, probably suffering from his chronic hemorrhoid condition.

Soldiers streamed in for hours and their behavior was mixed. Confederate supplies and the railway depot were burned, as well as the office of the *Iredell Express*, the local newspaper. It was not spared, despite pleas from the citizens who even offered to dismantle the building. Some citizens were treated courteously while others were abused and mistreated, even beaten, to make them disclose where gold might be hidden.[74]

Stoneman was pleased with the availability of supplies. Horses and mules were taken and Stoneman boasted: "We are much better mounted than when we left Knoxville." Some prisoners and up to 1,000 "contrabands" (freed slaves) were mounted and followed the bluecoats on their march west.[75]

In addition to the destruction of the industrial institutions of the towns, the movement of freed slaves appeared to be part of a strategy designed to force southern whites to turn to manual labor once the slaves were removed by force or went voluntarily. Black families were divided, as there appears to have been little effort to keep them together.[76] It seems that neither Stoneman nor his officers were sensitive to their plight. In fact, Stoneman hardly mentions them at all, except to refer to them as an encumbrance. With the war almost over, they probably would have been better off remaining where they were, rather than accompanying the Federals to an uncertain future.

Stoneman left Statesville on April 14, but Palmer's brigade arrived about midnight and the Yankee occupation continued. Confederates from Lee's army were now returning to their homes, telling the Union troopers about Lee's surrender and the fall of Richmond. The Confederates reported that it was "Phil Sheridan and his cavalry that did the mischief" which led to a wry comment, made after the war, by a member of the 15th Pennsylvania that "They [Sheridan's men] never saw any fighting equal to what our cavalry did on that campaign."[77]

Stoneman concluded by April 14 that he had accomplished what he had set out to do. The Virginia and Tennessee Railroad had been severed and made useless. General Lee's line of retreat had been cut off, which helped to force his surrender. Salisbury had been

Ten. Payment of a Debt

rendered militarily worthless and the hated prison burned. He had ridden some five hundred miles and the campaign had taken its toll on the veteran soldier. It was clear that the Confederacy was doomed and he could now return to the comforts of Knoxville. His reputation, which had been besmirched by his perceived failures at Chancellorsville, the Atlanta campaign, his imprisonment, and bureaucratic wrangling in Washington, had been restored. His command was turned over to General Gillem.

Stoneman's departure did not bode well for North Carolinians who would yet suffer from the wrath of the invaders. Gillem headed for Asheville by the roundabout way of Hendersonville. Palmer's advance guard entered the pretty village of Lincolnton and the main column arrived shortly afterwards. The Federals found the citizens "extremely rebellious — bitterly so — but with it all are refined and intelligent."[78] Despite the hostility, the troopers were invited to meals and enjoyed "southern hospitality." Biscuits and cakes were baked for the men and cigars were plentiful. One Federal trooper, Corporal George French, was killed by a bushwhacker while he was on sentry duty. He was buried in the Episcopal Cemetery with full military honors and the ladies of the town placed flowers on the grave, an act that was greatly appreciated by the Northerners.[79]

The Federals at Lincolnton learned of Lincoln's assassination on April 14. The word came from returning Confederate officers who had heard about it in camp. "Its truthfulness was doubted, but, on being confirmed, it is safe to say that if any citizen of Lincolnton had expressed himself in sympathy with the assassin, it might have resulted in the destruction of the town and many of its inhabitants," Captain Weand observed.[80]

The pleasant state of affairs at Lincolnton did not prevail as the raid progressed. Stoneman was accompanied by the brigades of Miller and Brown as far as Lenoir, a town described by Gillem as a "rebellious little hole," where he departed for Knoxville on April 17, by way of Blowing Rock and Boone. Federal discipline deteriorated rapidly under Gillem, and nine hundred Confederate prisoners brought to Lenoir were not treated well. Many were old men or teenage boys captured in their homes, and Gillem issued orders to shoot anyone who tried to escape, further earning his reputation in North Carolina as "a man supercilious, insulting, and unfeeling."[81]

The raiders, after a sharp encounter with Confederates at the Catawba River, swept into Morgantown and, according to the townspeople, there was destruction and plunder in retaliation for the fight along the Catawba. Most people, anticipating the arrival of the Federals, buried their valuables, but the raiders searched homes, grounds, and gardens for loot.[82] Townspeople reported that drunken soldiers held pistols to ladies' heads, stole horses, mules and foodstuffs, and pillaged houses. The worst offenders were "rear guards" of local mountain people who, under the pretense of supporting the Union cause, looted and robbed at will.[83]

Gillem continued toward Asheville on April 15 by way of the Swannanoa Gap, but passage was effectively blocked by five hundred Confederates with four pieces of artillery. Gillem knew that passage through the gap would be costly, indeed, so he headed instead toward Rutherfordton and eventually to Hendersonville. Word came of a truce that had been signed between Sherman and Johnston, and the Confederate commander at Asheville, General James Martin, asked for a meeting with Gillem under a flag of truce on April 24.

Believing that hostilities had ceased, Gillem and Martin, who had been West Point classmates, agreed that Gillem could travel through Asheville to Greenville and that Martin would provide three days' rations "to avoid the necessity of stripping the citizens of their scant supplies."[84]

It was a false truce. General Sherman's agreement with General Johnston was rescinded by President Johnson and Secretary of War Stanton, and this led to a bitter controversy between Sherman and Stanton in which orders to Stoneman played a prominent part. In the negotiations between Sherman and Johnston that began on April 14 while Stoneman was still raiding in North Carolina, Sherman told the Confederate commander, "General Stoneman is still under my command and will suspend any devastation or destruction contemplated by him."[85] Sherman sent Stoneman the following dispatch on April 18:

> General Johnston and I have agreed to maintain a truce in the nature of status quo by which each is to stand fast till certain propositions looking to a general peace are referred to our respective principals. You may therefore cease hostilities but for supplies may come to me near Raleigh. Keep your command well in hand and approach Durham's Station or Chapel Hill, and I will supply you by our railroad.[86]

This order was accompanied by an order from Johnston to Confederate units not to interfere with Stoneman's march.

This order to Stoneman, in addition to the text of the Sherman/Johnston surrender agreement, hit Washington like a bombshell. First of all, Stanton and others in Washington were convinced that Jefferson Davis was headed south through North Carolina and Georgia with millions of dollars in currency and gold. General Henry W. Halleck, on duty in Richmond, had informed Stanton that "respectable parties" in Richmond had informed him that Davis had taken the "plunder of Richmond banks" with which he hoped to make terms with Sherman "or some other Southern [Federal] commander." Johnston's negotiations with Sherman, Halleck warned, were to accomplish this purpose and then go to Mexico or Europe. "Would it not be well to put Sherman and all other commanding officers on their guard in this respect?" Halleck suggested.[87]

Sherman's order to Stoneman drove Stanton, who was in virtual control of the government in Washington in the wake of the Lincoln assassination, into a frenzy. He apparently believed that Sherman was trying to order Stoneman away from the pursuit of Jefferson Davis who was fleeing from Greensboro, an unlikely assumption since Stoneman was at Statesville moving west, approximately seventy miles from Greensboro when Sherman's order was issued and not in the path of Davis's assumed flight to the south. It seems clear that Sherman's intent was to stop the destruction by Stoneman's raiders and had nothing to do with capturing Jefferson Davis. In any case, Stoneman never received the message, sent over Confederate wires. Stanton further inflamed the situation by hinting to New York newspapers that Sherman might have been bribed by the Confederates.

Sherman was outraged. He read the northern newspapers that had printed the Stanton outburst and he bitterly resented Stanton's "comments that I was a common traitor and a public enemy, and high officials have even instructed my own subordinates to disobey my lawful orders."[88] This was a reference to Thomas's order to Stoneman to disregard any instructions except those from himself or Grant. Stoneman, who had reached

Knoxville, sent Brown's marauding Tennesseans and Kentuckians to head for Augusta, Georgia, to pursue Davis and "follow him to the ends of the earth, if possible, and never give him up."[89] Palmer was ordered to join his brigade with the other two and assume command of the manhunt.

The other confrontation between Sherman and Stanton concerned the ceasefire agreement with Johnston. Grant saw immediately, upon receiving the text, that it was disastrous. An urgent cabinet meeting was assembled at Grant's request and Sherman's terms were read. It was more than a military convention; it was a political treaty as well, and went far beyond Lincoln's instructions to Grant of March 3 forbidding him to discuss any political questions in his negotiations with Lee. Sherman had not seen Lincoln's orders. Had he done so, Sherman remarked later, it would have saved a world of trouble.

The treaty recognized the legality of state governments and even insurrection. Immunity was granted to those who had taken part in the rebellion, and the legality of Union state governments established under Lincoln's reconstruction policy was questioned. Slavery was not even mentioned. The president and all members of the cabinet strongly disapproved of Sherman's agreement, and Grant was dispatched to Raleigh to inform Sherman that his treaty was null and void.[90]

Palmer was in the vicinity of the Cowpens revolutionary war battlefield in South Carolina when he received Stoneman's orders of April 29. He headed for Spartanburg to meet the other two brigades, marching from Asheville. The Federals knew that Davis was traveling with four brigades of cavalry, and Palmer thought Davis would try to cross the Savannah at Petersburg. Perhaps he could be intercepted at Athens. The 15th Pennsylvania crossed the South Carolina border and marched to Spartanburg, where the citizens were expecting the worst from Yankee cavalry. Strict orders were issued not to disturb the private property of citizens, much to their relief.[91]

The First brigade moved on to the town of Anderson, where they met Brown's and Miller's brigades and the hunt continued in earnest. Palmer complained to Stoneman that these two brigades were out of control. "A large number of the men and some of the officers devote themselves exclusively to pillaging and destroying property," Palmer observed.[92] Rabun County, Georgia, and the western counties of North Carolina had long been strongholds of Union sentiment, and scores were settled by the "home Yankees" of Brown and Miller.[93]

Discipline did not improve when the bluecoats found a vast store of fine old Madeira and port wine that the wealthy people of Charleston had sent to Anderson for safekeeping. Palmer's men filled their canteens, but barrels of it were dumped in the street in compliance with Stoneman's standing orders. Gillem's men had captured a distillery in North Carolina just before they reached Wilkesboro on March 30, an episode Stoneman did not want repeated.[94]

Palmer's command crossed the Savannah on May 3 and entered Georgia. They learned that most of the Confederate cavalry had disbanded and a small force accompanying Davis and the cabinet were reported to be at Washington, Georgia, about eighteen miles away. The 13th Tennessee cavalry was sent to investigate. When they were close, a party of Confederates appeared, under Colonel Breckenridge, carrying a white flag of truce. When asked to surrender, they asked for time to think it over. It was a hoax. The colonel in charge of the 13th sent a message back to Palmer asking for instructions, giving Davis and his party time to continue.[95]

The 15th Pennsylvania did find a major prize. Pursuing General Bragg, the Federals marched to the Appalachee River and found seven wagons of the old "Conestoga" type. They also found four iron-bound kegs containing $188,500 in gold, $4,265,500 in Confederate money, $645,000 in bonds and securities of several southern states, $480,000 in bonds and securities of the Central Railroad and Banking Company of Georgia, and $460,500 in notes and bonds of the bank of Macon. There was an additional $68,000 in specie and boxes of silver and other valuables. All told, about $2,000,000 in valuables and a large amount of Confederate money were captured. The entire cache was sent to the commanding officer of U.S. Forces in Augusta.[96]

Stoneman must have had a moment of satisfaction when Palmer reported the capture of General Joseph Wheeler, who had forged parole papers and tried to pass himself off as a Lieutenant Sharp. Another old adversary, General Iverson, was also captured by the 12th Ohio.[97] The debt of Sunshine Church had finally been paid in full.

Palmer and his men followed every lead, but the honor of capturing Jefferson Davis was not to be theirs. On May 15, a courier from the 10th Michigan brought word that Davis had been captured at Irwinville by the 4th Michigan cavalry. The tired and disappointed men of Palmer's division made the best of it:

> The news caused great cheering by the men of each company as the word passed down our line of march. It was mortifying to lose our prey after all our hard marches and sleepless nights and our only consolation was that we made his capture easy for others to accomplish. It was as General Geo. H. Thomas remarked to his staff at the time. "General Wilson held the bag and Palmer drove the game into it...."[98]

Except for mopping-up operations in South Carolina and Georgia, Stoneman's raid was over, the longest of any raid by either side in the war, extending over 2,000 miles. General Thomas was quick to praise Stoneman in his report to Washington, noting that Stoneman "spiritfully" executed the orders given to him before he started on the expedition. Grant proved harder to please. His *Memoirs* included the following in his discussion of the raids of Canby, Wilson, and Stoneman (emphasis mine):

> They were all eminently successful, but without any good result. Indeed much valuable property was destroyed and many lives lost at a time we would have liked to spare them. The war was practically over before their victories were gained. They were so late in commencing operations, that they did not hold any troops away that otherwise would have been operating against the armies which were gradually forcing the Confederate armies to surrender. *The only possible good that we may have experienced from these raids was by Stoneman getting near Lynchburg about the time the armies of the Potomac and the James were closing in on Lee at Appomattox.*[99]

Grant's comments were grossly unfair. He minimized the problems involved in providing 3,000 cavalrymen with horses and acquiring 2,000 extra horses and 600 Spencer carbines, and he forgot that he had ordered "destroying the railroad and military resources of the country...."[100] Widely separated regiments had to be assembled right after the arduous Saltville campaign and three raids were being equipped at the same time. Finally, rain was once again a factor in delaying the operation.

Ten. Payment of a Debt

The raid was a major military accomplishment, carried out in compliance with Sherman's concept of destroying the ability of the south to wage war. Whereas many, including Grant, questioned the destruction of military supplies, food, and industrial facilities, the destruction at Salisbury alone drastically curtailed the ability of surviving Confederate units to continue the war.

The downside of the raid was the pillaging and depredations carried out by the "home Yankees" in the Tennessee and Kentucky regiments. Stoneman's message to Gillem, referring to his men as a "fine body of Cossacks," proved to be prophetic. They willfully robbed and pillaged, despite the best efforts of Stoneman and Palmer to control them. Stoneman can be faulted for leaving his command on April 17 to return to Knoxville, as the record clearly shows his presence helped to maintain discipline. He was, no doubt, worn out by two back-to-back campaigns, but this absence was catastrophic for the people of North Carolina.

Stoneman's raid broke the back of the Confederacy. General Luther S. Trowbridge, of the 10th Michigan cavalry, noted:

> From the beginning to the end, the expedition was managed with rare judgment and skill. While its movements were so directed as to constantly deceive the enemy as to the real point of attack, its quick and heavy blows were delivered in unexpected quarters, working immense damage to the waning hopes of the Confederacy.[101]

Riots and Reconstruction

The defeated South in 1865 was a scene of destruction and despair. Confederate authority had collapsed and thousands of refugees, black and white, wandered through the countryside, looking for food and shelter. The task of providing law and order and essential services fell to the occupying Union army. Even basic sanitary services were enforced by army commanders. When government was entrusted to loyal citizens, they were subject to military supervision.

A primary concern of the Federal government was providing assistance to the hundreds of thousands of freedmen throughout the South. The Freedmen's Bureau, established during the war to provide assistance to freed slaves, was extended in 1866, and its powers increased, despite a veto by President Johnson. A Civil Rights Act, also vetoed by Johnson, was passed by Congress. This act protected the civil rights for all persons in the United States.

As the struggle for control of Reconstruction was waged in Washington between the President and Congress, army commanders found themselves in a political crossfire. Reconstruction policy was the subject of bitter controversy and military officers, who were the principal administrators of reconstruction, were often forced to declare a political allegiance.[1]

George Stoneman would have preferred an appointment to a regular regiment rather than occupation duty, perhaps even fighting Indians in the Plains, were it not for his family. Despite his preference for active duty, he was assigned to the Department of the Tennessee under General George H. Thomas. Unlike some of his fellow officers, Thomas, a moderate Republican, took a conciliatory approach to the states in his division. Thomas believed that civil officials, such as judges and law enforcement officers, should remain in place and continue to perform their duties. Military aid and protection were promised and "loyal people" were asked to hold elections and select officers to uphold the authority of civil law.[2]

Stoneman wrote his father on June 14, 1865, and expressed his pleasure that his family had finally joined him in Knoxville. "...Mary and baby [Cornelius] have joined me here.... Mollie[3] is also enjoying most excellent health and *the boy* your grandson is improving every day."[4] Stoneman expressed his satisfaction with his contribution to the war. "I feel satisfied that in this war I have done my full share and come out of it with a fair reputation and with a creditable record. My prospects for the future were never brighter. I am contented with the present and satisfied with the past."[5]

The problem of encouraging local control was complicated by the Southern states' rejection of the Fourteenth Amendment, which defined citizenship and prohibited states from depriving "any person of life, liberty, or property" without due process of law. It also called for the reduction of congressional representation of any state that withheld suffrage from male citizens and disqualified any person who had held federal or state office, taken an oath to support the constitution, and later broke that oath by engaging in rebellion. This disqualified most Southern officials in office during the war.[6]

Refusal of Southern states to support black suffrage, the enactment of "Black Codes" which severely restricted the freedom of blacks, opposition to the Freedmen's Bureau, and resentment of Federal occupation all contributed to a seething discontent in the South and led to violence that eventually broke out in Memphis and later in New Orleans.

George Stoneman was named Commanding Officer of the Department of the Tennessee under George Thomas on June 27, 1865. He also aligned himself with the Democratic Party at this time, a decision that was consistent with his conservative and moderate views. It was never said that he was partisan in his administration,[7] and he worked to promote Thomas's liberal policies, but less than a year later, the city of Memphis, where Stoneman maintained his headquarters, was engulfed in a riot that plunged the city into anarchy. The riot would have a profound effect on Reconstruction policy and would place Stoneman at the center of controversy.

Racial tension had been building in Memphis due to the rapid growth of population, as well as economic and social factors. The city had grown in three years from 35,000 to 60,000. Between 1860 and 1865, the black population had increased from 3,000 to 25,000, of whom many were refugees, living in shacks close to Fort Pickering in an area known as South Memphis. This area was the base of the 3rd United States Heavy Artillery, a black regiment which had been formed in 1863, when Memphis had been occupied by Union forces. Although it was said that the 3rd was not known for its discipline, a charge that was used by those who resented the presence of black troops, it was also recorded that they were used to patrol the city and were complimented by their officers for using extraordinary restraint when they were subjected to verbal threats and abuse.[8]

In addition to black refugees, Irish immigrants had flocked to Memphis as well, many of them establishing themselves in South Memphis where they operated grog shops and grocery stores and fenced stolen goods, often exploiting blacks when they had the chance and contributing to the crime and disease of the area.[9] The burgeoning black population competed with the Irish for manual labor jobs, and friction between the two groups was particularly acute. The police force was an instrument of oppression against the black community, as testimony before a Congressional committee investigating the riot clearly shows. One hundred sixty-three of the 180 men on the Memphis police force were Irishmen. Police brutality was common and arrests for even a minor charge resulted in a beating.[10]

Other factors increased racial tension. The Freedmen's Bureau built schools and hospitals for blacks and these government programs were resented by lower-income whites. Some Memphis newspapers also contributed to racial hatred and attacked black residents. The Memphis *Argus*, two days before the riot, commented: "Would to God they were back in Africa, or some other seaport town, anywhere but here."[11]

Stoneman was not happy with his position in Memphis. He was known to be a conservative, opposed to radical solutions to the Reconstruction process, but he and his fellow officers had very little contact socially with Memphis society, and they felt the hostility of the community. Stoneman felt that Memphians did not admit that they were wrong about secession, but had simply accepted Union authority because they had no choice. They recognized the facts as they existed. Stoneman's isolation from the community, and his suspicion of local officials, may explain why he misjudged the situation once trouble started, but he could hardly have been unaware of the racial tension that mounted in the months before the riot.

Tension in Memphis had been building up for months before the riots in May. Black soldiers in Union blue were a special target for the police, as they were living symbols of the defeat of the Southern economic and social system. Some of the police were so ignorant of the law that they didn't realize that the curfew laws under slavery were no longer in effect.[12]

South Memphis was also the scene of lawlessness and disorder. Burglars, including a gang of youths called "Mackerels," terrorized the city, and thousands of dope addicts, gamblers, and prostitutes all formed the criminal element.[13] The police were unable to maintain law and order and, in the weeks before the riot, racial tensions increased, due in part to the conduct of black soldiers, but also as a result of police violence and brutality.

The series of events leading up to the riot began on Monday, April 30, 1866, when black soldiers were mustered out of active service. Unfortunately, they were not paid immediately but remained near the fort, waiting for their money. No longer on duty and looking for entertainment, the discharged soldiers gravitated to the saloons on South Street. Although muskets had been reclaimed by the army, many of the men were able to retain their sidearms.[14] On Monday afternoon, four policemen and three or four blacks had an altercation which involved fists and clubs, but not gunfire. The stage was now set for the mayhem that followed.[15]

On the following day, May 1, a crowd of 100 blacks[16] gathered on South Street. Their behavior, according to witnesses, was loud and disorderly, but not violent. The police arrived and arrested two blacks for disorderly conduct. The prisoners were "forcibly rescued"[17] by the discharged soldiers and the group returned to the saloon for more merrymaking. The police returned with reinforcements and two soldiers were arrested, again on a disorderly conduct charge, and were led away. The police were pursued by a large number of blacks, many of them armed, who began to shout "Shoot them! Kill them!" Although there are discrepancies in accounts of what follows, most agreed that the blacks began firing into the air and the unnerved police, thinking they were the targets, fired into the crowd. The blacks returned the fire and two police officers and four or five black soldiers were killed and a number wounded.[18]

An hour later, what one historian referred to as a "quasi-military skirmish between police and soldiers ensued with witnesses later disagreeing as to which group initiated the shooting."[19] The black veterans retreated to Fort Pickering at nightfall, and Stoneman ordered that the men be disarmed, separated from whites, and confined to the base.

Earlier on May 1, the second day of the riot, the sheriff of Shelby County, T.M. Winters, and several other leading citizens came to Stoneman's office and asked him to use Federal troops to quell the disturbances. He had approximately 150 men of the 16th United States Infantry at his disposal, used primarily to guard U.S. property in the city. Two considerations seemed to influence Stoneman at this critical point. Community leaders had pressed him to turn over the city to civil authorities and the press had clamored for the withdrawal of Federal troops. Stoneman responded to Winters's request as follows:

> I asked him if he had made use of the means at his disposal in quelling the riot; if he had summoned a sheriff's posse for that purpose. He told me he had not. I then told him that I had turned the city and the section of the country over to the civil authorities as far as it was possible and that I held them responsible for the good order and quiet of the city of Memphis.[20]

Stoneman noted that the people of Memphis had been "exceedingly anxious" to get rid of United States troops, insisting that they were competent to take care of themselves. This was a test of their ability to do so. He also insisted that any request for assistance should be "in black and white." He would not act on a verbal request.[21] Stoneman told the congressional committee that "he preferred ... to test the question whether they were competent to keep order, and waited for an application in writing from the city authorities before using the troops stationed here to interfere."[22]

A written request for assistance, sent by Mayor John Park, was delivered to Stoneman on May 1. "There is uneasiness in the public mind," the mayor wrote, "growing out of the occurrences of the day, which would be materially calmed if there was an assurance of military cooperation with the civilian police in suppressing all disturbances of the public peace."[23] Stoneman still equivocated. Instead of ordering troops into the riot area, Stoneman advised Parks that a "small force of infantry stationed at this post, in all not more than one hundred and fifty strong, will be directed to hold itself in readiness to cooperate with the civil authorities of Memphis 'in case of further lawlessness.'"[24] Park was advised to communicate directly with the commanding officer in case assistance was needed. "I should prefer that the troops be called upon only in case of extreme necessity, of which you must be the judge."[25]

Stoneman also ordered Captain Arthur W. Allyn, commanding officer of the 16th U.S. Infantry, to hold his command in readiness and to cooperate with the Memphis police in case of further lawlessness "on the part of persons white or black." He also advised Allyn to use firearms only in case of extreme necessity. He further ordered Allyn to see that all arms belonging to the U.S. were kept from "improper persons" and that all muskets should be taken from the black enlisted men.[26]

While these messages were flying back and forth, full-scale rioting broke out Tuesday night. Acting on his own authority, Captain Allyn sent two squads of troops into South Memphis, where they met Winters and his posse at the corner of Vance and Linden streets.

The troops tried to disperse and disarm anyone who had a weapon, even the police. These arms, however, were returned to the police once they identified themselves. This was done despite the fact that the police were beating blacks whenever they were encountered and, according to Allyn, one black was shot in cold blood. Blacks who had been arrested were turned loose to the crowd and some were killed. About 11:00 P.M., order was temporarily restored by the troops, the rioters were disarmed, and the crowd dispersed. The troops were withdrawn but were held in readiness in case they were needed.[27]

The night's mayhem was not over. Reports of the violence circulated through the city, and late in the evening, a crowd of about 200 gathered on South Street. All was quiet, but the posse split into smaller groups and, according to the minority report of the congressional committee:

> commenced an indiscriminate slaughter of innocent, unoffending, and helpless Negroes whenever found, and without regard to age, sex, or condition, visiting the humble houses of colored people, under the pretext of searching for arms; breaking open their houses when admission was not speedily granted by the inmates; shooting, beating and killing them in the most cruel manner without cause or provocation ... some of the colored females were violated by some of these fiends in human shape.[28]

The morning of May 2 was quiet after a night of murder, rape, robbery, and burnings, and blacks hoped that the worst had passed, but it was not to be. Around noon, police officers, firemen, and "quite a number of the lower and disorderly part of the population"[29] gathered on South Street to continue the violence of the previous night. Some black soldiers escaped from Fort Pickering and fired on the mob, but the evidence is conflicting as to how many were involved. Although they had little effect on the white mob, their presence served to spread rumors that the soldiers intended to invade Memphis, thus further inflaming the mob.[30]

Stoneman finally acted on the afternoon of May 3. He toured South Memphis and belatedly issued the following order to the mayor, the City Council, and civil authorities in the county of Shelby and Memphis:

> Gentlemen: Circumstances compel the undersigned to interfere with civil affairs in the city of Memphis. It is forbidden for any person, without the authority of these headquarters, to assemble together any posse, armed or unarmed, white or colored. This does not include the police force of the city, and will not so long as they can be relied upon as preservers of the peace.
> George Stoneman, Major General Commanding.[31]

Stoneman's orders stopped the rioting as troops patrolled the city, but the cost to life and property was tragically high. Forty-six blacks had been killed, the great majority in the first two days when there was no Federal protection. Most of the worst offenders were identified by witnesses. One of the most brutal was named John Pendergrast, a grocer well known to the black community. A witness named Lucy Tibbs saw Pendergrast shoot a black soldier in the mouth while he was trying to escape the mob. Another was beaten, while the men loaded their pistols and then shot him in the head three times. Pendergrast and his son set houses on fire, barred the doors, and "told the folks to stay in there."[32] As men, women, and children ran out, "They shot at them as fast as they could while they were running."³³ A black girl named Rachel ran out and was shot in the mouth. Her body fell between two houses and was burned.

A white policeman named Roach was another offender who shot blacks in cold blood in front of witnesses. Cynthia Townsend told the congressional committee that Roach shot a black who was driving a dray as well as a black soldier and was heard to say "This is a white man's day."³⁴

Testimony to the congressional committee was replete with accounts of dreadful atrocities against defenseless blacks. Most disturbing was the evidence that high-ranking civil officials encouraged and even participated in the riot. Attorney General William Wallace led a mob of citizens, many of them drunk, who killed blacks and burned shanties. Wallace harangued the mob, urging them to arm, and in fact provided ammunition, shotguns, and rifles. Wallace admitted he was on South Street on Wednesday morning but claimed he saw no disturbances or blacks. Witnesses placed him, however, at the scene of fires and killings and heard him inciting the mob.³⁵

John C. Creighton, Judge of the Recorder's Court, was one of the early provocateurs of the violence. A witness heard Creighton address the crowd, saying "Boys, I want you to go ahead and kill the last damn one of the nigger race and burn up the cradle...."³⁶

In addition to the 46 blacks killed, 75 were wounded. There were five rapes and over 100 robberies; 91 homes and shanties were burned. In addition, four black churches and 12 schools, run by the Freedmen's Bureau and missionary organizations, were destroyed.³⁷

Stoneman was culpable for failing to take decisive action at several crucial moments in the chronology of the rioting. Informing Sheriff Winters on the first day of the riot that civil officials were responsible for maintaining order and that he should form a posse may have been a rational decision for a minor disturbance, but this was a full-scale riot, directed against blacks. Although the conduct of discharged black soldiers substantially contributed to the disturbances, most of the victims were black civilians who deserved Federal protection. Winters's posse turned into a murderous mob. Stoneman, after receiving a written request from Mayor Parks, placed his troops on a state of alert, but Federal troops were not used except for two squads Allyn ordered into town on the evening of May 1. These troops did not effectively disarm the mob and returned to their base. It was only after two days and two nights of rioting that Stoneman finally declared martial law and sent in the troops in force.

One historian raised the question of whether racism influenced Stoneman's delay in taking decisive action. We have seen that Stoneman was not sensitive to the plight of black Union prisoners of war and was willing to sacrifice them in order to get prisoner of war exchanges started up again while he himself was a prisoner. He also separated "contrabands" from their families during the North Carolina raids in 1865. Stoneman's conduct in this regard, like many of his contemporaries, was not enlightened, and the charge that he was willing to defer to the white leaders of Memphis for racist reasons may have some credence. Support for this argument can be found in the white supremacist newspaper, the *Daily Avalanche*, which, two days after the riot, observed that Stoneman:

> has been reducing the negro force here.... He has not made himself a fanatic. He has acted upon the idea that if troops are necessary here to protect the rights of the blacks ever, white

troops can do this with less offense to our people than black ones. He knows the wants of the country, and sees that the Negro can do the country more good in the cotton field than in the camp. Under his military rule our people are about to obtain what they have so often petitioned for — the rule of the white man.[38]

Stoneman's actions immediately following the riot seem appropriate and forceful. He formed a commission to investigate the riot and determine who was involved, prepare a list of casualties, and calculate the damage. He also wrote a strong letter to Mayor John Park asking him to state what steps were being taken to "bring to trial and punishment the perpetrators of the outrages which have disgraced the city of Memphis during the past week, and what assurances can be given me that the murderers and incendiaries will be arrested and punished."[39] Stoneman also asked the mayor to indicate the steps taken to secure the rights and privileges of blacks in Memphis and what was to be done with black prisoners arrested in the past week. Stoneman concluded with a blunt threat:

> In conclusion, I have to assure you, and through you the people of Memphis, that if they cannot govern themselves as a law-abiding and Christian community, they will be governed, and that hereafter it will be my duty and privilege to see that there are no more riotous proceedings or conduct either on the part of whites or blacks or civil authorities.[40]

The mayor apparently had an alcohol problem and was "three quarters drunk" during the disturbances, according to a witness before the congressional committee. The majority report charged that he "had done nothing to suppress the riot" and was "utterly unequal to the occasion."[41]

The mayor's reply to Stoneman was evasive. After concluding that the police and army had effectively suppressed the riot, omitting the fact that forty-eight people had been killed, he observed that Stoneman had appointed a commission and Parks was sure that "the murders and incendiaries will be arrested and punished," quoting Stoneman. Parks went on to say that his "duties [were] restricted by statute" and that he could not give assurances that the rioters would be punished, "which could only be made good by the exercise of an usurped power upheld by military force, with which my constituents, the people of Memphis, have had a long time experience, even unto nausea." As far as losses were concerned, the mayor was not aware of any "statute or law authorizing any such appropriation of money."[42]

William Hunter, judge of the criminal court and a former Union officer, testified that no steps had been taken by local civil authority to bring the rioters to justice. Furthermore, he believed that "the chances of conviction would be very remote with the material we have."[43]

The congressional committee began its investigation three weeks after the riot and interviewed 170 witnesses before adjournment. Radical Republicans on the committee included E.B. Washburne, the chair, and John M. Broomall. The minority member was George Shanklin of Kentucky. The radicals followed a political agenda, focusing on what they considered to be terrorist activities of white Southerners. The state of affairs in Memphis, the majority argued, was much the same as it was before the rebellion. Their report concluded that "there will be no safety to loyal men, either white or black, should the troops be withdrawn and no military protection offered." The riots in Memphis are an example of what could happen throughout the South should military protection be withdrawn. The minority report stressed the participation of the "rowdy and rabble population of the city," in the riot, including blacks and the Irish. The better classes of Memphis, who were disenfranchised and prohibited from holding any office, should have their political rights restored. That was the best way to guard against a repetition of the Memphis tragedy. Both reports accepted the argument made by the elite of Memphis that the main cause of the riot was competition for unskilled jobs by the Irish and blacks.[44]

Stoneman was treated gently by the congressional committee. The majority report, after thanking Stoneman for extending every possible assistance, delivered a mild rebuke. After stating that his reluctance to intervene early in the disturbance was understandable in view of the insistence by Memphis officials that they could control the city by themselves, the committee did find his initial response inadequate:

> It is to be regretted, however, that he did not at an earlier period of the lawless and murderous proceedings taken the same resolute steps that he subsequently adopted, as he, no doubt, would have done, had he comprehended the full proportions of the riot and the true character of the city government of Memphis, and of controlling influences of that city.[45]

The committee went on to say that "General Stoneman is deserving of the highest commendation for his prompt and determined action" when he delivered his ultimatum to the mayor on May 5 threatening to govern the city if they could not do it themselves. The Minority Report was even more effusive in its praise of Stoneman:

> General Stoneman, in whose skill, prudence, and discretion I have great confidence, was upon the ground, and, no doubt, used all means at his control to collect the necessary information and facts to form a correct conclusion, and acted thereon according to his own convictions of right and duty.[46]

Northern reaction to the riot was angry and bitter. The *Chicago Tribune* called it "The Memphis Massacre" and said, "In downright brutality, and wanton, unprovoked diabolism, it makes the atrocities of the great New York anti-negro riot seem honorable and the massacre of Fort Pillow an innocent affair."[47] The *New York Tribune* said it should be determined "whether there was public restraint in the South that will demand and enforce the protection of Blacks from similar outrages in the future." The paper wondered if "further legislation by Congress is necessary to protect Blacks from butchery and rapine."[48]

The *New York Times* printed a scathing account of the disturbances:

> The conduct of a great number of the city police, who are generally composed of the lower class of whites, selected without reference to their qualifications for the position, was brutal in the extreme. Instead of protecting the rights of persons and property, as is their duty, they were chiefly concerned as murderers, incendiaries, and robbers....[49]

The *Times* went on to report that no public meeting had been held by the citizens in the three weeks following the riot "to express their approbation or condemnation of the mob, thus by their silence appearing to approve of their conduct."[50]

The riot in Memphis, and the even worse racial disturbances in New Orleans on July 30, set the stage for the congressional elections of 1866. Former military officers, and some still on active duty, participated, sometimes unwillingly, in the vitriolic campaigning that characterized the political battle between Radical Republicans and Democrats supporting President Johnson. Democratic supporters of the President in the military included General George Custer, who had served in the reconstruction government of Texas, General James Blair Steedman, who had headed the department in Georgia, and General Lovell H. Rousseau, who was not on active duty.[51]

The disturbances in the South provided the radicals with ample ammunition to support their contention that all opponents to radical reconstruction were "Copperheads" who wanted to dismantle the fruits of the Union victory and that Blacks were not safe from Southern savagery. Radical leaders like Charles Sumner proclaimed that, with the death of Lincoln, "the rebellion vaulted into the Presidential chair." Although Jefferson Davis was in the casements at Fortress Monroe, "Andrew Johnson was doing his work.... Witness Memphis, witness New Orleans. Who can doubt that the President is the author of these tragedies?... The blood of Memphis and New Orleans must cry out until it is heard...."[52]

The riots were also used by Democrats to justify their lenient reconstruction policies. The editor of the *Memphis Bulletin* wrote Johnson that the riot:

> was a literal verification of your prophecy to Fred Douglas that Negro suffrage would beget an irrepressible conflict between the non-slave holding whites of the South and the blacks. This is the real cause of our difficulties here. Our police are all Irish. The negro soldiers are particularly down on the poor whites and Irish. Several skirmishes had occurred between them, and when the negro soldier no longer had an officer to "obey," he was betrayed into unusual violence. The better class of citizens had nothing to do with the "mess."[53]

As political rhetoric involving the riots intensified, President Johnson became convinced that if he could talk directly to the people, he could win them over. Accordingly, he planned a trip along the eastern seaboard and through the Midwest, an unusual decision in the days when presidents were not expected to actively participate in campaigning. The prestige and dignity of the office had precluded such partisan activity.

President Johnson began his famous Swing Around the Circle on August 28. His party included some 50 people, including military heroes such as Grant, Admiral Farragut, and Custer. George Stoneman, fresh from the disruptions in Tennessee, was added to the party as a witness to the dangers of disenfranchising moderate Southern leaders and leaving the governing of the South in the hands of loyal, but ineffective, elements favored by Radical Republicans.

Some of the military men in the president's entourage, like Grant, were unwilling participants and did not speak but were present to add prestige to the proceedings. Johnson gave basically the same speech over and over again at each stop of the tour that included Philadelphia, New York, Albany, Chicago, Cleveland, Detroit, Springfield, St. Louis, and Louisville.[54]

Often using intemperate language, Johnson spoke of his humble beginnings, his occupation as a tailor, and his rise from village alderman to the presidency. The crowds were friendly at the first few stops. He was well received in New York by both officials and the general public, but as the trip progressed, the crowds became hostile, often incited by paid

Republican hecklers. They provoked him into angry exchanges with the crowds, particularly at Cleveland, where, at a reception in his honor, he flayed his political opponents in a fashion totally inappropriate for the occasion, to the dismay of Grant and Stoneman.

Matters were worse in St. Louis when someone in the crowed yelled "New Orleans," and Johnson blamed the riot on Congress. When Thaddeus Stevens called him a second Judas, he responded by saying if he was a Judas than Congress must consider themselves to be the Christ. In Indianapolis, local political leaders failed to show up to meet the president and there were violent encounters with partisans in the crowds. Grant became increasingly disenchanted. "I am disgusted with this trip. I am disgusted at hearing a man make speeches on the way to his funeral," Grant told a reporter from the *New York Herald Tribune*.[55]

Stoneman had departed Memphis before he had joined the president on his ill-fated trip and was ordered to command the Department of the Cumberland in June 1866. It is not clear whether this was a punitive transfer, but it took place a month after the Memphis riots. His stay at his new assignment was brief and by December, Stoneman was once again to serve under his mentor and benefactor, General John M. Schofield. On December 17, Stoneman reported for duty at the First Military District of Virginia, commanding the sub-district of Petersburg.

Stoneman wrote his father on December 27, 1866 with news of his family and his impressions of Petersburg. "As to myself and mine we are all well. Mollie & the babies are still in Baltimore but will join me here in the first part of Jany [sic] next."[56] Stoneman explained they would board "and not go to keeping house" as the future was uncertain. "Petersburg is an old town of about ten thousand inhabitants," Stoneman explained to his father, "quite a rail road center and considerable of a depot for cotton and tobacco. It was not injured during the war as much one would have thought." Stoneman noted that the holes in the walls of houses caused by cannon fire had been repaired and the houses were all occupied.[57]

Stoneman announced to his father that he had been promoted to full colonel and wrote that he had been "put above every man who graduated in my class at West Point which graduated in 1846 — with fair prospects of being a full general before long."[58] His predictions of a promotion proved to be optimistic.

The congressional elections of the previous November resulted in a series of stunning victories for the anti–Johnson radicals in congress, and the Republicans were now in full control. They were now in a position to develop a Southern strategy and to provide for "the more efficient government of the Rebel states." The second session of the 39th Congress met in December 1866, just as Stoneman arrived in Petersburg. The most significant proposal put before the Congress came from Thaddeus Stevens. His bill, which was referred to committee and went through several compromises, declared that the governments of the ten unreconstructed states were illegal and did not protect life and property. The first section of the bill divided the South into five military districts. Army officers, not below the rank of brigadier general, were to be in charge and were assigned sweeping powers. The military commanders were "to protect all persons in their rights of person and property, to suppress insurrection, disorder, and violence, and to punish, or cause to be punished, all disturbers of the public peace and criminals." The commanding general could permit existing courts to punish offenders, although military commissions could be established if necessary.

The bill was rigorously debated, and the wisdom of placing the South under virtual military rule questioned, but the main objection centered around the lack of a procedure for the Southern states to end military occupation. A "plan" was therefore added to the bill that outlined a series of steps that a state must take to end military rule. A convention must be held, a new constitution drawn up, and the Fourteenth Amendment ratified. Congress also established requirements for voting and for holding public office. With their majorities intact, the radicals quickly overcame the expected presidential veto, and the bill became law on March 2, 1867.[59]

Congressional Reconstruction was a radical departure from the role of the army before the March acts. Previously, the military exercised limited authority. Now they exercised direct political control over Southern states. How successful the exercise of this authority was to be depended on the competence and prudence of the men who exercised this power.[60]

General Schofield, who had commanded Federal troops in Virginia since the previous August, was named commander of the First Military District. Stoneman was his second-in-command and would succeed him on June 2, 1868. The two men supported a moderate policy that was to ease Virginia through this difficult period with a minimum of disruption and chaos.

Schofield was opposed to the Fourteenth Amendment, which he termed unjust and unwise, especially the third section which disqualified anyone from public office who had taken an oath to uphold the Constitution and then engaged in rebellion. This eliminated, in Schofield's view, almost any competent leader in Virginia who might have the confidence of the people. In a major speech, he expressed his convictions:

> It is folly to bring back a revolted people by disfranchising all the leaders in whom they trust and confide. These leaders, if they will act in good faith, can bring their people back to their allegiance. Without them it cannot be done in the existing generation. The question is simply can we trust the leaders of public opinion in the South when they say "we are honestly loyal to the Union and willing to do all in our power to effect a complete restoration?" If we cannot trust them there is nothing left but to hold the Southern states under military government, until a new generation can be educated.[61]

Schofield was hardly a champion of freedmen's rights, and he opposed suffrage for blacks, holding that they were in an "ignorant and degraded condition," a position that endeared him to Virginia conservatives. In fact, the General Assembly had requested that President Johnson appoint Schofield as military commander in view of his racial policy.[62]

Nonetheless, Schofield moved to carry out the directives of the Reconstruction Acts. Voter registration boards were established throughout the state. Biracial panels of loyal citizens were established to challenge anyone who could not legally register to vote under the Reconstruction Acts, namely those who had sworn allegiance to the United States and then fought against the Union. The Freedmen's Bureau encouraged black voter registration, and thousands of black voters were added to the rolls, most of them Republicans. Meetings of freedmen were held throughout the state, applauding speakers like James W. Hunnicutt, editor of the *New Nation*, who, as a white Republican, benefited from the emerging black political power. Hunnicutt was a clergyman and former slave owner from Fredericksburg who became a radical Republican at the beginning of Reconstruction.[63]

Schofield and Stoneman rarely intervened in the administration of the state except to moderate the actions of radical leaders. Both cooperated with conservative leaders and viewed growing black and Republican political power with suspicion. Military courts in general were stricter with blacks than were Republican civil officials.[64]

Political activity intensified following the passage of the Reconstruction Acts, and the Acts provided for an election in which voters would vote for or against holding a constitutional convention and would also elect delegates to the convention if it was approved. Three major political groups were competing for power: a left that supported the Reconstruction Acts and wanted to depart from the Confederate past, a right that opposed the Reconstruction program, particularly black suffrage, and a center looking for a middle path in the tradition of the Virginia Whigs.[65] The left, represented by Republican Radicals, championed a new government that would enfranchise blacks and remove former Confederates from state offices and voting rolls. Other objectives included free schools, economic development, and women's suffrage.

The Republicans held their political convention in April and drew strength from the growing number of black voters who were anxious to demonstrate their new freedom by registering to vote and forcibly integrating public transportation in major cities such as Richmond. Although the party was split between radical and conservative factions, the radicals prevailed and the convention adopted a radical platform for its time, demanding civil and political rights for blacks, calling for a progressive tax structure and state aid to transportation. The Republicans appealed to the laboring class and the poor and appeared to be one of the most radical political parties of the South.[66]

Traditionalists or conservatives enjoyed certain advantages over their political rivals, as they controlled most of the press and were adamantly opposed to black suffrage. That was a popular position with most white Virginians. The radicals made little headway with middle-class whites, particularly in the northern Piedmont region and the Shenandoah Valley, but white voters were divided and thousands of white voters wanted no part of a biracial election held under the Reconstruction Acts.[67]

Centrists, looking for a middle path between the two extremes, were disproportionately strong because of their influence in business and the press, and most importantly, they had strong support from Federal military commanders. Both Schofied and Stoneman wanted civil rights and fair trials for blacks, but they did not support universal suffrage or loyalty tests for civil officials. They were basically elitist in attitude and felt that qualified former Confederates were preferable as candidates for public office then unqualified blacks and poorly educated whites.

Schofield announced on September 12 that the election on whether a convention should be convened and delegates chosen would be held on October 22. Voting was by ballot, separate boxes for blacks and whites, supervised by army officers and Freedmen's Bureau agents. Radicals won a decisive victory in the election, helped by the fact that one-third of registered white voters failed to vote. The convention was approved and 73 radicals, and those Republicans sympathetic to them, were elected as delegates, as opposed to 32 conservatives.[68]

The convention, which included 24 black delegates, met from December 3, 1867, to April 7, 1868. The conservative press ridiculed the proceedings, referring to them as the mulatto convention, the "Bones and Banjo Convention," the "black and tan convention," and the "Black Bird Convention." As radicals were in control of the convention proceedings, the constitution it produced was unacceptable to most whites. The so-called Underwood Constitution, named after Judge Underwood, the presiding official, disenfranchised anyone who had held any state or federal office and had taken an oath in support of that office, and had later participated in a rebellion. Moreover, no one could hold public office unless he took an iron-clad oath that he had never willingly served the Confederacy.[69]

Except for the disqualifying clauses, there was much in the new charter to admire. The new constitution established free public schools, enacted uniform taxation of property, proclaimed universal manhood suffrage (except for the disenfranchised), prevented discrimination in jury selection, protected debtors in hard economic times, and established a New England-style township system, designed to increase participation in local government.[70]

General Schofield addressed the convention on April 17 and asked the delegates to repeal the test-oath condition for holding state office, saying that its enactment would deprive the state of qualified office holders. With so few qualified candidates available, state offices would be filled with poorly educated and inexperienced men. Schofield also opposed the disfranchisement of former office holders and the township system. He told General Grant that he hoped the new constitution would die and not be submitted to the citizens of the state. Failing that, he hoped that the test-oath provision would be submitted separately so that the constitution could be approved without the oath.[71]

Despite Schofield's advice, the constitution was adopted as it had been drafted. Schofield later described his reception. "I was listened to with cold restraint, my advice was disregarded, and promptly after my departure, the Constitution was adopted, and the Convention adjourned...."[72] Schofield complained to Grant about the "baneful influence" of "ignorant blacks and equally ignorant or unprincipled whites" who controlled the Convention. "They could only hope to obtain office by disqualifying everybody in the state who is capable of discharging official duties...."[73]

Nonetheless, Virginia had taken a number of key steps that would readmit her representatives in Congress. It remained for the commonwealth to ratify the new constitution, which Schofield continued to oppose, elect state officers, and adopt the Fourteenth Amendment. These steps were crucial for the restoration process to be complete, and it would fall to George Stoneman to guide Virginia through this critical period.

The national scene now dictated events in Virginia. President Johnson was acquitted of impeachment charges on May 26. While the proceedings were going on, a group of moderate Republicans reportedly made an agreement with Johnson that, in the case of acquittal, Schofield, who could be counted on to carry out congressional reconstruction, would be named Secretary of War. Schofield was nominated on April 24 and confirmed by the Senate after Johnson's acquittal. Schofield was relieved on June 1, 1868, and Stoneman assumed command of the First Military District on the following day.

Stoneman had won the respect and admiration of Virginians in the sub-district of Petersburg during his tenure, and his appointment was met with relief by state and community leaders. The Petersburg correspondent of the *Richmond Enquirer* expressed his admiration for Stoneman's leadership:

> We cannot permit the opportunity to pass without expressing our regret at General Stoneman's departure. His administration of affairs at this sub-district has been marked by a singular wisdom, delicacy, and devotion. During his sojourn in our midst he has envinced [sic] a dignity of character, both in social and official intercourse, alike honorable to himself and gratifying to the people. If Virginia must remain under military rule, we should be glad always to receive the affliction at the hands of such officers, while true to the service to which they are engaged can administer justice with an impartial hand.[74]

The *Richmond Dispatch* was equally enthusiastic:

> Brig. General Stoneman succeeds General Schofield in command in this district. He was second in command in this district, has been stationed in Petersburg, and won the regard of the people of that city by the kind and considerate manner in which he discharged the delicate duties of his position. Not having been involved in the partisan politics of the day, it is believed he will impartially perform the duties of his new station. This is all we can ask of an officer placed over us in these strange and adverse times. We cannot expect to escape the bitter and painful formalities prescribed by the faction of the Government which holds sway at Washington. It is no more than reasonable, however, that we should expect them to be conducted with order and fairness. We should be protected from frauds, and should have such guarantees as fair and open proceedings can give. From all that is known of General Stoneman, it is believed our people will not have cause to regret that he succeeds General Schofield.[75]

Stoneman inherited a difficult situation from Schofield, due primarily to the adoption of the Fourteenth Amendment. Using his discretionary powers, Schofield had appointed some five hundred officials to civil offices who were able to meet the requirements of their office. With the ratification of the Fourteenth Amendment on July 28, 1868, all office holders who could not meet the requirements of the amendment would be removed from office. Stoneman was faced with the monumental task of finding thousands of qualified officials for state and municipal offices. "You are very well aware," he wrote Schofield in August, "that before you left you had pretty nearly exhausted the material proper to be used ... and that I have had to cull over the rubbish."[76]

Thousands of positions were unfilled and Stoneman was forced to compromise. Those "not disloyal" to the Federal government and "were not opposed to reconstruction" were appointed until more suitable candidates could be found.[77] Since so few white Virginians were qualified to hold public office, Stoneman at first continued Schofield's policy to buy more time and retained most civil servants in their posts. He was opposed to appointing unqualified blacks, and he resisted appointing radicals, despite pressure to do so, particularly from the governor, Henry H. Wells.

One of Schofield's last major acts before he departed Richmond was to appoint Wells, a carpetbagger from Michigan, governor, replacing Francis H. Pierpont, who had been installed as governor by the Federal military after the demise of the Confederacy. Pierpont had been governor for seven years by 1868, since he had been governor of Union-occupied areas of the state since 1861, and he wanted to see the normalization process through.

He could have been reappointed, even though his term was up, but Schofield decided that Wells represented the best hope for the success of reconstruction and to blunt the radical movement.

Stoneman's policy to fill state offices put him on a collision course with Governor Wells, who was anxious to control state patronage. Wells, although he was considered to be a conservative when appointed, adopted an increasingly radical posture by the time Stoneman assumed command of the district. Wells also frequently used his pardoning powers to free offenders, especially blacks, who had been convicted by military courts. Stoneman was convinced that many of these pardons were politically motivated. To blunt the appointive power of the governor, and the Republican Party which he distrusted, Stoneman appointed a military commission on February 1, 1869, which was charged with making recommendations to district headquarters "with the view of enabling the commanding general to make a proper selection of competent persons to fill the vacancies now existing."[78]

Military officers were dispatched throughout the commonwealth to find qualified candidates for a wide range of positions, from justices of the peace and sheriffs up to executive state offices at the capital. Stoneman instructed his military commissioners in no uncertain terms:

> It is my desire that every inducement be held out and every opportunity given to loyal and competent men to present themselves in order that there may be no excuse hereafter if the offices are not filled and filled with proper persons.[79]

Stoneman's report to the Adjutant General illustrated the extent of the problem. There were 5,446 vacancies to be filled. Schofield had appointed a small number, 532. By February 1869, Stoneman had appointed 1,972, but 329 of these appointees could not take the test oath. As of February, 2,613 positions needed to be filled.[80]

Stoneman explained the problem to Washington:

> In accounting for the very small number of persons in the State who can take the test oath of office it must be taken into consideration that Virginia was one great battlefield during the war, that there was small chance of escape from the rigors of the conscript law, that nearly every man was directly under the eye and control of the Confederate government and that at some time or other nearly everyone gave 'aid, countenance, or encouragement to persons engaged in armed hostility' to the government of the United States, and besides once having been engaged in the war, probably no frontier of the Southern people, old and young, male and female were more earnest in its prosecution.[81]

As Stoneman grappled with the problem of filling state offices, politics were heating up in the commonwealth. The constitutional convention had set the date of June 2, 1868, for the referendum on the proposed constitution, but Schofield had postponed it indefinitely on the grounds that funds were not available to meet expenses. He was opposed to the proscription clauses and he wanted to give moderates and conservatives time to organize and effectively oppose the radicals. Despite the suspension of the election, the political parties began extensive campaigning, assuming that Congress would eventually authorize one.[82] The Republicans, meeting in Richmond, nominated H.H. Wells for governor, defeating the more radical Hunnicutt, and the Conservatives nominated Robert E. Withers. In blazing summer heat, so hot that Stoneman authorized the troops to wear straw hats except on parades and reviews,[83] candidates campaigned throughout the state.

As Wells moved to a more radical position, his relations with Stoneman deteriorated. He pressed Stoneman to appoint more blacks, a policy that both Schofield and Stoneman opposed. Stoneman's appointment of a military commission to recommend applicants for civil positions was a major blow to Wells, who previously had assumed that role. Stoneman had also used his powers to assist business leaders, especially to promote the plan of William Mahone to consolidate Virginia railways. Mahone was an engineer by training, a graduate of the Virginia Military Institute, who became president of the Norfolk and Petersburg Railway in 1860. He was a highly successful brigadier general in Lee's Army of Northern Virginia.

When the war ended, Mahone lived in Petersburg for about four years, where he doubtless knew George Stoneman when Stoneman was commander of the sub-district.[84] Mahone was elected to the presidency of the Virginia and Tennessee Railroad after expressing his interest to consolidate with several smaller railroads into one railway system leading to the West. The powerful Baltimore and Ohio Railroad was opposed to consolidation because the consolidated system would be an important competitor in the drive for western trade. An agent of the Baltimore and Ohio Railroad, R.T. Wilson, arrived in Richmond on October 25, 1868, for the express purpose of fighting the merger. He convinced Governor Wells that the state should sell its interest in the Virginia and Tennessee to the Baltimore and Ohio, a deal which would personally benefit the governor. Wells tried to persuade State Treasurer George Rye, but Rye refused, and made the offer public. Stoneman was also approached and strongly disapproved of the proposal. Public opinion was equally opposed to a sell-out to Northern interests, and Wells's popularity with the public and with Stoneman plummeted. Stoneman would not permit the Board of Public Works to interfere with the state's railroads and said that he would remove the governor and state treasurer if necessary to prevent it. This was good news for the Mahone camp, and Mahone was advised by his Richmond banker, James R. Branch, to "get the ear & influence of Genl. Stoneman before the opposition prejudice him, & you should lose no time in securing him."[85] Branch had called on Stoneman shortly after his appointment and found him to be "a frank and straight-forward soldier" who would support consolidation. The railroad consolidation convinced Mahone to politically overthrow Wells, and provided him with an important ally in Stoneman.

Stoneman sought the advice of Schofield in the fall of 1868, and the two exchanged letters on the future of Virginia's railroads. Schofield thought that the ultimate solution was to transfer the state's interest to private parties but, as long as Virginia was under military control, Stoneman was obliged to protect its commercial interests. Schofield cautioned Stoneman to remain politically neutral. "You may be sure of one thing," Schofield wrote, "that political interests are at the bottom of the present question *on both sides*." As long as the state maintained part-ownership of the railroads, "their management will be ... in the interest of one party or the other." Schofield remarked:

> You must decide which party shall reap the benefit, or else leave it to chance without any interference on your part, or, as a last resort, assume personal control of the whole matter and try to

conduct railroad affairs on a neutral basis.... Under the present condition of Virginia it would be desirable if it were possible, to conduct all affairs, Governmental as well as financial, independently of party politics. But that is impossible, since all citizens of character have decided convictions and sympathies one way or the other. Hence the only just policy practicable is a fair division between the two parties. If you can accomplish this you will do well. But if by action or failure to act, you give or leave the control of any important matter to one party alone, you may be sure of serious trouble.[86]

Bipartisanship was difficult to achieve as political divisions in Virginia intensified over an acceptable institution. The Conservative party opposed black suffrage and could not accept the Underwood Constitution, while the Republicans supported the constitution and the Wells administration. There were moderates in each party who looked for a way to accept a modified constitution that would permit black suffrage, while not disqualifying former Confederates. As 1868 closed, the moderates were in a position to make a bid for power.[87]

Early in 1869, an association of moderate Republicans and Conservatives was formed, known as the New Movement, encouraged by General William Mahone. It was an attempt to embrace the proposed constitution, but remove the disfranchisement and disqualification sections. They also called for the separate submission to the voters of Virginia of the test oath and disfranchisement provisions.[88]

Under the leadership of Alexander H.H. Stuart, a statesman and cabinet minister in the Fillmore administration, a "Committee of Nine" was formed to draft the compromise resolutions. Stoneman gave his imprimatur to the movement, as he saw it as a countering force to the radicalism of the Republicans.

The basic views of the New Movement were published in a letter written by Stuart to the *Richmond Dispatch,* under the pseudonym of "Senex," in which he said the only way to escape the disfranchisement and the test oaths in the Underwood Constitution was to accept Negro suffrage. "Is it not better to surrender 'half' a loaf than lose all?"[89] asked "Senex."

As Stuart predicted, many in Virginia were not ready to make such a bargain:

I knew full well, however, that in the condition of public opinion which then existed in Virginia, in regard to the granting the right of suffrage to the ignorant Negroes, the simple announcement of that proposed basis of compromise would arouse a storm of fierce indignation throughout the state, and drawn down on him who had the hardihood to suggest it a torrent of denunciation and oloquy which few men have been called upon to endure.[90]

There were moderate voices in Virginia who realized that "universal suffrage" and "universal amnesty" were the best ways to ensure that the affairs of the state would not "pass into the hands of strangers and adventurers."[91] A meeting of prominent citizens was held on December 31, 1868, at the Exchange Hotel in Richmond. From this group, the "Committee of Nine" was to travel to Washington and present their petition to Congress. The committee felt that "freedmen of the Southern states, in their present uneducated position are not prepared for the intelligent exercise of the elective franchise ... and are, therefore, at this time, unsafe depositaries of political power." The participants felt, however, that it was time to make an offering "on the alter [sic] of peace, in the hope that union and harmony may be restored on the basis of universal suffrage and universal amnesty."[92]

Although Stoneman had his doubts about universal suffrage, he invited the committee to a New Year's reception where, according to Stuart, he "expressed sympathy with the objects of their meeting and hoped it might prove successful."[93]

One member of the committee, Colonel John B. Baldwin, Stuart's brother-in-law and business partner, expressed grave doubts about Stoneman in a letter to Stuart:

> I am afraid of General Stoneman. They say he has no instructions from Washington, and yet he goes on to kick and cuff our people as if he were a very radical, aiming at political objects. Truly, we are fallen on evil times, and I fear worse are coming.

Despite Baldwin's misgivings, Stoneman supported the "New Movement." He saw it as a means to dilute the power of Governor Wells, whom he continued to mistrust. On January 19, 1869, Stoneman advised Schofield that the New Movement "would soon swallow up the Wells and Underwood party."[94] A week later, Stoneman established the military board that recommended candidates for state and local offices, a move which effectively removed Wells's powers of patronage. The radical press was outraged. The *Winchester Journal* commented:

> General Stoneman has been far more successful in his attempts to destroy the republican party in Virginia and turn the state government over to the conservatives then we can imagine.... If nature had given Stoneman an understanding to keep pace with the principles — the malignity — the depravity of his heart — he would have made perhaps the most formidable agent ever employed in Virginia to destroy the very vestige of her republican institutions.[95]

The *Journal* went on to describe one of Stoneman's appointees to the bench, Edward Pendleton, as "a base and infamous liar," and his appointment was "an infamous outrage upon the purity and dignity of our courts of justice ... like all traitors, he [Stoneman] seeks now to ruin what he could not rule."[96]

As the political situation heated up, the antagonism between Stoneman and Wells intensified. Efforts were made, through Schofield, to mediate the dispute, but the break was complete. Relations became even worse when Wells was accused of tampering with the U.S. mails. A letter from a political opponent, urging action against Wells's policy of attempting to fill state offices with radicals, turned up in Wells's office. Although the charges were eventually dropped, the case convinced Stoneman that Wells should be removed from office. Stoneman was convinced that Wells did not have moderate Republican support and that the New Movement represented a coalition of moderates in both parties, particularly the Republicans, which is what he assumed Grant and Schofied desired. Accordingly, on March 27, he asked Wells to resign, ostensibly because Wells used his pardoning power for political purposes.[97] Wells's political opponents were delighted. The *Lexington Gazette* observed that Stoneman's decision was met with "universal satisfaction" and proposed that Wells go to prison "to keep company with his betters."[98]

Stoneman accepted the advice of General Mahone and was prepared to appoint Franklin Stearns as governor. Stearns had been a member of the moderate Republican committee that had urged a compromise on the Underwood Constitution before the

Reconstruction Committee of Congress. Mahone strongly urged Stoneman to appoint Stearns as governor and the order removing Wells was written out and signed.[99] However, Wells refused to resign and began a campaign in Washington to have Stoneman's order nullified. Wells had a strong ally who proved to be the deciding factor in the dispute. Dr. Alexander Sharp, a close friend of President Grant and Mrs. Grant's brother-in-law, interceded on behalf of Wells. Sharp was also a member of Grant's staff during the war and had been appointed Deputy Postmaster in Richmond by President Johnson. His influence with Grant was considerable.[100]

Grant was displeased with Stoneman, believing that he had interfered in Virginia state politics, and there is no evidence that Schofield intervened on Stoneman's behalf. Bowing to pressure from Sharp and Wells, Grant not only reinstated Wells as governor, but relieved Stoneman from his command of the First Military District as well, ordering him to join his regiment and proceed to California. He was replaced by General Alexander S. Webb on April 2, but a few days later, Stoneman's former comrade-in-arms, Major General Edward R. Canby, assumed command of the district.

The decision to remove Stoneman was certainly political. His refusal to appoint Radical Republicans to state offices, his decision to create a military board to recommend suitable candidates, and his feud with Wells were all factors. Furthermore, Stoneman did not have the political skills to buttress his position in Washington, particularly with Grant, and to avoid the shoals of Virginia politics. For once, his friendship with Schofield did not save him.

Conservatives in Virginia genuinely regretted his departure. "He will take with him the cordial respect and esteem of all those whose good opinion is worth having," commented the *Richmond Whig*. *The Enquirer* was effusive:

> He has manifested a tender consideration for the feelings of our people and as far as possible has abated the full measure that has been dealt out to us. He has spared us whenever he could spare us, and has helped us where he could help us. He will leave us with the kind feelings of our people — and will have the consciousness of having acquitted himself like a gentleman and a soldier in a most trying situation.[101]

As Stoneman took his leave, the political parties prepared for the coming election. A tumultuous Republican convention at Petersburg nominated Wells for governor and Dr. J.B. Harris, a black West Indian physician, for lieutenant governor. Since the Wells ticket would not appeal to many whites, centrist Republicans, under the influence of Mahone, formed a "True Republican" ticket with Gilbert C. Walker for governor. Walker was a Northerner who had come to Virginia in 1864 from New York and Chicago. A Douglas Democrat turned Republican, he was supported by conservatives who decided that he would further their political and business objectives. The conservative party withdrew their ticket in order to consolidate support behind the Walker candidacy.[102]

Grant set the election for July 6 and ordered that the disfranchising and test oath clauses be voted on separately. Over 220,000 Virginians voted and overwhelmingly ratified the proposed constitution. The proscriptive clauses were defeated by 40,000 votes. Walker won 54 percent of the vote, defeating Wells. Conservatives and "True Republicans" were in control of the Virginia house and senate.[103]

Commentators in the North hailed the vote in Virginia as an example of ideal Reconstruction, noting the fertile climate for Northern investment. Grant belatedly issued the order to remove Wells from office and appoint Walker after Malone persuaded Horace Greely to intervene with Grant.[104] Conservative ascendancy in Virginia had begun and the commonwealth moved toward readmission to Congress which was finally accomplished in 1870.

The ratification of the constitution and a Conservative victory over the Wells radicals were in large part due to the moderate policies of Schofield and Stoneman. Stoneman made the machinery of local government function effectively and advocated the New Movement that led to the enactment of political reform, including black suffrage. The editor of the *Petersburg Index* recalled that under Schofield and Stoneman, "Virginians knew none of the dreaded horrors of military despotism and that the officers' honest and efficient administration contrasted markedly with the incompetent, corrupt, Radical governments of other states."[105] Unlike Schofield, Stoneman did not have Grant's personal friendship. Nonetheless, Stoneman's performance in Virginia contributed greatly to the success of the reconstruction process, especially his determination to find competent men for public office. His major weakness was a lack of tact and political skills, which made it difficult for him to support moderate factions while not offending other factions of the political spectrum.

Arizona Territory

George Stoneman may well have been relieved when he was ordered to return to his regiment in April 1869. The regiment was soon dispatched to the District of Arizona with Stoneman in command at his permanent rank of colonel. This was banishment to the outer reaches in one sense, but Stoneman was not displeased. As a junior officer 20 years earlier, he had made a vow to return to California and had selected his retirement site in the San Gabriel Valley. Arizona was a frontier post, with all its attendant hardships, but it was close to the land of his dreams.

Stoneman arrived at Camp McDowell, northeast of present-day Phoenix, on August 16, 1869. The heat and discomfort did not appeal to Stoneman and his family, and he persuaded his commanding officer, General George H. Thomas, Commander of the Department of the Pacific, to extend the District of Arizona to include Drum Barracks, at Wilmington, Southern California, a much more moderate and comfortable locale. Although Stoneman's motive was obviously designed to place himself and his family in more comfortable circumstances, the request had some logic behind it. Drum Barracks served as a staging and supply area for action against the Apaches and other "hostiles" in the Southwest, and the district included San Diego, San Bernardino, and Los Angeles counties. Moreover, Stoneman had the services of capable subordinates commanding sub-districts in Arizona, including Colonel Frank Wheaton at Prescott. Stoneman's request was approved and he administered his district from afar, a fact that was not unnoticed by the settlers in Arizona. Orders flowed up and down the chain of command with little comment from Stoneman. There is no evidence of direct orders by Stoneman to his subordinates in the endorsement book, and he rarely intervened in routine administration. He initially did not visit the district that he commanded, but constant problems between Native Americans and the settlers finally forced Stoneman into a more active role.[1]

The governor of Arizona Territory, Anson Peacely-Killen Safford, the third territorial governor, became increasingly concerned by Native American attacks on settlers, especially the Apaches. He was vexed by the apparent inability of the army to protect the rapidly increasing white population of the territory. Part of the governor's problem stemmed from the primitive communications between far-off Arizona and Washington. Railroads and telegraph facilities had not yet connected the nation's capital with the territorial authorities and, consequently, they had little political influence with the Grant administration and Congress. The Arizonians faced a dilemma. They wanted a larger and more aggressive military in the territory, but did not want to discourage immigration and commercial investment. Nonetheless, the territorial legislature decided to memorialize Congress and request protection. Admitting that the territory lacked communications and had limited political influence, the legislators informed Congress that "the suffering and death which have attended the settlement of this Territory in consequence of the hostility of the Apache Indians are but little known and appreciated beyond our borders."[2] Testimony by citizens and army officers was forwarded to Congress, which showed that a "savage war still exists here, causing the murder of hundreds of our citizens and the loss of a vast amount of property ... that the hostility of the Apache Indians and the want of protection have led to the abandonment of many valuable mines, and that large farming settlements have been, and are being, abandoned for like causes." After praising the "genial climate" and the "pastoral, agricultural, and mineral resources," of Arizona, the memorialists informed Congress that "they have endured the hardships and braved the dangers incident to pioneer life with a fortitude that should command the admiration of a brave people." Hundreds had been killed by the scalping knife and suffered torture, and assistance and protection were urgently requested.[3]

The Apaches had been a concern of the U.S. Army in Arizona since the United States government acquired the territory from Mexico through the Treaty of Guadalupe Hildago in 1848. According to the terms of that treaty, the United States was obliged to prevent Indian raids across the new boundary. The U.S. had no military base between Santa Fe and San Diego, but the army patrolled southern Arizona as best it could, protecting isolated settlements.[4] There was little the army could do during the Civil War, but after Appomattox, settlements were rapidly established and the Apaches, faced with increasing competition for land and hunting rights, committed raid after raid, with murder an inevitable consequence. Stoneman and his army colleagues were obliged to fight the Apaches, while they were also subject to increasing pressure from the Grant administration to bring the Apaches onto reservations peacefully by providing food and land on which the Apaches were free to settle. There they would be protected from the wrath of white settlers. This policy was nothing short of appeasement in the eyes of territorial citizens and government.[5]

As the situation in Arizona became more critical, Governor Safford made the long trip to Washington to plead his case for more military intervention directly with the president, the secretary of war, and General Sherman, Commanding General of the Army. His trip was also necessitated by a judge's ruling that the second, third, and fourth territorial legislatures had been illegally convened. Hence, all legislation that had been enacted was invalid. While waiting for Congress to legalize the legislature, Safford lobbied for the creation of a military department in Arizona.[6]

Sherman had previously discussed creating the new department with General Thomas, who favored the proposal. Major General George Crook was offered the post, but he declined, informing Thomas that he "was tired of Indian work, that it only entailed hard work without any corresponding benefits." Like Stoneman, Crook disliked the climate of Arizona, and Thomas reluctantly agreed that Crook could remain in command of the Department of the Columbia.[7] Thomas may have felt that Stoneman was not up to the job of department commander, but on March 28, he was stricken with apoplexy and died suddenly. His successor was Stoneman's old friend and mentor General John Schofield, who once again helped the career of his fellow Chautauquan. George Stoneman was given command of the new department with his brevet rank of major general. The district included Arizona Territory and "so much of California as lies south of a line from the northeast corner of Arizona to Point Conception."[8] Headquarters was established at Fort Whipple, near Prescott. Stoneman could no longer administer his command from the relative comforts of Drum Barracks.

Prior to the announcement of Stoneman's appointment, Governor Safford met Stoneman in Washington to discuss future actions against the Apaches. Safford urged Stoneman to pursue a vigorous and active campaign against the Apaches and tried to appeal to his vanity by remarking that fame would certainly be in store for any officer who conquered a foe "who had held their own against the governments of Spain, Mexico and for twelve years against the United States."[9] To the governor's displeasure, Stoneman replied that he did not consider that there was any credit to be gained in fighting Indians and that the greatest mistake the government had made "was in taking away from the Indians such a desert and worthless country as Arizona and New Mexico."[10] The governor later expressed his disappointment with Stoneman's attitude:

> I saw at a glance that if Stoneman was forced upon us, we could expect but little relief and no sympathy. I went to General Sherman and mildly suggested that perhaps a younger and more ambitious man might be sent in his place, but in effect I was informed that the military authorities at Washington were capable of managing their own affairs.[11]

Stoneman assumed his command on May 3, 1870, and advised division headquarters that he would first organize the equipment and men "necessary to put the Department of Arizona in operation." He hoped that the division commander would not change the location of department headquarters from Fort Whipple to Tucson or Camp McDowell, which were even less suitable in Stoneman's eyes.[12] Stoneman abolished the subdistricts on May 31, depriving himself of deputies, but he instructed post commanders to suppress Indians in areas "over which they will naturally be supposed to have control ... failing in which they must expect to give place to those who can and will." Citizens and immigrants will be given aid and encouragement "consistent with public service."[13] Stoneman then outlined his policy toward Native Americans:

> In their intercourse with Indians the troops will treat as friendly those who are positively known to be such; the most vigorous and persistent efforts will be made to pursue and chastise those not so considered — and to this end both Cavalry and Infantry will be employed either separately or jointly and in large or small parties, as may be thought most advisable.[14]

Stoneman and his staff arrived in Prescott on July 3, traveling from California via the Mojave route. As the party entered the territorial capital, citizens lined the streets and cheered, guns were fired, and full military honors, as elaborate as the frontier outpost could muster, were rendered to the new department commander.

Governor Safford put aside his dislike of Stoneman and observed the necessary protocol by holding a welcoming reception for Stoneman and his staff at the residence of U.S. Collector Bashford upon arrival on July 3. It was a pleasant affair, according to the *Weekly Arizona Miner*, and Stoneman, in his remarks reported by the paper, noted the kind reception he had received which he felt "could not do otherwise than produce a feeling of gratification, and stimulate a purpose of his to do all that it was possible with his available means to give safety and security to life and property, and develop the resources of the Territory."[15] He suggested that the paramount concern was the settlement of the country so that the people could protect themselves. To that end, he sought to open up more and better wagon roads, improve mail service, and subdue the Apaches. He made a totally unrealistic suggestion that farmers and miners settle near one another so that they could protect themselves. If they did so, he could move his troops into the mountains where the Native Americans lived. He could not possibly guard every farming and mining camp, and he wished to concentrate his forces and not restrict them to camp duty. It was his intention to make a concentrated movement against the Apaches with all his available force in the fall. He invited citizens to join with the army to protect the country, and he would provide rations for them if they did so. Stoneman's first order to post commanders was "to regard as hostile all Indians not known to be friendly." His confidence in the future of the Territory was great, and he noted that he had first visited the area some 20 years before. The grazing was unsurpassed in the national domain, and he believed Arizona would be in the first rank as a gold- and silver-producing state. He concluded by assuring the people that if his relations with them, so pleasantly begun, did not continue, it would not be his fault.[16]

Although Stoneman's remarks were at variance with his views allegedly expressed in private to Safford, he told the settlers what they wanted to hear in his first public appearance at Prescott. A journalist from *The Arizona Miner* met with Stoneman a few days after his arrival and reported to his readers that he "came away satisfied with him and fully convinced he is the right man in the right job. He will do everything in his power to bring about peace and advance the interests of the territory."[17] The newspaper editorially welcomed the new department commander, referring to him as "the gallant and accomplished General Stoneman...." While noting that Stoneman had been attached to the Department of California with headquarters at San Francisco nearly 1000 miles away, "and our Indian affairs all the time being no better, it is no wonder that our people welcome the gallant General with hearts full of hope and confidence."[18] The newspaper concluded with a ringing endorsement of Stoneman and a message to Washington:

> For in General Stoneman we do not recognize the mere military adventurer, but the able and accomplished chieftain, around whose honored brow already circle laurels sufficient to satisfy the ambition of any man; for his fame is part of the history of his country. His energy and determination are well known; and it only remains for the authorities in Washington to do their part, in furnishing him with the necessary troops, and he will put an end to our Indian troubles.[19]

The affable public exchanges between Governor Safford and Stoneman masked an intense disagreement over the policies to be pursued toward Native Americans and the disposition of military resources in the department. The two met privately in Prescott shortly after Stoneman's arrival. Safford advised Stoneman of the feuds that existed between various Apache bands and suggested that he could turn one band against another. Stoneman, according to Safford, abruptly rejected his advice. "He replied to me in that self-confident, commanding tone he so frequently assumed, that the government of the United States was capable of fighting its own battles."[20]

As Stoneman formulated plans for his department, it became clear that he was placed in an impossible position by conflicting interests in Washington and Arizona. A peace policy toward Native Americans was popular within the Grant administration and Stoneman was ordered to establish "feeding stations" where Native Americans who had surrendered were provided with food, shelter, and protection.[21] At the same time, he was expected to reduce expenditures. Acting on orders from the War Department, he reduced the number of clerks to four and civilian employees to 61 and limited their salaries to 150 dollars a month. Soldiers were not to perform the duties that had been carried out by discharged civilians.[22]

Stoneman issued orders to consolidate his troops at three or four central points in the interest of economy and efficiency and, although Safford complained about "breezy proclamations" that did not lead to action, there was some activity. Two infantry companies were moved to Camp Grant, and Troop F, 3rd Cavalry, was detached from Camp Grant for service in the field under civilian control. Safford was consulted about where the troops should operate, and Stoneman, true to his word, issued rations to a militia company.[23]

Stoneman decided to make an inspection trip of his district in August and was accompanied by John Marion, editor of the *Prescott Miner*. Marion had welcomed Stoneman as "the savior of Arizona who would deal sternly with the Apaches and free the settlers from constant dread of fire, mutilation, and death."[24] The party was comprised of Major M. Cogswell of the 21st Infantry, Surgeon H.R. Wirtz, three servants, one cook, and 12 enlisted men of the 3rd Cavalry, 25 men in all. Four wagons and two ambulances, drawn by mules, transported supplies and equipment.

It was, as Marion reported in his detailed narrative of the expedition, "a dangerous undertaking." Friends of the travelers had serious misgivings toward the venture, as the party traveled through the heart of Apache country "peopled with savages, the most treacherous on the continent,"[25] but Stoneman was determined to inspect the military installations under his command and to see the situation firsthand.

The party left Fort Whipple on August 29 and almost immediately suffered damage to one of the wagons. Surprisingly, repairs were made by Stoneman himself, despite the fact that presumably he had men along for that purpose. The party headed northeast through the Chino Valley toward the San Francisco and Bill Williams mountains. They passed through Leroux Springs, named after a French explorer, about seven miles from present-day Flagstaff. Crossing the Little Colorado River, they turned south toward the first post to be inspected, Camp Mogollon.[26] The route was extremely difficult to transverse, some of the most formidable country on the continent, Marion observed. Once again, Stoneman showed his resourcefulness by "rigging a purchase" which enabled them to move an ambulance after a wheel refused to turn. The spindle was heated "and made as good as new."²⁷ Making about 27 to 30 miles a day, sometimes over mountainous terrain, the expedition passed through the rugged but spectacular territory.

Camp Mogollon was garrisoned by three small companies. An inspection followed Stoneman's arrival, but another reason for the visit was to consult with the Coyotero Apaches who were present in the region. Stoneman wanted a pow-wow with the four principal chiefs to convince them that, if they were peaceful, the army would protect them. Marion heartily approved of Stoneman's policy of feeding and "civilizing" the Apaches, a position he later changed after Stoneman's report of his trip was published. At this point, the two were of one mind:

> We know it to be the fixed opinion of most Arizonians that the Apaches cannot be tamed, but proper measures for doing so have never been taken, and it may be that this opinion will soon be abandoned. We hope so, at all events, for it is cheaper, better for the country to feed and civilize them than it is to fight them, which latter mode of dealing with them has so far proved an expensive, ineffectual way of subduing them.²⁸

Marion recorded that one of the Apache chiefs told Stoneman that God had made men differently; "the white man He made rich, the red poor." The chief had "heard a good deal about Stoneman, and was glad to see him. God had brought them together to smoke in peace, (a gentle hint for some cigaritoes....)" Although the Apaches were grateful for the meat the army had given them, they asked for powder and lead "to kill game with."²⁹ The Apaches said they were tired of war and wanted peace with the Americans. Marion described Stoneman's reply:

> "God," he said, "wants all people to live together in peace. Away to the east were myriads of white men, and in one big city lived the Great Father of all Indians and Americans (meaning Ulysses) who would do right by both." This appeared to please the reds, who grunted their approval.³⁰

Stoneman offered other inducements to the Apaches. If their traditional enemy, the Navajos, continued to make war on them, he would send troops against them. The Apaches would receive meat and perhaps flour if they remained peaceful and assisted the army to hunt down and kill bad Indians. The business of the soldiers was to kill bad Indians and protect settlers. If Indians did not behave themselves and stop stealing, they would be killed, but if they cooperated with the government, Stoneman would provide medicine and would request the appointment of an Indian Agent to represent them.

Stoneman's first parlay with the Apaches was typical of his carrot-and-stick approach to Native Americans in his district, and his inspection tour confirmed to him the wisdom of his policies. He and his party met no hostile Indians on his tour, although he did see examples of depredations that had so upset the settlers. The party moved south to Camp Goodwin, which Stoneman ordered abandoned after finding every man, women, and child sick with fever, and moved on to Camp Bowie along a route that Stoneman had traveled over twenty years before. He had been one of the first white Americans to travel through the region, and he recognized Stein's Peak and Cathedral Rock in the San Simeon Valley. Near Camp Bowie, the party saw a graveyard where the remains of settlers killed by the Apaches were buried. When they were within forty miles of Tucson, the temporary capital of the Territory, Stoneman passed the crossing of La Cienega, where Apaches had recently captured a mail party and murdered those escorting it. The sight of torn letters and papers and freshly dug graves deeply affected Stoneman's group. Soon afterwards, they came upon a deserted adobe house where the inhabitants had been murdered by Apaches.[31] Stoneman could not have been unaware that such incidents were still a feature of life for the settlers in southern Arizona.

While "mooding over the dangers incident to a trip through Arizona," Marion described Stoneman's arrival at Tucson, which consisted of about 400 adobe houses, built with rafters of cottonwood and mesquite poles, covered with hay or straw with a thick coating of mud. Marion reported that saloons were a feature of the town but were "fixed up in splendid style," and the lager was reported as excellent. The census gave the town population of 3,200, which Marion thought was slightly exaggerated. Nonetheless, it was the largest town in the territory.[32]

Stoneman's party departed Tucson on Sunday, September 25, and headed northeast toward Camp Grant. It stood on high ground in a delta formed by the San Pedro and Aravaipa rivers[33] in the heart of Pinal-Apache country and was garrisoned by three small companies. After departing Camp Grant, the party reached the Gila River at Florence and followed the Salt River to Camp McDowell. An arduous trek followed over the Black Canyon to Camp Whipple at Prescott, which was reached on October 5 after a journey of 800 miles.[34]

Stoneman decided it was time to confer with his friend, Division Commander General Schofield, and received permission to travel to Drum Barracks. He departed Prescott on October 14, and upon reaching California, he sailed by steamer to San Francisco, where he met Schofield at the Presidio. He remained there a full two months, which seems excessive even for the standards of the day, given the situation in Arizona. He took the opportunity to again complain about the lack of quarters at Fort Whipple and argued that his headquarters should be "temporarily" located at Drum Barracks which, of course, was close to where he hoped to eventually retire. "It is respectfully suggested," Stoneman wrote in his official report, "that authority be granted for a temporary location of heaqrs at Drum Barracks, to remain there until spring, when we can return to Prescott and spend the summer in tents."[35] Schofield deferred his decision at first, but on January 12, 1871, Stoneman announced that his headquarters would be "temporarily located at Drum Barracks."[36] They would remain there as long as Stoneman was department commander. Stoneman was the senior officer present at Drum Barracks, "on detached service" status, but Colonel Frank Wheaton commanded the barracks and signed the returns.[37]

Stoneman's absences from Arizona, and the fact that he established his headquarters hundreds of miles from the scene of an increasing level of Indian attacks, created a public relations disaster. Territorial officials and settlers clamored for action, and Stoneman reacted by ordering "a vigorous, persistent, and relentless winter campaign against the Pinal and Tonto branches of the Apache tribes of Indians." His order established an infantry camp to function as a depot of supplies in the Pinal country for troops operating against them. Scouting parties were sent into areas occupied by the Pinal and Tonto Apaches, but Stoneman confided, in a private letter to Sherman, that they were intended for the "Arizona market," in other words, for local consumption.³⁸ In the same letter, Stoneman called for Peace Commissioners to "take this arduous and dangerous duty out of our hands, and to protect the lives of the people of Arizona by an exercise of moral and religious influence."³⁹ This was a remarkable statement from a professional soldier and clearly reflects disenchantment with the use of force. It must have caused Grant and Sherman to question Stoneman's determination to act decisively.

Events soon led to one of the most tragic incidents in the history of encounters between Native Americans and white settlers, the massacre at Camp Grant on April 30, 1871. In December of 1870, several young officers rode into Tucson to report for duty in the territory. Lieutenant Royal Emerson Whitman was among them, assigned to "H" troop of the 3rd Cavalry stationed at Camp Grant. Whitman was a New Englander of integrity and conscience with a distinguished record in the Civil War, but he was unfamiliar with the West and had little understanding of the depth of feeling against the Apaches in white settlers.

In February 1871, five old Apache women, hungry and poorly clothed, came into Camp Grant, looking for one of their sons who had been taken prisoner by the army several months before. Whitman treated the women kindly, fed them, and let them leave, giving them permission to return with other members of their band. They returned after eight days, accompanied by other Apaches, and with articles for sale. Again they were well treated and Whitman urged them to tell their chiefs to come to the camp to talk.⁴⁰ A few days later, a young Apache chief named Eskiminzin rode into camp and told Whitman that he was tired of war and wanted to settle peacefully along Aravaipa Creek with 25 of his braves. Whitman did not have the authority to place them on a reservation, but promised to feed and protect them while he waited for approval from higher authority. The Apaches were disarmed and camped about a half-mile from the fort.⁴¹ Whitman wrote two letters to Stoneman at Drum Barracks, requesting instructions. The first was sent on February 24, followed by a more detailed second letter on the 28th, sent by special messenger who took it to Sacaton on the Gila, the closest mail station on the route to Drum Barracks in California. While Whitman waited for a reply, more Apaches came in. The camp held 300 by March 5, and the number soon swelled to 500 at the "rancheria."⁴² When the Aravaipa dried up, Whitman authorized the Indians to move five miles into the mountains, but he kept the settlement under surveillance. He was pleased and excited over the success of his program. He bought hay from the Indians, giving them a source of hard cash, and even arranged for them to be hired by white settlers as field hands. As they were guaranteed protection, they sold their bows and arrows. They were not expecting a fight.⁴³

Six weeks after he dispatched his letter of February 28, Whitman finally received a reply from Drum Barracks. His disappointment can be imagined as he read a note from a clerk informing him that he had not written a brief on the envelope of his original communication, a formality that was required in those days. There was no response to his original request to permit the Apaches to raise crops and to receive protection.⁴⁴

This example of army red tape at its worst has been subject to various interpretations by historians. James Hastings, in his analysis of the Camp Grant tragedy, argues that Stoneman used the briefing requirement as a pretext to return it without taking any action.

Hastings believes that Stoneman knew about the situation at Camp Grant and, in fact, gave oral instructions to the new commandant at Camp Grant, Stanwood, as he passed through Drum Barracks en route to his new assignment, to continue supplying food to the Apaches. It is likely that Stoneman had read Whitman's letter of February 28 and was aware of what was being done at Camp Grant, which seemed to comply with Stoneman's expressed policies. However, Stoneman was under intense criticism for his "feeding stations" policy and may have simply wanted to evade responsibility for creating another one. Jerone Stone, in *The History of Camp Grant*, believes that it was a case of bureaucratic bumbling and the letter may never have reached Stoneman.[45]

Despite Whitman's conciliatory policies, tensions increased in Southern Arizona and Whitman came under increasing criticism. On March 10, Apaches attacked a baggage train that had departed Camp Grant headed for the Pinal Mountains. A soldier and a Mexican civilian were killed and 16 mules were captured. On March 20, a rancher named L.B. Wooster was killed by Apaches at Tubac and a woman, Trinidad Aggera, was carried off. Other incidents convinced the settlers that the Apaches at Camp Grant were out of control. All told, 19 settlers had been killed and ten wounded between March 7 and 29, allegedly by Apaches within close proximity of Camp Grant.[46] The attitude on the frontier that all Indians should be exterminated became pervasive in Tucson, and Camp Grant was a convenient target.

As emotions among the settlers intensified, a Committee of Public Safety was formed at a mass meeting in Tucson, headed by William Sanders Oury, a colorful Virginian who had fought with Sam Houston at the battle of San Jacinto and had later joined the Texas Rangers before settling in Tucson. The committee decided to meet with Stoneman at Florence, and they rode 90 miles in 18 hours.[47] The mood of Oury and two others who accompanied him, S.R. Delong and John W. Hopkins,[48] was not improved by their reception from Stoneman, who met them coolly. He told the committee that he had received a memorial from settlers in the Santa Cruz Valley, signed by 250 and said to represent 500. The department commander, according to Oury, told the committee that they should be able to look after themselves, an unfortunate comment because Oury and his followers later claimed that Stoneman had given them carte blanche to do whatever they felt necessary to protect themselves. Stoneman went on to say that the Santa Cruz petitioners were illegal squatters on old Spanish land grants who had no right for further protection. Stoneman told his three visitors that he had been criticized by his superiors in Washington for his aggressive campaign against the Apaches. Stoneman was referring to Grant's suggestion to Sherman that Stoneman's orders should be modified to comply with administration policy, which was "one of moral suasion and kindness, looking to their Christianization." Sherman, in turn, had written Schofield and advised, "The President has no desire to revoke or qualify General Stoneman's orders, but he wishes General Stoneman to know that his general policy toward the savages is to treat them justly and kindly."[49]

Oury later reported to his committee that Stoneman had given him a detailed account of the constraints placed on him by budget limitations. He could only mount one man in five due to the limited number of horses available to him and there were no funds to supply remounts. The Third Cavalry had been sent from the east but were mounted on broken-down horses unfit for mountain service. They replaced the Eighth Cavalry, who were "admirably mounted on young California horses peculiarly adapted for the work required of them."[50] Stoneman told Oury that previously he had an appropriation of $130 per soldier in the Territory but that had been reduced to $33. He observed that one-tenth of the entire army was now stationed in Arizona, which was a greater proportion than they had a right to expect, and he cautioned the people of Tucson "that a continuance of their complaints of the lack of protection by the military would have the effect to withdraw the troops entirely; that the subject had been seriously contemplated and might yet be acted upon."[51]

Oury ended his report, which was published in the *Arizona Citizen*, with an ominous conclusion:

> The pith and substance of the whole matter as your Committee understands it from Gen. Stoneman is: That we can expect nothing more from him than has been done, and if anything further is expected we must depend upon our own efforts for its consummation.[52]

As mass meetings in Tucson continued, an additional incitement of settler violence against Apaches emerged when the *Citizen* acquired a copy of Stoneman's annual report, issued the previous December. Excerpts from the report had been published by both Arizona newspapers, but when the full impact of Stoneman's recommendations was examined by the press on April 15, a firestorm followed that led to an increasing scale of violence.

Since he assumed command on May 3, 1870, Stoneman reported that he had made a thorough inspection of the department. There were 18 posts in the department in May, but three had been discontinued. He now recommended a concentration of troops at eight posts: Camps Verde, Thomas, Grant, Bowie, Hualpai [sic], Date Creek, Mojave, and Yuma, listed in order of importance. The first three were located in "the heart of hostile Indians,"[53] the next three were close to mail routes and highways, and the last two, located on the Colorado River, would serve to control "River Indians."

Stoneman expressed his ire at suppliers who continually defrauded the government:

> The posts and depots recommended to be discontinued are expensive, and can be dispensed with advantageously to the Government, and without detriment than a pecuniary one to the people of the Territory in their immediate vicinity, who, of course, will object, as they will be unable, as heretofore, to dispose of their hay, grain, etc., to the Government, at the usual exorbitant prices.[54]

Stoneman alluded to the practice of contractors who took advantage of the situation and charged exorbitant prices for fuel, forage, and beef. The poorest kind of red oak was provided for the repair of wagons. Glass was "blistered, warped, and discolored." Water buckets invoiced as "gutta percha" turned out to have been made of paper. Blankets marked as woolen were actually made of buffalo hair.[55]

Stoneman's condemnation of unscrupulous contractors who defrauded the government, sometimes with the collaboration of Stoneman's troopers, was justified. Historian Frank C. Lockwood, in his work, *The Apache Indians*, describes how an army inspector discovered that out of a garrison of 86 men, 54 had deserted and sold their horses and arms to local citizens. Other profiteers cheated the government shamelessly. Few of them remained in the Territory, usually departing for San Francisco once they had made their money.[56]

Stoneman was on firm ground with his denunciation of profiteering, and his call for reform was supported by the press. But his analysis of the Indian situation, which he raised "with no little reluctance, fearing that the authorities at headquarters in San Francisco, as well as Washington, may have already been surfeited and wearied with its consideration,"[57] infuriated many Arizonians. Stoneman asserted in his report that the Hualpais [sic], Mojaves or Yavapais, and Coyotero Apaches were quiet and were fast becoming domesticated. Cachies (Cochise), who had caused a great deal of trouble over the past eight years, "has expressed a wish to go on a reservation, become quiet, and be left alone." Only two branches of the great Apache nation, the Tontos and the Pinals, were openly hostile, and steps were being taken to bring them to terms. Stoneman referred to his long experience in the region:

> The Apache nation in this region, as compared with what I knew of it more than twenty years ago, is nearly harmless, and their destitution is great in the extreme. They must either starve, steal, or be fed, and as they are unwilling to do the former, it becomes simply a question as to which is the best policy—feed them, or continue the endeavor to prevent them from stealing.[58]

Stoneman ended his report with optimism that put him directly at odds with Territorial officials and settlers. "In conclusion, it gives me pleasure to express the opinion that Indians, as well as other affairs in the Department are in as satisfactory a condition as can reasonably be expected."[59]

The *Citizen* published a bitter denunciation of Stoneman's optimistic summation of the state of affairs in Arizona. "Since the organization of the Territory in 1863, no act of any military officer has so unnerved the hearts of the brave settlers of Arizona as this same report of Col. George Stoneman," the paper thundered. The people, the paper continued, had hoped for a *real* war against "the cursed Apaches," and that troops would carry continuous, effective, operations until the "wretches would sue for peace that would be permanent." The writer noted that a separate department had been established for Arizona, but the settlers were like the frogs of Aesop's fable, who, when they got a king, were worse off than they were before. The commander's comments were "astounding" and "sickening"[60] and Stoneman's phrase introducing the subject closest to the settlers, to wit "The all absorbing topic in Arizona, the irrepressible Indian, is approached with no little reluctance..." was particularly offensive to the *Citizen*:

> But when the Col. apologizes for mentioning the cause which brought him here, which keeps U.S. troops here, which makes the producers of the country ask such high prices for forage, fuel, and beef, he causes each man, woman, and child in Arizona to shudder with distrust of him and his intentions.[61]

This inflammatory rhetoric, combined with news items reporting the theft of cattle, attacks on mail riders and settlers, and Oury's public speeches in which he said the settlers were on their own, led to a mass meeting in Tucson. The ineffectual speechmaking of the meeting convinced Oury and his accomplice, Juan Elias, that community action would not solve the Apache problem. Convinced that the Camp Grant Apaches were responsible for Indian attacks in March and April, Oury agreed to contact the Americans and Elias would approach the Mexicans for the purpose of organizing a punitive expedition against Camp Grant. Both men would also enlist the aid of Francisco, the most influential Papago chief.[62]

On the morning of April 28, 94 Papagos, 48 Mexicans, and six Americans met at Rillito Creek near Tucson. The Adjutant General of the Territory, Samuel Hughes, agreed to provide guns and ammunition for the expedition, an act that implicated the administration of Governor Safford in the massacre of the unsuspecting Apaches at Camp Grant.[63] The expedition reached Camp Grant on April 30, a Sunday morning, and, after clubbing to death two Apache sentries, attacked the camp. Most of the victims were women and children, although 27 Apache children were spared and taken back to Tucson to be slaves of the Papagos who did most of the killing. They advanced in a skirmish line, clubbing their victims to death. Those who escaped the Papagos were shot by the Mexicans and the Americans. By eight o'clock the attack was over and the war party rested, according to Oury, "a few miles above the fort in the full satisfaction of a work well done."[64]

Whitman, who learned of the attack while at breakfast, sent a medical team to render assistance, but no survivors were found. Bodies of women and children were strewn around the campsite. Most of the dead were mutilated, and two of the squaws had been raped and then shot. Estimates of how many Indians were killed vary widely. Whitman reported 125 killed and wounded. Others reported a figure as low as 35 and as high as 144.[65]

Reaction from the east was swift. President Grant called the attack "pure murder" and told reporters that it would be thoroughly investigated. The president told Governor Safford that martial law would be declared if the participants were not brought to trial. A five-day trial was held, but the jury released the defendants after deliberating for 19 minutes. Stoneman, who had left Fort Whipple on May 8, en route to Drum Barracks, called the attack a dastardly outrage.[66]

Typical of the reaction by newspapers in Arizona was that of the *Arizona Miner*:

> Again and Again during the past bloody years, has the *Miner* urged upon the settlers to organize and carry the war home to the villages of the redskins. Now should we faint at the result of our teaching? Shall we apologize?... No! a thousand times no. the blood of our relatives and friends, spilled on nearly every road and trail, in every farming settlement and mining district in Arizona cries out to us from the ground to rejoice that they are partially avenged.[67]

A chain of events, now led by Governor Safford and the Territorial legislature, as well as public opinion in Arizona, inflamed by Stoneman's policies of moderate treatment of Native Americans which were endorsed by the president, led to an ultimately successful campaign to remove Stoneman from command of the department. The legislature prepared a pamphlet citing the depredations of the Indians that included a resolution calling for Stoneman's removal. Safford counseled against the resolution, telling the legislators that it would put Stoneman on notice of their intentions and give him time to "muster all his forces to prevent removal."[68] After the legislature adjourned, Safford met Stoneman in San Diego. Safford described the meeting:

> He at once proceeded to show me the difficulties of his position. He pulled from his pocket eastern papers denouncing him for a very sanguinary proclamation he had issued sometime before. 'Now,' said he, 'you can see I am between two fires, if I pursue a relentless war against the Apaches, as prescribed by this proclamation, then the peace party attack me, if I don't do it then the Arizonians attack me.' I replied that his proclamation had not placed a soldier in the

field nor had it killed an Indian. He replied that the proclamation was intended for the Arizona market.[69]

Safford later recounted that he made up his mind at that moment "that a man who would trifle with the lives and property of a people he was sent to defend should not hold the place if I could prevent it."[70] He left for the east on March 21 and while in Washington, read Stoneman's annual report. He wrote Secretary of War Belknap complaining that Indian depredations had steadily increased and that Stoneman had lost the confidence and esteem of the people. "I make this statement without feeling as my personal relations with Col. Stoneman have been friendly," Safford concluded.[71]

Safford, accompanied by Senator William M. Stewart, a close friend, went to see President Grant and asked him to replace Stoneman with Lieutenant Colonel George Crook. According to Safford's account, Grant listened attentively and replied that all Safford said was true. Grant also said that Crook was the best Indian fighter in the army but it would require "the cutting of a great deal of red tape to send Crook, for he was only a lieutenant colonel, and pretty well down the list at that...."[72] Safford told the president that the frontier expected protection, and if it was necessary to cut red tape, they believed he would do it.

> After a moments thought the President said "I believe I can send him on his brevet rank of Major General." He called the Secretary of War and in a moment it was agreed upon and Stoneman's head rolled into the basket....[73]

Stoneman was furious. He blamed the people of Tucson and may have spread the story that he was removed because of the massacre at Camp Grant. This was impossible, however, as the order for his removal was issued on May 2, 1871, and the Camp Grant tragedy took place on April 30. Information did not travel that quickly.

It must have seemed to Stoneman that his relations with Grant had taken a paradoxical twist. In his last great raid of the Civil War, Stoneman had carried out Grant's orders to destroy the railroads and military resources of the Confederacy only to have Grant write, after the war, that while successful, the raids were without any good result. In Arizona, Stoneman followed Grant's "peace policy" of setting up "feeding stations" where Native Americans could be issued rations and protected. The Apaches were to be pacified and the settlers protected while expenditures were to be drastically reduced, from $3,000,000 to $1,000,000.

Although Stoneman was placed in an impossible situation, his own lack of political judgment contributed to his removal. He was unable to placate his political and military superiors in Washington, while satisfying the recalcitrant settlers in Arizona, particularly in Tucson. Stoneman also consistently mishandled delegations of citizens who clamored for more protection, stiff-arming them in effect, and made an implacable foe of Governor Safford, who had good connections in Washington, including General Sherman. Moreover, moving the department's headquarters from Fort Whipple to Drum Barracks was a fatal blunder and gave ammunition to his critics who maintained that he had a totally unrealistic view of the situation in Arizona.

Stoneman referred to his political problems in his final report, and his comments proved to be prophetic:

Any officer of the Army, who has had the opportunity, must have learned, that of all the duties he has been called upon to perform, that of a reformer, is a most thankless; and he is fortunate if he has not also learned that there is such a thing as political necessity, that knows no law, human or divine.[74]

As protocol dictated, Stoneman received his successor at Fort Drum and invited Colonel Crook to dinner. Crook was obliged to accept, but it was a long and uncomfortable evening for him. As Crook noted in his autobiography:

While at Wilmington, I was invited to dinner at the Stoneman's (when he was relieved of command). I had to accept out of politeness, but never passed through such an ordeal. Mrs. Stoneman, while trying to be polite, could not help showing in every action that she would like to tear me to pieces ... and there I had to sit and sit, and if she only knew how I hated to go to Arizona, she might feel differently. This assignment had made me the innocent cause of a great deal of heartburning and jealousy.[75]

It was time for the old soldier to retire, embittered by yet another rejection by Grant and weary of the bureaucratic and political struggles. After 29 years of service and at age 49, his military career was clearly at an end and he was ready to acquire his ranch and vineyard at Los Robles and enjoy life with his family. Although he did not know it at the time, he was to reach the pinnacle of his civilian career in his adopted state of California, but not before he was once again involved in controversy, this time over the terms of his retirement.

Governor Stoneman

Stoneman lost no time in notifying the retirement board sitting in San Francisco, as well as the army, of his intention to retire, effective August 16, 1871. His old friend John Schofield was chairman of the Board to retire Disabled Officers, established by an act of Congress on August 3, 1861. The Board examined the requests of officers claiming disability due to wounds in action. The board examining Stoneman's case convened in June, 1871, in San Francisco. Stoneman's old comrade-in-arms on the North Carolina raid, Colonel Alvin Gillem, was on the board along with Lieutenant Colonel Marcus Simpson. Two surgeons also served, Assistant Medical Purveyor Lieutenant Colonel Robert Murray and Surgeon Charles M. McCormick.

Stoneman requested that the board retire him at his brevet rank of Major General, based on an act of Congress, July 28 1866, section 32, which states in part:

> And be it further enacted that officers of the regular Army, entitled to be retired on account of a disability occasioned by wounds received in battle, may be retired upon the full rank of command held by them, whether in the regular or volunteer service at the time such wounds were received.

Stoneman suffered from a severe case of hemorrhoids, which he argued with some justification were caused and aggravated by years of arduous duty as a cavalry officer. The board saw the merit of his request and recommended that Stoneman be retired with the full rank of major general. Based on the board's recommendation, Special Order 317 was issued by the War Department on August 16, 1871, in which President Grant directed that Stoneman's name be "placed on the list of retired officers of that class in which the disability resulted from long and faithful service, or from wounds or injury received in the line of duty...."[1] Stoneman was retired at the full rank of major general.

Just as John Schofield played a major role in Stoneman's life, so it was with U.S. Grant. On August 19, just three days after Special Order 317 was issued, Special Order 322 was issued by the War Department. It specified that since Special Order 317 was "made under a misconception of the law, [it] is by direction of the President hereby revoked."[2] Stoneman was retired at the rank of colonel, "it not appearing that he was wounded in battle, and the law requiring in explicit terms, that an officer be disabled by wounds,"[3] not by disease.

This began a ten-year battle that Stoneman was destined to lose. The retirement board reopened Stoneman's case and forwarded a protest to the secretary of war. The medical members pointed out that they concluded that "the disability he now labors under was occasioned by a continuous series of contused wounds from the jolting in the saddle during his raids in Tennessee, Virginia, North Carolina, and Georgia. This was no misconception of the law."[4] The board went on to argue that the law authorizing retirement at the rank held while wounded applied to Stoneman:

> At the commencement of his campaigns he was suffering severely from piles, and under this hard service occurred an extreme falling of the rectum, amounting to an extreme protrusion of the bowel which yet with great difficulty [was] returned and kept in place.[5]

The medical members of the board discussed the meaning of the word "wounds" used in the law. A wound is "to hurt by violence, as to wound the head, arm, etc. (or any other part of the body.)" The word "contusion" means "a bruise, a hurt, or injury of the flesh." Wounds are "incised, punctured, contused, etc. Colonel Stoneman suffered and is now suffering from a series of contused wounds.... Death itself is preferable to the injuries he has sustained."[6]

The decision by Grant to overcome the board's recommendation was probably the result of political intrigue. Stoneman was an avowed Democrat, out of favor with Grant and Republicans in Congress. His problems with Grant dated back to the war and his command in Virginia when he opposed radical reconstruction. His policies in Arizona led to his removal.

Stoneman protested the decision to reduce his pay and grade, and pointed out that this was the first case in which a local retirement board had been overturned. He wrote a personal letter to Sherman, referring to the virtue of honesty in the service, but to no avail. His only consolation was the fact that he was always referred to as general for the rest of his life.[7]

The demotion in rank and pay galled Stoneman, and he continued the fight for years after his retirement. He wrote President James Garfield as late as January 23, 1881, shortly after his election, pleading his case to the new president. He pointed out that the retirement board "found that I, George Stoneman, Col. 21st Infantry was incapacitated for active service by means of command wounds received in the line of duty and in Battles with the enemy during the time I held the rank *of* a Major General in the Army of the U.S."[8] He wrote the president that Order No. 317, retiring him as a major general, was changed "for some reason or from some inner cause,"[9] and his retirement rank was reduced to colonel. Stoneman believed that the last proceedings never reached the president's office, and he asked that they again be considered. Order 317 was "legal, just, and final in my case," Stoneman wrote. "This, I believe, is the first case on record where the Executive [went] behind and act[ed] contrary to the recommendations of the retiring or returning board, and is therefore exceptional and without precedent."[10]

The president referred the letter to the Attorney General, Charles Devens, who was unmoved. "The report clearly shows that the injuries received by Col. Stoneman were not wounds received in battle, but were the ordinary series of contusions from the jolting of the saddle which aggravated and perhaps occasioned the disease from which he was suffering," Devens advised.[11] This judgment was the end of the matter.

Stoneman realized his lifelong dream in 1872. He eventually purchased 400 acres for the bargain price of $17.50 an acre, for a total of $7,000,[12] from Benjamin D. Wilson and John C. Downey in the rich San Gabriel Valley. This was the site that he had seen when he first arrived in California as a young second lieutenant over 30 years before. The ranch, named Los Robles (The Oaks), was to become a prosperous vineyard and orange grove, carefully supervised by the retired soldier. Stoneman settled in with his wife and his four children: Cornelius, his eldest son, another son, George, who was to become a prominent attorney in Los Angeles and Arizona, and two daughters, Katharine Cheney and Adele, who was born in the military hospital at Drum Barracks in 1870.[13]

He wrote his father that Cornelius, the eldest, was about ten years old and "is perfectly healthy, very active, quite bright. And is very much like his grandfather." He was under the instruction of an Aunt Rebecca who lived with the Stonemans. Stoneman described his son George as "a gnat awkward, good natured, unselfish, truthful affectionate fellow, whom everyone admires and loves and calls 'a very fine boy.' He will not make a very brilliant, but will make a brave and honorable man."[14] Stoneman's favorite child was Katherine Cheney, known as "Kitty." She suffered from a curvature of the spine and was

General Stoneman, standing in the driveway, and his family at his ranch, Los Robles, in San Gabriel, California. He purchased the ranch after his retirement from the army. It is probably Mrs. Stoneman standing on the porch next to Stoneman's sister, who tutored the Stonemans' four children. A fifth child is visiting the family (courtesy of George B. Stoneman, M.D.).

in the east for treatment in 1872. "Dear little Kitty ... is one of the sweetest children and has one of the most lovable character[s] of any child I ever knew and is very bright ... the prospect now is that a permanent and radical cure will be affected in her." Adele, the Stoneman's youngest child, was two in 1872 and "is a fine, large, healthy child and has a will of her own I can tell you, and if she ever grow[s] to be a women will make some man toe the mark."[15]

Although Stoneman had not purchased the property until early in 1872,[16] after his retirement, it had been an article of faith among the settlers in Arizona that Stoneman had spent much of his time away from Arizona residing on his ranch when he commanded the Arizona Department, an inaccuracy that is perpetuated in historical accounts and in fiction.[17]

Stoneman wrote his father with his news on May 15, 1872, writing from San Pasualito. "I suppose you know that I have gone on the 'Retired List,' that is I am one of the officers of the Army who are not liable to be called upon to perform any duties whatsoever, and get $3,500 a year for the privilege to tending to my own business and this last for as long as I live. This is for 'long and faithful service, and disease contracted in the line of duty.'"[18]

Stoneman informed his father that he had purchased a home "consisting of 300 acres of the finest land you ever saw, being a rich deep gravelly loam and without an acre of waste land upon the whole place." Stoneman exulted in the fact there were three large springs "on the upper or north end" which furnished five times the amount of water he would need. He wrote that over 100 acres were covered with a "fine vineyard which will produce year by year 500,000 lbs. of grapes and ten acres are with fruit trees of almost every variety...."[19] Stoneman described a veritable Garden of Eden: "orange, lemon, lime, fig, apple, pear, peach, cheery, plum, quince, pomegranate, apricot, nectarine, mulberry, olive" were all available. For nuts, Stoneman wrote, "I have the filbert almond, English and walnut, and hazlenut, and will soon have all the different varieties of berrys.... The ripe oranges and limes are still hanging on the trees & will last until the figs, pears, and apricots are ripe...."

Stoneman reported to his father that he was six miles from Los Angeles and 20 from the sea. The mountains were five miles to the north and protected his land from the "cold northerly winds." His estate was about 1,000 feet above sea level, where he "expected to enjoy the rest of my days, be they few or many, and be free of the annoyances, the cares and anxieties, the pains and penalties incident to an active public life."[20]

Stoneman expressed his contempt for the post–Civil War army and the politics he endured in Virginia and Arizona. "Formerly, an officer of the army could take some pride in his profession, and some satisfaction in the performance of his duties but now everything ... is made subservient to a political necessity which know no law human or divine, and to which everything right or wrong must bend or be broken."[21]

Stoneman soon developed a bountiful vineyard in the rich California soil, but his temper destroyed his relations with his nearest neighbor, James De Barth Shorb. Stoneman thought that his agreement with Wilson included control of an adobe house on the edge of the property that Stoneman ordered removed, since it was an eyesore. It turned out that Wilson, who apparently conducted his affairs informally, had leased the house to a Mr.

Palmer. Wilson and Shorb, who was looking after Wilson's affairs, told Stoneman that the lease had a year to run, a development that infuriated Stoneman, who launched into a tirade that, according to a witness "made the most blackguard speech he ever knew a white man guilty of."[22] Shorb was deeply offended and demanded an apology that was never received. As a result, Shorb remained an implacable foe and later a political enemy.[23]

Despite this altercation, Stoneman prospered and enjoyed the respect of the community. By 1874, Stoneman told his visiting former army colleague, General John C. Fremont, that he expected a harvest of 25,000 gallons of wine and that he could market all that he could produce.[24] A journalist visiting the Stonemans described a bucolic, if austere, scene. The house, isolated from public roads and surrounded by semi-tropical trees and plants, was "a large, plain, square-box house of weather stained red wood, almost black with age, two stories high." The upper story was reached by an outside stairway. The house was covered with flowers, especially roses of all shades. The interior was plain, "devoid of plaster and wall-paper," but the rooms were supported by polished redwood. Modest paintings adorned the walls, and some "very fine paintings" were displayed.[25]

George Stoneman, despite his altercations with his neighbors, was a happy man. "I never was more self satisfied or better *controlled* in my life than I have been since I became an honest farmer sitting, under my own vine and fig tree with none to trouble or make afraid, indifferent to presidential frowns and independent of presidential favors."[26] Stoneman told his father that he had a large library "of valuable and selected works by the best authors ... so that I have all the reading I want and more than I can master."[27]

Stoneman is described as a benign patriarch who breakfasted with his family, invariably eating two eggs and bacon but never liver. "Liver, no, I never eat deadly organs," he once told his daughter, Adele. He never talked at meal time.[28] After breakfast, he supervised his workers, who did not include "Chinamen" as a matter of principle, although the family had a faithful Chinese servant, Charlie Feng. Stoneman told his visitor how he first saw the ranch site:

> Right down there at the foot of the hill, just where you see that grove of live oaks is where I first camped with a squadron of dragoons about 33 years ago. I was quite a young man then and had recently made a march across the continent to assist General Kearny and Commodore Stockton to make a conquest of California.[29]

Stoneman had been a lieutenant of the 1st Dragoons when he first saw Los Robles. He had been ordered to the St. Gabriel Mission "on a little business connected with some of Col. Fremont's volunteers who were camped at the Mission."[30] As young as Stoneman was, he resolved to make his home in the San Gabriel Valley. "It was more than twenty years afterward before I was able to carry out my determination. But I did so at last and here I expect to live and die."[31]

Stoneman adopted an old-fashioned patriarchal system, employing Spanish-speaking workers, most of them born on the property, who lived in cottages near springs. Each family had a plot of land on which they could grow vegetables such as potatoes, frijoles, peppers, and melons. According to accounts written when Stoneman entered political life, his workers revered the old general, never calling him by any name except "Padrone."

Stoneman occupied himself with the ranch following his retirement from military service, but he did perform a few civic duties. In 1873, he became president of the Los Angeles Branch of the Veterans of the Mexican War. On July 4, 1876, the 100th anniversary of the Declaration of Independence, which was also the 95th year of the founding of Los Angeles, and the 105th year of the founding of the San Gabriel Mission, Stoneman appeared with the veterans of the Mexican War. Stoneman was the Grand Marshal of Los Angeles's first centenary on September 5, 1881.[32]

As the population of California expanded, an issue emerged that was to propel Stoneman into public life and dominate his political agenda: the regulation of powerful railroads. In 1876, state commissioners of transportation were appointed, primarily to devise equitable tax regulations for railroads and to control freight and passenger rates. Governor William Irwin appointed Stoneman as one of the three commissioners, a puzzling move. Nothing in Stoneman's background seemed to qualify him for such an appointment and it isn't clear why he accepted it, preoccupied as he was with his ranch. Moreover, he lived in the Los Angeles area, which was not favored with a major rail connection until 1876, when the Southern Pacific Line was completed, four months after Stoneman became a commissioner.[33] The three-man board met and decided there should be a permanent body to study the railroads and propose legislation to correct abuses, but the authority of the board was limited to the investigation of railroad rates.[34]

Stoneman was a member of the commission until 1878, when it was combined with the office of the Commissioner of Transportation. In the two years he served, Stoneman found ample evidence that the railroads in California were a monopoly, guilty of inflating fixed capital illegally, misleading stockholders concerning the average charge per mile, and most importantly for the average citizen, charging passengers more than comparable roads in the east. As a result, railroad giants like the Central Pacific were earning lucrative profits despite an extensive construction program.[35] Unfair practices by the railroads became a *cause celebre* for Stoneman, who developed a public policy that he embraced throughout his political career. Although he was a "Jeffersonian Democrat" by inclination, he believed the state should defend the people against special interests and the power of the state should be used to regulate economic interests, regardless of their power and influence.[36]

Following a brief stint as an Indian commissioner, appointed by Republican president Rutherford B. Hayes in 1878, Stoneman sought his first elective office in 1879, running for the office of railroad commissioner which had been authorized by the second state constitution. His fame as a critic of the railroads had spread and he was endorsed by the Workingmen's Party, the New Constitution Party, and the Democratic Party. He decisively defeated his Republican opponent, receiving 35,518 votes to 19,410. The annual salary of $4,000 was generous for the time, designed to discourage bribes from rich rail corporations.[37]

Although the Railroad Commission was empowered to fix maximum rates and prohibit unfair practices, only Stoneman of the three commissioners was experienced with railroad matters, especially rate regulation. Although the commission had authority to examine railroad books, the mass of data was confusing to the inexperienced investigators. Staff support was not available, and the other two commissioners were ineffective and pawns of railroad interests. The railroads were able to continue their domination of state politics, but as Stoneman traveled throughout the state, he developed strong convictions concerning abuses by powerful railroad interests. Over Stoneman's objections, the commissioners set rates favored by the Central Pacific.[38] Stoneman was a voice in the wilderness, but as public awareness of abuses by the railroads increased, he became a symbol of rectitude and populist anger. The Democrats realized they had a potent issue and a war hero to champion it.

Stoneman attracted the attention of Democratic politicians as the gubernatorial election of 1882 approached, notably Judge David S. Terry and Stephen M. White.[39] Another early and influential supporter was Colonel James T. Ayers, who had come to Los Angeles in 1872, a pioneer of the gold rush days. He was editor and later owner of the *Evening Express*, a Democratic paper opposing special interests. Ayers was a representative from Los Angeles County to the Constitutional Convention of 1878–1879, a reform-minded body that had created the railroad commission "to curb the monopolizing tendencies of the Southern Pacific Railroad."[40] Ayers and other reform-minded Democrats prevailed on Stoneman to seek the Democratic nomination for governor.

Despite his growing fame as a foe of railroad interests, Stoneman had political negatives as well. He was a relative newcomer to California politics and not a favorite of the Democratic inner circle. His popularity was rurally based. He was not an effective public speaker and appeared to some as an honest but uninspiring leader. Colonel Ayers described him as follows:

> He was not a keen, sharp man, but he was a man of noble purposes, true as steel, and steadfast in his determination to do the right thing according to his lights. His weaknesses were those of a loyal and unsuspicious nature. He was too apt to be imposed upon by designing men who had wormed their way into his confidence....[41]

Stoneman's principal opponent for the nomination was George Hurst, who owned his own newspaper, the *San Francisco Examiner*, and was the favorite of the party machine. A wealthy man, Hurst expected to be nominated by an early ballot at the Democratic convention in San Jose.[42]

Hurst led in the early balloting, but Stoneman steadily gained strength as his rural supporters rallied around him. In grueling proceedings that lasted for ten days, the 11th ballot saw Hurst and Stoneman about even. On the 12th ballot, Stoneman took the lead accompanied by "enthusiastic cheering and confusion," according to newspaper accounts. Stoneman was nominated on the 14th ballot.[43]

Stoneman's acceptance speech was brief and pointed. "My experience in life is that four politicians out of five ruin themselves by talking and writing.... The great General Grant did neither," Stoneman observed, and then said he did not follow Grant in all things, a rather pointed jab.

> I have made a record — I hope I have — during my past life. I have no other security to offer in the future.... I have made no pledges, no promises ... I have met defeat often, I hope I can say I have met with victory, and oftener, during my past life; but there is no victory that I have ever gained — in fact all put together — that gives me more satisfaction than this.[44]

It was a moment of redemption. As he stood at the podium before the cheering delegates, he must have felt that all the hurt from his critics over his war record and his tenure in Arizona, all his troubles with Grant, his bitter dispute over his retirement, all of this was superseded by his nomination to the office of governor of one of the most important and fastest-growing states in the Union. Now, in the winter of his life, it was sweet vindication.

Stoneman set the tone for the campaign. His was a victory for the people and the railroads were their enemy. He told the delegates, "Go down to the street and see the railroad agents. The order had gone forth. Crush this man Stoneman."[45]

Mary Oliver Hardisty Stoneman was not comfortable with politics or politicians. She kept a diary for the years 1882 to 1887, and may have kept one for other years as well, but in these years she revealed her thoughts about California life and her family relationships. In August 1882, she went with her husband to have a campaign photograph taken. She referred to him as "GenS" or, in more affectionate moments, "Stony." Her entry records her dismay at the campaign. "Went with GenS to the city to have his photo taken — stupid vanity to see his face out of every shop window. Oh how I hate this political move. So many sacrifices and no compensation."[46]

The Republicans nominated Morris M. Estee, an experienced politician who also opposed the power of the railroads. A member of the Second Constitutional Convention and Speaker of the Assembly, Estee was supported by those who felt that Stoneman was inexperienced and not ready to manage the problems facing California. Stoneman's executive ability was challenged. The editor of the *Daily Alta* claimed that "his heart is all right but his mouth is a scatter gun."[47]

Chinese immigration was an issue and Stoneman allied himself with the anti–Chinese prejudice of the time. The pro–Stoneman *San Francisco Daily Examiner*, appealing to the anti–Chinese vote, commented:

> He hires principally native Californians. Having always recognized the fact that Mongolian immigration would ultimately bring the state to ruin, he puts precepts into practice and rigidly abstains from employing Chinese, even in the lowest menial work about him.[48]

Stoneman campaigned throughout the state, hampered by his poor speaking ability and rigid style, but he hammered on the railroad issue and other populist themes. His wife Mary continued to deplore the rigors of the campaign. "Stony returned from Martinez having had a very successful meeting there. He is feeling sick and used up. Oh why did he enter into this dirty political contest?"[49] On August 18, she went even further. "to think GenS being one of them [California politicians] makes me sick."[50] After a long summer of campaigning, Election Day finally arrived. "Today is the fateful election ... have been nervous as a cat ... not much doubt of the result yet nothing is absolutely certain until vote is counted."[51] Stoneman overcame his political shortcomings and overwhelmed his opponents, receiving 67,175 votes or 40 percent of the total of the 164,661 votes cast for four candidates.[52]

Mary Stoneman exulted in the results: "Slept badly woke to hear by all the papers of Gen.S's success!! Hurrah, hurrah to think of *our* [italics mine] being Governor of

Mary Oliver Hardisty (Mrs. George) Stoneman, the First Lady of California (courtesy of George B. Stoneman, M.D.).

California!!... Sent telegram to girls and papa — dear old fellow."[53] Her entry the next day continued to reflect her buoyant mood despite her distaste for politics:

> Every paper speaks of the Grand Democratic Victory all over the United States. This promises a Dem President in 1884. Who knows what may come? 15,000!! majority beyond anyone's expectation. I seem to be carried along by a resistless [sic] fate to what I have never contemplated or prepared for. I trust I may do credit to the position.[54]

When Stoneman accepted the nomination of the Democratic Party, he was unaware of a provision in the state constitution that prohibited an officer of the U.S. Army from being a candidate for governor. When he was advised that this provision applied to retired officers as well, he resigned from the retirement list. This would cause him grief later after he left office, as it would take a special act of Congress to restore him to the retirement list and this was not easily arranged.[55]

Stoneman delivered his inaugural address on January 10, 1883. True to his Jeffersonian convictions, he expressed his philosophy of government. "The people are the sovereigns and we are the servants." He concentrated on the issue that got him elected. The farmers had harvested bumper crops, but the railroads charged exorbitant freight rates to get the crops to market. The people had spoken against special interest groups, Stoneman concluded. A new commission should establish fares and rates.

The new governor addressed other issues. The state penal system should work to reform prisoners and all prisoners should be received at San Quentin. Unnecessary governmental expenses should be cut to the bone. Railroad taxes should be increased. Chinese immigration should be restricted, although Stoneman conceded that this was primarily a federal matter.

Mary Stoneman recorded the inauguration but ended her comments on a sour note:

> Genl Stoneman inaugurated as Governor of California today — the children were all present — quite a crowd — he acquitted with dignity and delivered or rather read a very good inaugural address — perhaps the proudest moment of his life — he has gained it by being totally thoughtless for anything but his own wishes and ambition.[56]

Her sardonic view of her husband on his day of triumph reflected long-standing tension between the reticent George Stoneman and his sensitive, emotional wife, who had deep feelings of resentment toward him. She frequently recorded her distress in her diary. "He is the most unsympathetic man — has the least tenderness of anyone I ever saw — but demands the most for himself.... I might as well live with a post for companionship — truly he is an iceberg — no heart, none."[57] Yet, on another occasion, she was pleased when her husband paid her a compliment shortly after the election:

> Oh how charming he can be when he chooses — he paid me a very pretty compliment. Today I was speaking rather timidly of fulfilling my new duties. [He said] "I wish I might be as sure of doing credit to my place as I am that you will in every way fulfill yours. [There] is no doubt whatever about you." it was particularly sweet after these last years.[58]

Stoneman as governor soon ran into frustration in dealing with a lethargic and compromised legislature. He saw his office as an instrument of activism, unlike most 19th-century governors who viewed their role as facilitators, rather than administrators, of legislative programs. The *Sacramento Daily Union* called Stoneman a demagogue "when he speaks so pompously of 'my policy.' Since when we may ask was the executive required to have a 'policy?'"[59]

There were successes. Laws dealing with roads and the incorporation of cities were passed. The state was reapportioned and California's irrigation problems were studied by the state engineer. However, Stoneman was unable to solve the great question that had brought him to office. The issue of delinquent taxes from railways was heard by the federal circuit court, which had decided against the state, but the case went to the U.S. Supreme Court. Stoneman expected to win, but the California Attorney General made an out-of-court settlement with the railroads, an arrangement that Stoneman never accepted. Only part of the tax bill was paid by the railroads and the penalties were minimal. Stoneman's frustrations continued when he called a special session of the state legislature to consider the railroad tax issue. The assembly passed his recommendation, but it failed in the senate. Stoneman was never able to resolve the question.[60]

Despite his problems with the railroads, Stoneman's record as governor was remarkably progressive. Two new state hospitals were established in 1885. A home for the blind was established. A board of forestry was created for the first time, as well as a mining bureau board of trustees. Regulations of food and drugs were adopted and care for additional mental and blind patients.[61]

On July 17, 1885, tragedy struck the Stoneman household at Los Robles. Fire destroyed the ranch house, and although there were no injuries, as the family was absent, Stoneman's papers and personal effects were destroyed.

The press was convinced that the house had been burned by Stoneman's enemies. In a story datelined Los Angeles, July 17, a newspaper account noted that the fire had started in a second story storeroom and that the house was a total loss. "The Governor's library, pictures, piano, jewelry and a number of war relics, including his uniforms, saddle, sword, etc. were destroyed." The newspaper went on to say that it was "hardly a question but the fire was the work of an incendiary."[62]

Newspaper accounts pointed out that Stoneman had permitted the execution of two Mexican murderers a short time before the fire, but he had commuted the sentence of a white murderer named Lenox, described as "the most brutal murderer of all," to a life sentence. "It is thought that some terrible revenge will be taken on the Governor and that the burning of the house is just a starter. It is certain that he has aroused the deadly enmity of a people who are good haters...."[63]

Stoneman tried to discourage insinuations that the fire was a deliberate act by political enemies. W.W. Moreland, a Stoneman intimate, asked Stephen M. White, a prominent Democrat, to investigate the newspaper allegations. White reported that "No one here ever hinted as far as I know that the Governor's house was burned by incendiary hands. It was an old building and may have caught fire in many ways independent of direct human agency."[64]

Whatever the cause, the family was devastated by the loss, especially daughter Kitty. Mary Stoneman lamented: "So we are houseless and homeless — not a souvenir left of home — noth(ing) of my children's youth-nothing. Well, we shall never go back to that house anyway—Kitty was dreadfully grieved over the loss."[65] Apparently, Stoneman did not discuss the loss with his wife but she was appalled to learn that the house was uninsured. She wrote: "Stony came home—but was still and dumb—such carelessness to have let the insurance die out."[66]

This was the second loss of Stoneman's papers, the first having taken place as a result of a train fire in New York state.

Stoneman issued a new pardoning policy which called for appeals to first go to prison directors, but appeals eventually came to his desk. Between 1883 and 1885, Stoneman extended clemency in 162 cases. According to his daughter Adele, this compassion was characteristic of Stoneman, despite his rather severe appearance and manner. "Though seemingly stern and very silent, every time he had to sign a death warrant he was sick for a day or two and he pardoned so many that his enemies censured him."[67]

Although control of the railroads was his major concern, another important question was that of water rights for all citizens, especially those employed in California's agricultural industry. The courts had upheld the riparian rights of those who lived on riverbanks, but Stoneman argued that those living inland had a right to the source of supply as well. Stoneman favored water rights for all, but vested interests opposed the free use of flowing water. The issue was important enough for Stoneman to call a special session of the legislature in July 18, 1886. In his proclamation, Stoneman referred to "the ruin and disaster which seems likely to flow from the enforcement of the doctrine recently announced by the Supreme Court as to water rights...."[68] Once again, he was defeated and the special session adjourned in September without acting on his recommendations to permit the political nominating conventions to convene.[69]

As the Democrats met to consider who would be the next candidate for governor, Stoneman faced strong opposition from his own party. There was feeling against him for a series of non-partisan appointments he had made, his crusade against special interests, and the issue of water rights. He lacked the political skills to build a core of support within the party. Consequently, he wasn't considered for renomination and his record as governor was hardly mentioned.[70] Stoneman denounced his political enemies in a letter to his wife:

> I find that public sentiment is fast tending in the right direction & I will be endorsed by the people if I was not by the yelping crew of traitors ... all of whom have been rejected by the people of California.[71]

Since he was soon to leave office, Stoneman's biennial message of 1887 was his last public pronouncement. He regretted the increase in state expenditures and warned that they should not exceed revenues. He admitted that he had not succeeded in his campaign against the railroads, but he pointed with pride to the healthy condition of the state's agricultural industry. He re-affirmed his position on irrigation and hoped that another session of the legislature would be held to solve the problem.[72]

Of note was Stoneman's progressive stand on rehabilitation of prisoners, his support of the parole system, and his proposal for financial aid to prisoners to help their reform and rehabilitation. He believed that young offenders should be placed in reform schools, separate from older prisoners.[73]

Stoneman was on familiar ground when he called for new uniforms and equipment for the state's National Guard. Young men must be attracted to the guard, he said, and most could not afford the expenses of equipping themselves.[74]

Upon leaving office and public life, Stoneman returned to Southern California. His political influence, never strong with Democratic regulars, soon faded, and Stoneman, his ranch gone, lived with his wife at their residence on Grand Avenue in Los Angeles. Financial difficulties soon followed, as Stoneman no longer had revenue from his ranch or from public office, and his pension had terminated when he resigned from the retirement list. It was necessary to appeal to Congress to reinstate him on the retirement rolls.

Although his friends gathered around him, it was a difficult procedure. In April 1890, he memorialized the Congress to pass a special act of relief, appointing him as a colonel. He reviewed his military record in his declaration and pointed out that when he had accepted the nomination as governor, he was advised by the secretary of war that his rank and commission would be forfeited if he served as governor. This interpretation of the law was now subject to "grave doubts," Stoneman alleged.[75]

His old friend General John Schofield intervened in his behalf:

> All who know General Stoneman know him to be a man of the very highest sense of honor; more than usually scrupulous in the matter of veracity. He cannot possibly, in my judgement, have intended to make any representation in his memorial not strictly in accordance with the facts.[76]

It took a year for Congress to act. An exasperated Mary Hardisty Stoneman wrote President Harrison, without her husband's knowledge, asking him to intervene on behalf of "so willing and faithful an officer and defender of the country as George Stoneman of cavalry renown."[77] Pointing out that the bill failed to pass because it was introduced at the end of a session, Mary Stoneman alluded to her husband's frail health caused by his military service. She implored the president to act "to comfort

Stoneman shortly after he left the office of Governor of California in 1887 (from the collection of Andrew J. Potts).

and bless the honorable and conscientious soldier whose best years, health, and spirits have been given to his country's service."[78] Finally, on February 9, 1891, Congress appointed him colonel of infantry.[79]

Stoneman was broken in health and finances and faced domestic problems, as well. His wife, who was considerably younger than he, was the object of much unfavorable gossip due to her active social life. In contrast to the taciturn general, she was vivacious and musically inclined, once entertaining Los Angeles society by singing "Cavatina" from *Ernani* and "Coming Through the Rye."[80] Newspaper accounts described her receptions in Sacramento while her husband was governor as memorable occasions, but she "could not escape the tongue of slander." She was linked to the governor's private secretary, Harry Dam, and, in 1892, she was named as a co-respondent in a sensational divorce case against Judge A.E. Bronson, a prominent attorney from Southern California. The *Los Angeles Times* reported that the scandal was "an open secret for months past, and has been a lively topic of conversation in society circles, not only in this city, but also in the Northern metropolis, on account of the high social standing of the parties...."[81] Mrs. Bronson claimed she was in possession of evidence in the form of hotel registers where Judge Bronson and Mary Stoneman allegedly visited. A damning letter was published, denounced as a forgery by Mary Stoneman, which spoke of her wanting to be "clasped in those loving, tender, protective arms and held close to your faithful heart."[82] The article went on to describe the Stoneman's financial difficulties and reported that the general moved to a downtown hotel for some weeks after learning of the scandal. Although she was exonerated, the attendant publicity apparently convinced Stoneman that he should travel across the continent to visit his sister, Mrs. Benjamin Williams, in Buffalo, New

Mary Stoneman later in life, in a photograph taken in Los Angeles. She was a vivacious, high-spirited lady, quite different from her reserved husband (courtesy of George B. Stoneman, M.D.).

York.[83] He was never to return to California. His friend Colonel James J. Ayers lamented Stoneman's departure:

> It is sad to think that Governor Stoneman, after a career so distinguished and services so valuable to his country and his chosen State, should have closed it so far away from the scenes of the campaigns of his youth, his civic successes in mature life and the beautiful retreat in San Gabriel Valley where he fondly hoped to spend his declining years....[84]

Epilogue

What was initially planned as a three-month visit with his sister, Mrs. Benjamin Williams, turned out to be a permanent exile from California for George Stoneman. His health continued to deteriorate and he became a recluse, withdrawing completely from public life. He suffered a stroke in April 1894, from which he never recovered. Death came to the old soldier early in the morning of September 5, 1894. The attending doctor attributed his death to "paresis" as the "chief and determining" cause of death due to "exposure and hardship of army life."[1]

A solemn service, conducted by a Unitarian minister, was held at the home of his sister in Buffalo, which was followed by full military honors, including a guard of arms of the 21st Infantry, Stoneman's old unit. In all, over 800 men in full dress uniform were in attendance. The services were the first in the city of Buffalo for a major general who had fought in the Civil War. Flags were at half mast throughout the city as the hearse and carriages were driven to Erie station where the casket was taken to Jamestown, New York, by a military escort and Harris Stoneman Williams, a nephew of the general.

The body of the old soldier lay in state at the armory in Jamestown before it was taken to the village of Lakewood, close to the general's birthplace at Busti. The final ceremony at Bentley Cemetery was attended by the general's brother and sister, Judge John. T. Stoneman of the Supreme Court of Iowa, and Kate Stoneman of Albany, New York. A poem from Wordsworth entitled *Character of the Happy Warrior* was read, as well as an excerpt from Browning's *Epilogue*:

> One who never turned his back, but marched, breast forward:
> Never doubted clouds would break;
> Never dreamed, though right were worsted,
> wrong would triumph.
> Held, we fall to rise, are baffled to fight better.
> Sleep to wake.

Top: Stoneman family burial site in Lakewood, New York, close to Stoneman's birthplace in Busti, New York. *Bottom:* Tombstone of General George Stoneman. The inscription reads: "Chief of Cavalry. Army of the Patomac [sic]. Commander of Third Army Corps at Fredericksburg. Pensioner of Mexican and Civil Wars" (J. David Petruzzi collection).

Mary Oliver Hardisty Stoneman moved to Brookline, Massachusetts, where she lived with her daughter, Katharine (Kitty) for ten years. She died in March 1915 at the age of 77.[2] There is no evidence that she saw her husband after he left California. There is also no evidence that she or her children attended George Stoneman's funeral.

Chapter Notes

Preface

1. H. Brett Melendy and Benjamin F. Gilbert, *The Governors of California: Peter H. Burnett to Edmund G. Brown*. Georgetown, California: The Talisman Press, 1965, 216.

Chapter One

1. Stephen Z. Starr, *The Union Cavalry in the Civil War: From Fort Sumter to Gettysburg, 1861–1863*, Vol. 1. Baton Rouge, Louisiana: Louisiana State University Press, 1979, 337–338.
2. *Official Records of the Union and Confederate Armies*. Vol. 25, Pt. 2, 51.
3. Carl Sandburg, *Abraham Lincoln: The War Years*, Vol. 2. New York: Harcourt, Brace, and Company, 1939, 84.
4. *Ibid.*, 86.
5. Joseph P. Cullen, "The Battle of Chancellorsville," *Civil War Times Illustrated*, reissued by Eastern Acorn Press, 1981, 4–5.
6. Newel Chaney, *History of the Ninth Regiment: New York Volunteer Cavalry, War of 1861–1865*. Poland Center, New York: Martin Merz and Son, 1901, 92.
7. *Ibid.*, 83.
8. Lt. John J. Parker, *History of the Twenty-Second Massachusetts and the Third Light Battery in the War of the Rebellion*. Rand and Avery Company Press, Published by the Regimental Association, 1887. Reference was found in an insert between pages 250–251, author unknown.
9. Sandburg, *The War Years*, 92.
10. John Hyde, *Historical Sketches of Old Berlin*, Vol. 1. N.Y: Unadilla Valley Historical Society, 1907.
11. *Ibid.*, 38.
12. O. Herbert Entwistle, Jr., *A History of New Berlin: New York to 1907*, master's thesis, Colgate University, 1953.
13. John Hyde, *Historical Sketches of Old New Berlin*, 13.
14. *Ibid.*, 15.
15. Floyd A. Wilber, "Early Glimpses of the New Berlin Area" and other articles. New Berlin Center History, New Berlin, N.Y. Revised Ed., 1964.
16. Lenora A. Snedeker, "Civil War Veteran Made His Mark," *The Evening Sun*, Norwich, N.Y., August 9, 1989, 3.
17. William J. Doty, Ed., *The Historical Annals of Southwestern New York*. New York, N.Y.: Lewis Historical Publishing Company, 1940, 46.
18. Undocumented paper on "The Stoneman Family," provided by Norman Carlson, historian of the town of Busti, N.Y.
19. Lucy Darrow Peake, *History of the Town of Busti*, July 1950, Chautauqua County Historical Society, file 158.001.
20. Andrew W. Young, *History of Chautauqua County*. Buffalo: Printing House of Matthews and Warren, 1875, 659.
21. John P. Downs and Fenwick Y. Hedley, Eds., *History of Chautauqua County and Its People*, Vol. 1. Boston, New York, Chicago: American Historical Society, Inc., 1921, 119.
22. *Ibid.*, 119.

Chapter Two

1. Letter from E.A. Dickinson, Jamestown Academy, to the Hon. John C. Spencer, Secretary of the Navy, November 10, 1841. United States Military Academy Library, Special Collections Division, hereinafter referred to as the USMA Archives.
2. Hugh J. Mohan, E.H. Clough, John C. Cosgraves, *Pen Pictures of Our Representative Men*. Sacramento: H.A. Weaver's Valley Press Printing House, 1880, XIX.
3. Letter from George Stoneman, Jr., to the Hon.

Abe Bell, Secretary of War, July 26, 1841, USMA Archives.

4. Letter from Samuel A. Brown and others to the Hon. John C. Spencer, Sec. of War, November 13, 1841, USMA Archives.

5. "Regulations Established for the Organization and Government of the Military Academy at West Point New York." New York: Wiley and Putnam, 1839, Article II, 29.

6. Letter from Dr. L. Hazeltine to the Hon. John C. Spencer, Secretary of War, November 17, 1841, USMA archives.

7. Darius Couch, *Twenty-Sixth Annual Reunion of the Association of Graduates of the United States Military Academy at West Point*, New York, June 10, 1895. Saginaw, Michigan: Seenann and Peters, Printers and Binders, 1895, 25.

8. Regulations, USMA, 1839, Article II, 9.

9. *Ibid.*, 10–16.

10. Official Register, Officers and Cadets of the U.S. Military Academy, 1843–46, USMA Archives.

11. Cadets Arranged in Order of Merit in Their Respective Classes, as Determined at the General Examination in June 1846. USMA Archives, 253.

12. U.S. Military Academy Staff Records, Vol. II, 1835–1842, USMA Archives, 253.

13. USMA Regulations, 1839, Article XII, "Discipline," 31–33.

14. *Ibid.*, 40, 41.

15. Letter from Stoneman to John Griffith, October 29, 1842. Courtesy of Norman Carlson, Town of Busti Historian.

16. *Register of Delinquency 1842–1846*, USMA Archives, 282.

17. *Ibid.*, 251.

18. Stephen W. Sears, *George B. McClellan: The Young Napoleon*. Ticknor and Fields, 1988, 11, quoting GBM to Elizabeth B. McClellan, March 18, 1846. George B. McClellan Papers, Library of Congress.

19. Brevet Major General George W. Cullum, *Biographical Register of the Officers and Graduates of the U.S. Military Academy at West Point, New York*, Third Edition, Vol. II. Boston and New York: Houghton, Mifflin and Company, 1891, 280.

Chapter Three

1. It was not unusual for West Point graduates at this time to receive a brevet or temporary commission while waiting for an opening in the regular ranks of the army.

2. James J. Polk, *The Diary of James K. Polk, 1845–1849*, Vol. 1, Ed. Milo Milton Quaife. Chicago: A.C. McClurg and Company, 1919, 445.

3. *Ibid.*, 445.

4. *Ibid.*, 446.

5. *Ibid.*, 449.

6. Sergeant Daniel Tyler, *A Concise History of the Mormon Battalion in the Mexican War, 1846–1847*. Glorieta, New Mexico: The Rio Grande Press, Inc., 113.

7. William Stegnel, *The Gathering of Zion: The Story of the Mormon Trail*. New York: McGraw Hill and Company, 1964, 76.

8. Tyler, *A Concise History of the Mormon Battalion*, 115.

9. *Ibid.*, 117.

10. M.R. Werner, *Brigham Young*. New York: Harcourt, Brace, and Company, 1925, 216.

11. Erwin G. Gudde, *Bigler's Chronicle of the West*. Berkeley, University of California Press, 1962, 17; Tyler, *A Concise History of the Mormon Battalion*, 117.

12. Susan Young Gates, *The Life Story of Brigham Young*. New York: The Macmillan Company, 1930, 75.

13. Lt. Col. (Ret.) Sherman L. Fleek, *History May Be Searched in Vain: A Military History of the Mormon Battalion*. Spokane: The Arthur H. Clark Company, 2006, 142.

14. Tyler, *A Concise History of the Mormon Battalion*, 81–82.

15. *Ibid.*, 136.

16. Erwin G. Gudde, *Bigler's Chronicle of the West*, quoting Huntington's journal, 22.

17. Tyler, *A Concise History of the Mormon Battalion*, 144.

18. Gudde, *Bigler's Chronicle of the West*, 23.

19. *Ibid.*, 24.

20. Bernard DeVoto, *The Year of Decision: 1846*. Boston, Mass: Little Brown and Company, 1943, 312.

21. Tyler, *A Concise History of the Mormon Battalion*, 164.

22. Tyler, quoting Orders No. 7 from Headquarters Mormon Battalion, Santa Fe, October 13, 1846, 166.

23. "Journal of the March of the Mormon Battalion under the Command of Col. P. St. George Cooke from Santa Fe New Mexico to San Diego California." U.S. Government Document, special session, 30th Congress, Senate Document No. 2, Washington D.C., 1849, October 19, 2.

24. *Ibid.*

25. Tyler, *A Concise History of the Mormon Battalion*, 177.

26. Cooke's "Journal of the March," 2.

27. Gudde, *Bigler's Chronicle of the West*, 28.

28. Tyler, *A Concise History of the Mormon Battalion*, 207.

29. Sherman L. Fleek, *History May Be Searched in Vain: A Military History of the Mormon Battalion*, 241.

30. Tyler, 180.

31. *Ibid.*, 180–181.

32. Cooke, "Journal of the March," December 10, 27.

33. John F. Yurtinus, "A Ram in the Thicket: The Mormon Battalion in the Mexican War, Vol. 1." Ph.D. diss., Brigham Young University, 1975, 396; Cooke, "Journal of the March," December 11, 37.

34. Gudde, *Bigler's Chronicle of the West*, 32; Yurtinus, "A Ram in the Thicket," Vol. I, 397–400.

35. Cooke's "Journal of the March," December 13, 39.

36. Cooke's "Journal of the March," December 18, 44.

37. Fleek, *History May Be Searched in Vain*....

38. Cooke, "Journal of the March," January 1, 59; Yurtinus, "A Ram in the Thicket," Vol. 1, 444.
39. Tyler, *A Concise History of the Mormon Battalion. 1846–1847*, 238.
40. Cooke's "Journal of the March," January 1, 59.
41. *Ibid*.
42. Tyler, *A Concise History of the Mormon Battalion*, 239.
43. Cooke's "Journal of the March," January 2, 60.
44. *Ibid*., January 5, 63.
45. Yurtinus, "A Ram in the Thicket," Vol. 1, 459.
46. Cooke's "Journal of the March," January 15, 72.
47. *Ibid*., January 23, 79.
48. Bernard Devoto, *The Year of Decision: 1846*, 368, 470; Sherman L. Fleek, *History May Be Searched in Vain...*, 278–279.
49. Yurtinus, "A Ram in the Thicket," Vol. 1, 478, quoting "Journal of Robert Bliss," 85.
50. Tyler, *A Concise History of the Mormon Battalion. 1846–1847*, 252.
51. Cooke's "Journal of the March," January 30, 84–85.

Chapter Four

1. Dwight L. Clarke, *Stephen Watts Kearny Soldier of the West*. Norman, Okla.: University of Oklahoma Press, 1961, 288.
2. *Ibid*., 289.
3. "The Journal of Lieutenant John McHenry Hollingsworth of the First New York Volunteers," September 1846–1849. San Francisco California Historical Society, 1923–29, 30.
4. *Ibid*., 32.
5. Darius Couch, *Twenty-Sixth Annual Reunion of the Association of Graduates of the United States Military Academy at West Point, New York*, June 10, 1895. Letter to Couch from Mr. J.C.L. Wadsworth. Saginaw, Mich.: Seemann and Peters, Printers and Binders, 1895, 27.
6. Hubert Howe Bancroft, *History of California*, Vol. 11, 1848–1859, 281.
7. J.W. Caughey, Ed., *The Indians of Southern California in 1852*, "The B.D. Wilson Report and a Selection of Contemporary Comment," 1952, The Huntington Library, San Marino, Calif., 22.
8. *Ibid*., 23.
9. Robert M. Utley, *Frontiersmen in Blue*: Lincoln, Nebraska: University of Nebraska Press, 1967, 29.
10. *Ibid*., 175–176.
11. Letter from Captain George Stoneman to Captain George Cullum from Cavalry Camp on the Rio Grande, Texas, September 28, 1860, USMA Archives.
12. Richard A. Bartlett, *Great Surveys of the American West: 1803–1863*. Norman, Okla.: University of Oklahoma Press, 1962, 11, 12.
13. William H. Goetzmann, *Army Exploration in the American West*. New Haven, Conn.: Yale University Press, 1959, 292–293.
14. *Ibid*., 290.

15. Utley, *Frontiersmen in Blue*, 178.
16. Carl Coke Rister, *Robert E. Lee in Texas*. Norman, Oklahoma: University of Oklahoma Press, 1946, 13.
17. *Ibid*., 14.
18. Rister, *Robert E. Lee in Texas*, 22, 23.
19. *Ibid*., 16. Douglas Southhall Freeman, *R.E. Lee: A Biography*, Vol. I. New York: Charles Scribner's Sons, 1934, 362.
20. George F. Price, *Across the Continent with the Fifth Cavalry*. New York: Antiquarian Press Ltd., 1959, 32–35.
21. *Ibid*., 363–364.
22. *Ibid*., 367–368.
23. Stoneman to J. Couts, June 1, 1856, collection of Stoneman correspondence from The Huntington Library, San Marino, Calif.
24. *Ibid*.
25. Carl Coke Rister, *Robert E. Lee in Texas*, 112–113.
26. National Archives, Second Cavalry Records, Military History of Officers, 1860, Entry 770.
27. Price, *Across the Continent with the Fifth Cavalry*, 85.
28. *Ibid*., 87.
29. *Ibid*., 87.
30. Letter from George Stoneman to Captain George Cullum, December 28, 1860, Special Collection, USMA Archives.
31. *Dallas Herald*, April 4, 1860. "From the Rio Grande."
32. Walter Prescott Webb, Ed., *The Handbook of Texas*, Vol. 2. Austin, Texas: The Texas State Historical Association, 1952, 812.
33. Freeman, Douglas Southhall, *R.E. Lee*, 416.
34. Letter from George Stoneman to Robert H. Ramsay, Brvt. Col., Nashville, Tennessee, July 1, 1866, National Archives, U.S. War Dept. "Service Record of George Stoneman."
35. *Ibid*.
36. *Official Records of the Union and Confederate Armies*, Vol. 1, 579. (Hereinafter referred to as the *Official Records*.)
37. *Ibid*., 580.
38. *Ibid*., 580.
39. *Ibid*., 504. Twiggs to Lt. Col. L. Thomas, Asst. Adjt, Gen., Headquarters of the Army, Washington D.C.
40. Price, 97.
41. *Official Records*, Report of Maj. C.C. Sibley, Vol. 1, 561.
42. *Official Records*, Brig. Gen. S. Cooper to Col. Earl Van Dorn, Vol. 1, 623.
43. Robert Underwood Johnson and Clarence Clough Buel, Eds., Caroline Baldwin Darrow, *Battles and Leaders of the Civil War*, Vol. 1, "Recollections of the Twiggs Surrender." Secaucus, N.J: Castle, 39.

Chapter Five

1. Shelby Foote, *The Civil War: A Narrative*, Vol. 1: *From Fort Sumter to Perryville*. New York: Random House, 1958, 51.

2. *Official Records*, Vol. 2, Report of Maj. Gen. S.P. Heintzelman, 40.
3. Stephen W. Sears, *George B. McClellan: The Young Napoleon*. New York: Ticknor and Fields, 1988, 72.
4. Bruce Catton, *The Coming Fury*, Vol. 1. Garden City, N.Y.: Doubleday and Company, Inc., 1961, 196, 330.
5. Stephen W. Sears, Ed., *The Civil War Papers of George B. McClellan: Selected Correspondence, 1860–1865*. New York: Ticknor and Fields, 1989, 25.
6. *Ibid.*, 26.
7. *Ibid.*, 80.
8. *The Civil War Papers of George B. McClellan*, McClellan to Lincoln, 28.
9. *Ibid.*, 35–36.
10. Jacob P. Cox, Maj. Gen., U.S.V., *Battles and Leaders of the Civil War*, Vol. 2, "McClellan in West Virginia." Secaucus, New Jersey: Castle, 129.
11. Sears, *George B. McClellan: The Young Napoleon*, 89.
12. *Ibid.*, 88.
13. Stephen W. Sears, Ed., *The Civil War Papers of George B. McClellan*, 59.
14. Stephen Z. Starr, *The Union Cavalry in the Civil War: From Ft. Sumter to Gettysburg*, Vol. 1. Baton Rouge: Louisiana State University Press, 1979, 236, quoting T.F. Thiele, "The Evolution of Cavalry in the American Civil War," Ph.D. diss., University of Michigan, 1951, 87.
15. Starr, *The Union Cavalry*, 237.
16. *Ibid.*
17. *Official Records*, General Reports, Series 1, Vol. 5, 55.
18. *Ibid.*, Series 1, Vol. 5, "Reconnaissance to Cedar Creek," Report of George Stoneman, 550.
19. *Ibid.*
20. Thomas F. Thiele, "The Evolution of Cavalry in the American Civil War," Ph.D. diss., University of Michigan, 1951, 265.
21. Price, *Across the Continent with the Fifth Cavalry*, 317–318.
22. *Official Records*, Series 1, Vol. 5, 550.
23. Sears, *George B. McClellan: The Young Napoleon*, 170, 171.
24. Sears, 168, quoting John Tucker of the War Department.
25. *Official Records*, Vol. 11, Pt. 3, 26.
26. Starr, *The Union Cavalry*, 265.
27. *Ibid.*, 265.
28. William W. Averell, Brevet Maj. Gen., USA, *Battles and Leaders of the Civil War*, "With the Cavalry on the Peninsula," Vol. 2, 429.
29. *Ibid.*, Vol. 2, George B. McClellan, Maj. Gen. USA, "The Peninsula Campaign," 173.
30. Starr, *The Union Cavalry*, 263.
31. Don E. Fehrenbacher, Ed., *Abraham Lincoln, Speeches, Letters, Miscellaneous Writings, Presidential Messages, and Proclamations*. New York: Literary Classics of the United States, 1989, 313.
32. Richard Wheeler, *Sword Over Richmond*. New York: Harper and Row, 1986, 144.
33. *Ibid.*, 151.

34. *Official Records*, Vol. 11, Part 2, 424–425.
35. *Ibid.*
36. Gen. Joseph Hooker, Report of Brigadier General F.J. Hooker, III Army Corps Headquarters, May 10, 1862, courtesy of the Williamsburg Foundation, Williamsburg, Va.
37. *Ibid.*, 425.
38. H.B. McClellan, *I Rode with Jeb Stuart: The Life and Campaigns of Major General J.E.B. Stuart*. Bloomington, Indiana: Indiana University Press, 1958), 48.
39. *Official Records*, Series 1, Pt. 3, footnote p. 270.
40. H.B. McClellan, 49.
41. *Ibid.*, 437.
42. Etat of Service of George Stoneman, Aug. 1866, Letter to Gen. George McCullum, Supt. Military Academy, West Point, New York. Special Collections Division, United States Military Academy Library.
43. Wheeler, *Sword Over Richmond*, 193.
44. *Ibid.*, 126.
45. Sears, *The Civil War Papers of George B. McClellan*, 235.
46. *Official Records*, Ser. 3, Vol. 3, 274.
47. Price, *Across the Continent with the Fifth Cavalry*, 318.
48. *Ibid.*
49. *Ibid.*, 199–201.
50. Emory M. Thomas, *Bold Dragoon: The Life of J.E.B. Stuart*. New York: Harper and Row, 1986, 113.
51. *Ibid.*, 117.
52. *Ibid.*, 123.
53. *Battles and Leaders of the Civil War*, "With the Cavalry in the Peninsula," by William W. Averill, Vol. 2, 430.
54. Sears, *George B. McClellan: The Young Napoleon*, 211.
55. *Ibid.*, 211.
56. Foote, *The Civil War: A Narrative, Vol. 1: Fort Sumter to Perryville*, 274–275.
57. *Ibid.*, 275.
58. *Battles and Leaders of the Civil War*, Vol. 2, 340–341.
59. *Official Records*, Vol. 2, Pt. 1, 61.
60. *Ibid.*, 61.
61. Sears, *George B. McClellan: The Young Napoleon*, 214–215.
62. Thomas F. Thiele, "The Evolution of Cavalry in the American Civil War," 294–295.
63. *Official Records*, Vol. 11, Part 2, Report of Brig. Gen. Silas Casey, 482–483.
64. H.B. McClellan, *I Rode with Jeb Stuart*, 78.
65. *Official Records*, Vol. 11, Pt. 2, 930.
66. Thiele, "The Evolution of Cavalry in the American Civil War," 494,

Chapter Six

1. George Alfred Townsend, *Rustics in Rebellion: A Yankee Reporter on the Road to Richmond, 1861–1865*. Chapel Hill: The University of North Carolina Press, 1950, 77.
2. Worthington Chaucey Ford, Ed., *A Cycle of*

Adams Letters, Vol. 2. Boston: Houghton Mifflin Company, 1920, 8.
 3. *The Baltimore Sun*, November 22, 1861.
 4. *Ibid*.
 5. Virginia Jean Lass, Ed., *The Civil War Letters of Elizabeth Blair Lee*. Urbana and Chicago, Illinois: University of Illinois Press, 194.
 6. *Official Records*, Vol. 19. Pt. 2, 55.
 7. *Ibid*., 55.
 8. H.B. McClellan, *I Rode with Jeb Stuart*, 142, quoting Col. A.K. McClure, resident of Chambersburg.
 9. *Ibid*., 148–149.
 10. *Official Records*, Vol. 19, Pt. 2, 43.
 11. *Ibid*., 43, Report of Brig. General George Stoneman.
 12. *Ibid*., 43.
 13. McClellan, *I Rode with Jeb Stuart*, 156.
 14. *Ibid*., 161.
 15. *Ibid*.
 16. *Official Records*, Vol. 19, Pt. 2, 38–41, Report of Brig. Gen. Alfred Pleasonton.
 17. *Ibid*., 44, Report of Brig. Gen. Stoneman to Gen. Williams, Adjutant General.
 18. *Ibid*., 44.
 19. *Ibid*., 77.
 20. *Ibid*., 30. Report of Maj. Gen. George B. McClellan.
 21. McClellan, 156.
 22. Henry Kyd Douglas, *I Rode with Stonewall*. Greenwich, Conn.: Fawcett Publications, Inc., 1961, 188.
 23. *Ibid*., 188.
 24. *Official Records*, Vol. 19, Pt. 2, 417.
 25. *Ibid*., 421.
 26. Starr, Vol. I, 319.
 27. *Official Records*, Series I, Vol. 19, Pt. 1, 74.
 28. Starr, Vol. I, 321, footnote 81.
 29. Richard B. Irwin, Lt. Col. and Assistant Adjutant General, "Washington Under Banks," *Battles and Leaders of the Civil War*, Vol. 2, 544.

Chapter Seven

 1. Don E. Fahrenbacher, Ed., *Abraham Lincoln: Speeches and Writings, 1859–1865*. New York: Literary Classics of the United States, 1989, 377.
 2. *Ibid*., 376–377.
 3. *Official Records*, Vol. XIX, Pt. 2, Orders to George Stoneman, 495–496.
 4. *Ibid*., 542.
 5. Stephen W. Sears, *George B. McClellan: The Young Napoleon*. New York: Ticknor and Fields, 1988, 337.
 6. Mark M. Boatner, *The Civil War Dictionary*. New York: Random House, Inc, 1988, 449; James C. Robertson, Jr., *General A.P. Hill: The Story of a Confederate Warrior*. New York: Random House, Inc., 1987, 128; *Battles and Leaders*, Vol. II, 538n.
 7. Sears, *George B. McClellan: The Young Napoleon*, 341.
 8. Vorin E. Whan, Jr., *Fiasco at Fredericksburg*. State College, Pa., The Pennsylvania State University press, 1961, 19.
 9. Edward J. Stackpole, *The Fredericksburg Campaign*. Harrisburg, Pa: Military Service Publishing Company, 1957, 97–98.
 10. *Ibid*., 80.
 11. *Official Records*, Vol. XXI, Series I, Bayard to Burnside, 6; James M. Chauker, "Opportunity Lost: William B. Franklin and the Battle of Fredericksburg," master's thesis, James Madison University, May 1990, Chap. I, 10.
 12. *Official Records*, Vol. XXI, Report of Maj. Gen. A.E. Burnside, 85.
 13. William F. Smith, "Franklin's Left Grand Division," *Battles and Leaders of the Civil War*, Vol. III, 128.
 14. Oliver O. Howard, *Autobiography of Oliver Otis Howard*. New York: The Baker and Taylor Company, 1907, 321.
 15. *Ibid*., 130–131.
 16. *Official Records*, Vol. XXI, Report of General Burnside, 87.
 17. Smith, "*Battles and Leaders of the Civil War*," Vol. III, 133.
 18. *Official Records*, Vol. XXI, 457.
 19. Smith, *Battles and Leaders*..., Vol. III, 134–135.
 20. Stackpole, *The Fredericksburg Campaign*, 182; Vorin E. Whan, *Fiasco at Fredericksburg*. State College, Pennsylvania: The Hines Printing Company, 196, 64.
 21. *Official Records*, Vol. XXI, Report of General George Stoneman, 359.
 22. Stackpole, *The Fredericksburg Campaign*, 192.
 23. *Ibid*., 361.
 24. *Official Records*, Vol. XXI, 361, Report of General George Stoneman; Chauker, 48.
 25. Maj. General Darius Couch, "Sumner's Right Grand Division," *Battles and Leaders of the Civil War*, Vol. III, 113.
 26. Stackpole, *The Fredericksburg Campaign*, 216–217.
 27. *Official Records*, Vol. XXI, Report of Gen. George Stoneman, 361.

Chapter Eight

 1. *Official Records of the Union and Confederate Armies*, Vol. 21, 815.
 2. *Ibid*.
 3. *Official Records*, Vol. 25, Pt. 2, 51.
 4. *Ibid*., 65–66.
 5. Stephen Z. Starr, *The Union Cavalry in the Civil War: From Fort Sumter to Gettysburg, 1861–1863*, Vol. I. Baton Rouge: Louisiana State University Press, 1979, 339. More recent research has revealed a letter, dated February 9, 1865, in the National Archives written by Buford to Stoneman in which he asked for an assignment with "Western troops" or "regulars." Stoneman agreed and assigned Buford to command the reserve brigade. See Michael Phipps and John S. Peterson, *The Devil's to Pay: General John Buford, USA*. Gettysburg, Pa.: Farnsworth Military Impressions, 1995, 28–29.
 6. John Edward Pierce, "Judson Kilpatrick in the

American Civil War." Ph.D. diss., Pennsylvania State University, 1983, 2.
　7. Edward G. Longacre, *The Cavalry at Gettysburg*. Lincoln, Nebraska: University of Nebraska Press, 1986, 54.
　8. Pierce, "General Hugh Judson Kilpatrick in the American Civil War: A New Appraisal," 84; Don Edward Alberts, "General Wesley Merritt: Nineteenth Century Cavalryman," Ph.D. diss., University of New Mexico, 1975, 53.
　9. *Official Records*, Vol. 25, Pt. 2, 199.
　10. Walter H. Hebert, *Fighting Joe Hooker*. Indianapolis: The Bobs-Merrill Company, 1944, 36.
　11. *Ibid.*, 225.
　12. *Ibid.*, 200.
　13. *Ibid.*, Vol. XXV, Pt. 1, 1066.
　14. *Ibid.*
　15. *Ibid.*
　16. *Ibid.*, 1067.
　17. Rev. Frederick Denison, *Sabers and Spurs: The First Regiment Rhode Island Cavalry in the Civil War, 1861–1865*. Central Falls, Rhode Island: E.L. Freeman and Co., 1876, 218–219.
　18. Allan Nevins, ed., *A Diary of Battle: The Personal Journals of Colonel Charles S. Wainwright, 1861–1865*. New York: Harcourt, Brace, and World, 1962, 181.
　19. *Official Records*, Vol. 25, Pt. 2, 214.
　20. *Ibid.*
　21. *Ibid.*, 221.
　22. Rev. S. L. Gracey, *Annals of the Sixth Pennsylvania Cavalry*. E.H. Butler and Company, 1868, 136.
　23. *Official Records*, Vol. 25, Pt. 2, 229.
　24. John Bigelow, Jr., *The Campaign of Chancellorsville, A Strategic and Tactical Study*. New Haven: Yale University Press, 1910, 443.
　25. Rev. Samuel L. Gracey, *Annals of the 6th Pennsylvania Cavalry*. Philadelphia: E.H. Butler and Co., 1868, 141.
　26. Bigelow, 443–444.
　27. *Official Records*, Vol. 25, Pt. 1, 1060.
　28. *Ibid.*, 1060.
　29. Samuel H. Merrill, *Campaigns of the First Maine and First District of Columbia Cavalry*. Portland: Bailey and Noyes, 1866, 98–99.
　30. Richard Bowles, Jr., "Shannon Hill Encounter," *Goochland County Historical Society Magazine*, Vol. 17, 1985, 41.
　31. *Ibid.*, 44–45.
　32. Malcolm H. Harris, *History of Louisa County* (Richmond: The Dietz Press, 1936), 97.
　33. *Ibid.*, 98.
　34. Willard Glazier, *Three Years in the Federal Cavalry*. New York: R.H. Ferguson, 1873, 180–181.
　35. *Official Records*, Vol. 25, Pt. 1, 1084.
　36. *Ibid.*, 1086–87.
　37. *Ibid.*, Pt. 2, 775.
　38. *Official Records*, Vol. 25, Pt. 2, 760.
　39. Clifford Downey, Ed., *The Wartime Papers of R.E. Lee*. Boston, Toronto: Little Brown and Company, 1961, 458.
　40. *Official Records*, Vol. 25, Pt. 2, 779.
　41. *Ibid.*, Vol. 18, 1050.
　42. *Richmond Daily Dispatch*, May 5 and 6, 1863.
　43. Tobie, *History of the First Maine Cavalry*, 141–142.
　44. *Official Records*, Vol. 25, Pt. 1, 1063.
　45. *Ibid.*, 1063.
　46. Bigelow, 456–457.
　47. *Official Records*, Vol. 25, Pt. 2, 785.
　48. *Ibid.*, 449.
　49. *Ibid.*, 782.
　50. "Fighting Joe Hooker," *San Francisco Chronicle*, May 23, 1872, 13.
　51. Newel Chaney, *History of the Ninth Regiment, New York Volunteer Cavalry, War of 1861–1865*. Poland Center, New York: Martin Merz and Son, 1901, 88.
　52. Colonel Hampton S. Thomas, *Some Personal Reminiscences of Service in the Cavalry of the Army of the Potomac*. Philadelphia: L.R. Hamersly and Co., 1889, 9.
　53. Starr, Vol. I, 364, quoting Henry P. Pyne, *The History of the First New Jersey Cavalry*. Trenton, N.J.: J.A. Beecher, 1871, 146–147.
　54. Edward P. Tobie, *History of the First Maine Cavalry, 1861–1865*. Boston: Press of Emery and Hughes, 1887, 143–144.
　55. *Official Records*, Vol. 25, Pt. 2, 463.
　56. Walter H. Hebert, *Fighting Joe Hooker*. Indianapolis: The Bobbs-Merrill Company, 1944,, 223.
　57. *Report of Joint Committee on the Conduct of the War*. Washington: Government Printing Office, 1865, Vol. I, 140.
　58. Longacre, *The Cavalry at Gettysburg*, 173.
　59. Douglas Southall Freeman, *Lee's Lieutenants: A Study in Command, Cedar Mountain to Chancellorsville*, Vol. 2. New York: Charles Scribner's Sons, 1944, 646.
　60. Worthington Chauncey Ford, Ed., Charles Francis Adams, *A Cycle of Adams Letters*. Boston and New York: Houghton Mifflin Company, 1920, Pt. II, 8.

Chapter Nine

　1. John Bigelow, Jr., *The Campaign of Chancellorsville*, 459. Stoneman's men abandoned 1000 horses, about half the total of those ridden in the raid. Many were shot so that they would not fall into the hands of the Confederates. Most of them were replaced by brood mares and mules collected from farmers along the path of the raid.
　2. Gary W. Gallagher, Ed., A. Wilson Greene, "Stoneman's Raid," quoting Joseph Hooker to Samuel P. Bates, December 24, 1878, Bates Papers, PSA, in *Chancellorsville. The Battle and Its Aftermath*. Chapel Hill: The University of North Carolina Press, 1996, 97, 98.
　3. Clark B. Hall, "The Battle of Brandy Station," *Civil War Times Illustrated*, June 1990, 34–35.
　4. The Sixth Pennsylvania Lancers abandoned that weapon before the Stoneman Raid because it proved to be unwieldy in combat.
　5. *Ibid.*, 36–37: Notes by Winston Wine.
　6. *Ibid.*, 37.

7. Edwin B. Coddington, *The Gettysburg Campaign: A Study in Command*. New York: Charles Scribner's Sons, 1984, 73–74.
8. *Official Records*, Vol.27, Part 3, 172.
9. Robert F. O'Neill, *The Cavalry Battles of Aldie, Middleburg, and Upperville*. Lynchburg, Va.: H.E. Howard, Inc., 1993, 16–17.
10. *Ibid.*, 69–76.
11. Starr, *The Union Cavalry in the Civil War*, Vol. I, 410, quoting George M. Neese, *My Three years in the Confederate Horse Artillery*. New York: Neale Publishing, 1911, 182–183.
12. U.S. War Department, "Service Record of George Stoneman." Adjutant General's Records, 3414, National Archives, Appointment Commission and Personnel Branch, 1871. Hereafter referred to as "Service Record of George Stoneman."
13. *Official Records*, Series 3, Vol. 3, 580.
14. Thiele, "The Evolution of Cavalry in the American Civil War," 112.
15. Starr, *The Union Cavalry in the Civil War*, Vol. II, 8.
16. *Official Records*, Vol. 32, Pt. 3, 269, 302, 361, 399, 500, 512.
17. Stoneman to J. Couts, August 27, 1863, Couts collection, The Huntington Library, San Marino, Calif., CT 2272 (1).
18. *Ibid.* Couts sent the saddle but Stoneman advised Couts after the war that it had been captured by the Confederates. "The Rebs got it when I had my horse shot and was captured down in the interior of Georgia on a raid last summer." Stoneman to Couts, Aug. 9, 1865, Couts collection, The Huntington Library, San Marino, Calif., CT 2274.
19. W.T. Sherman, *Memoirs of Gen. W.T. Sherman*, Vol. II. New York: Charles L. Webster and Co., 1892, 5.
20. Sergeant E. Tarrant, *The Wild Riders of the First Kentucky Cavalry*. Louisville, Kentucky: A Committee of the Regiment, 1894, 315–316.
21. *Ibid.*, 314.
22. *Ibid.*, 287, Starr, *The Union Cavalry in the Civil War*, Vol. III, 452.
23. Tarrant, 328–329.
24. *Official Records*, Vol. 38, Pt. 4, 507.
25. *Ibid.*, Pt. 5, 99, 133, 145; Starr, Vol. 3, 461.
26. *Official Records*, Vol. 38, Pt. 2, 915.
27. *Ibid.*, Pt. 1, 75.
28. *Ibid.*, 76.
29. W. L. Sanford, *History of the Fourteenth Illinois Cavalry*. Chicago: R.R. Donnelley & Sons, 1898, 184.
30. Lloyd Lewis, *Sherman: Fighting Prophet*. New York: Harcourt and Bruce and Company, 1932, 403.
31. Col. Thomas H. Butler, "The Stoneman Raid and Why It Was a Failure," Report of Reunion of the Fifth Indiana Cavalry, held at Indianapolis, Indiana, Oct. 10 and 11, 1883. Indianapolis: Hasselman Journal Co, Printers, 1887, 10.
32. David Evans, *Sherman's Horsemen: Union Cavalry Operations in the Atlanta Campaign*. Bloomington: University of Indiana Press, 1996, 208.
33. *Ibid.*, 212–213; *Official Records*, Vol. 38, Pt. 2, 804.
34. Tarrant, *The Wild Riders of the First Kentucky Cavalry*, 360; letter from Lt. Huffman to his brother; Evans, 292–293.
35. Sam R. Watkins, *Co. Aytch Maury Grays, First Tennessee Regiment or, A Side Show of the Big Show*. Jackson, Tenn.: McCowat-Mercer Press, repr., 1952, 191.
36. Butler, "Report of the Reunion of the Fifth Indiana Cavalry," 10.
37. Sanford, *History of the Fourteenth Illinois Cavalry*, 186, 187.
38. *Ibid.*, 915.
39. Tarrant, *The Wild Riders of the First Kentucky*, 362, letter of Lt. Richard E. Huffman.
40. *Official Records*, Vol. 38, Pt. 5, 913.
41. *Ibid.*, 917.
42. Evans, *Sherman's Horsemen*, 217.
43. *Official Records*, Vol. 38, Pt. 2, 762.
44. *Ibid.*, 774.
45. John P. Dyer, *Fighting Joe Wheeler* (University, Louisiana: Louisiana State University Press, 1941), 183–186. Starr, Vol. III, 470–473. 47. *Official Records*, Vol. 38, Pt. 2, 762–763.
46. Evans, *Sherman's Horsemen*, 310.
47. Evans, 313.
48. *Ibid.*, 313–314.
49. Major Myles Walter Keogh was born in Ireland in 1840, served as a lieutenant in the Papal army, came to the U.S. in 1862 and was commissioned Captain, USV in April. Keogh was assigned to General John Buford's staff and was with him at Second Bull Run and the Chancellorsville raid in April-May 1863. He was Buford's aide-de-camp at Gettysburg. Stoneman apparently asked for Keogh after Buford's death and was captured with him at Sunshine Church. He accompanied Stoneman after the Atlanta campaign in the raids to Southwestern Virginia and North Carolina in 1864-65. He was killed at Little Big Horn in June 1876. (Biography by James Drueke in private correspondence with the author.)
50. Butler, "Report of Reunion of Fifth Indiana Cavalry," 10.
51. Butler, "The Stoneman Raid and Why It Was a Failure," 10; Evans, *Sherman's Horsemen*, 319.
52. *Ibid.*, 11.
53. *Official Records*, Vol. 38, Pt. 2, 920.
54. Sanford, *History of the Fourteenth Illinois Cavalry*, 193.
55. Tarrant, *The Wild Riders of the First Kentucky Cavalry*, 363.
56. *Official Records*, Vol. 38, Pt. 2, 914.
57. Tarrant, *The Wild Riders of the First Kentucky*, 365.
58. *Ibid.*
59. *Ibid.*
60. *Official Records*, Vol. 38, Pt. 2, 917.
61. Colonel Butler of the Fifth Indiana recounted at the regimental reunion in 1886 that he asked Stoneman for permission to leave the field and head for Sherman's lines but Stoneman refused. Report of Reunion of the Fifth Indiana Cavalry, 11.
62. *Ibid.*, 920.
63. Butler, "Report of Reunion of the Fifth Indiana Cavalry," 11–12.

64. Evans, *Sherman's Horsemen*, 340.
65. Service Record of George Stoneman: An account of the surrender by Louis A. Brown, *The Salisbury Prison. A Case Study of Confederate Military Prisoners. 1861–1865*, Wilmington, North Carolina: Broadfoot Publishing Co., 1992, 64, quoted an unnamed source who reported that Stoneman was "broken by fatigue and grief, collapsed on a log and wept."
66. C.M. White, "The Prison Life," believed to have been published in the "National Tribune," date unknown. White's father was also with the Fifth Indiana Cavalry and captured at Sunshine Church.
67. *Ibid*.
68. *Ibid.*, 929; Henry L. Boies, *History of DeKalb County Illinois*. Chicago: O.P. Bassett, Printer, 1868, 313, 314.
69. *Official Records*, Vol. 38, Pt. 2, 914. Report of General George Stoneman.
70. Tarrant, *The Wild Riders of the First Kentucky*, 373.
71. Butler, "Report of Reunion of Fifth Indiana Cavalry," 12.
72. *Official Records*, Vol. 38, Pt. 2, 764.
73. *Ibid.*, 914.
74. Sherman, *Memoirs*, Vol. 2, 98.
75. *Official Records*, Series 2, Vol. 7, 616–617.

Chapter Ten

1. *Official Records*, Vol. 45, Pt. 2, 54.
2. Starr, *The Union Cavalry in the Civil War*, Vol. 3, 556.
3. *Ibid.*, 1074.
4. *Ibid.*, 80.
5. William Marvel, "The Battle of Saltville," *Blue and Gray Magazine*, August, 1991, 11; Mack J. Blackwell, *The Preston Salt Works: A Vital Link to Southwest Virginia's Industrial Beginning*. Abingdon, Va.: 1992. Published privately by the Author, 32.
6. William C. Davis, "The Massacre at Saltville," *Civil War Times Illustrated*, February 1971, 7–8; Marvel, 17.
7. Davis, 11.
8. *Official Records*, Vol. 39, Pt. 1, 554.
9. Marvel, "The Battle of Saltville," 52.
10. John S. Wise, *The End of an Era*. Boston and New York: Houghton, Mifflin and Company, 1900, 379.
11. Davis, "The Battle of Saltville." 48.
12. *Ibid.*, 45, Pt. 1, 809–810.
13. *Ibid*.
14. *Ibid.*, 811.
15. F.H. Mason, *The Twelfth Ohio Cavalry in the War of the Rebellion*. Cleveland: Nevins' Steam Printing House, 1871, 85.
16. Mary B. Kegley, *Wythe County Virginia: A Bicentennial History*, "The Battle of Wytheville." Marceline, Mo: Wallsworth Publishing Inc., 1989, 200.
17. *Ibid.*, 813.
18. *Battles and Leaders*, Vol. 4, "Operations in East Tennessee and South-West Virginia," 479.
19. F.H. Mason, *The Twelfth Ohio Cavalry in the War of the Rebellion*, 91.
20. *Official Records*, Vol. 45, Pt. 1, 813. There are conflicting reports about the burning of the town by Stoneman's men. Stoneman reported that "the town of Saltville was in flames," and that "the enemy had first burned and then evacuated the place the night before." A local history of Saltville states that "The Yankees did not molest private homes nor wilfully [sic] destroy. They took food, clothing, horses, and whatever they could find that was actually needed." See William B. Kent, *A History of Saltville*, June, 1955, available at the Saltville Library.
21. Shelby Foote, *The Civil War*, Vol. 3, 722; Gary Walker, author of *The War in Southwest Virginia, 1861–65*. Roanoke, Va.: Gurtner Graphics & Printing, 1985, argues that Stoneman's Raid at Saltville led to the fall of Richmond in 1865.
22. Mason, *The Twelfth Ohio Cavalry in the War of the Rebellion*, 91–93.
23. *Official Records*, Vol. 45, Pt. 2, 402.
24. *Ibid.*, 59.
25. *Ibid.*, Vol. 49, Pt. 1, 616.
26. *Ibid*.
27. *Ibid.*, 663.
28. *Ibid*.
29. Ina Woestemeyer Van Noppen, *Stoneman's Last Raid*. Raleigh, N.C.: North Carolina State College Print Shop, 1961, X.
30. *Official Records*, Vol. 49, Pt. 1, 325.
31. *Ibid.*, 777.
32. *Ibid.*, Pt. 1, 330; Starr, *The Union Cavalry in the Civil War*, Vol. III, 563; Luther S. Trowbridge, *The Stoneman Raid of 1865*, MOLLUS. Detroit, Michigan: Ostler Printing Company, 1888, 5.
33. Charles H. Kirk, Ed., *History of the Fifteenth Pennsylvania Cavalry, 1862–1865*. Capt. H.K. Weand, "Our Last Campaign and Pursuit of Jeff Davis," Philadelphia: Historical Committee of the Society of the Fifteenth Pennsylvania Cavalry, 1906, 493.
34. *Official Records*, Vol. 49, Pt. 2, 408.
35. Cornelia Phillips Spencer, *The Last Ninety Days of the War in North Carolina, 1866*. Reprint, Washington, N.C.: Broadfoot Publishing Company, 1993, 193.
36. John G. Barrett, *The Civil War in North Carolina*. Chapel Hill: The University of North Carolina Press, 1963, 351; Van Noppen, *Stoneman's Last Raid*, 17.
37. *Ibid.*, 550.
38. Van Noppen, *Stoneman's Last Raid*, 21, 22.
39. Spencer, *The Last Ninety Days of the War in North Carolina*, 196.
40. Van Noppen, *Stoneman's Last Raid*, 25, quoting diary of Mrs. G.W.F. Harper, Southern Historical Collection, University of North Carolina.
41. Chris J. Hartley, *To Restore the Old Flag*. Wilkesboro, N.C.: Old Wilkes, Inc., 1990, 27, quoting Calvin J. Cowles Papers, North Carolina Archives, Raleigh. The Federals searched the village and surrounding areas for forage and booty, but Cowles approached Stoneman and asked "for protection of public and private property, which were heeded."

42. Barrett, *The Civil War in North Carolina*, 353; *Official Records*, Vol. 49, Pt. 1, 331; *History of the Fifteenth Pennsylvania Volunteer Cavalry*, 494.

43. *History of the Fifteenth Pennsylvania Cavalry*, Howard A. Busby, Co. E, "With Gillem's Tennesseans on the Yadkin," 523–524.

44. *Ibid.*, 524.

45. *Ibid.*, 525.

46. A local historian, Ms. Marguerite Tise, believes that a group of Floyd County men, perhaps five, rode forward on April 3 to give Stoneman's men "some grape" on what is now Route 221, 12 miles south of Floyd. One was killed and it is said that Federal troopers rode over his dead body. An account in the *National Cyclopedia* ("Stoneman," p. 112) reported that Stoneman's column was fired upon by 200 men near Christiansburg as they rode to board the Virginia and Tennessee Railroad en route to Washington to participate in the Grand Review at the end of the war. This account said that the incident was the last armed encounter of the Civil War.

47. Mason, *The Twelfth Ohio Cavalry in the War of the Rebellion*, 99.

48. Brig. General Luther S. Trowbridge, "The Stoneman Raid of 1865," a reprint from "The Journal of the United States Cavalry Association," Vol. IV, No. 13, June 1891. *The Cavalry Journal*, No. 4. Vol. XXIV, 1 December 1999.

49. *Official Records*, Vol. 49. Pt. 1, 324, 331.

50. Weand, *History of the Fifteenth Pennsylvania Cavalry*, 496.

51. Mason, *The Twelfth Ohio Cavalry in the War of the Rebellion*, 100.

52. Shelby Foote, *The Civil War*, Vol. 3, 965; William C. Davis, *Jefferson Davis: The Man and His Hour*. New York: Harper Collins Publishers, 1991, 612.

53. Trowbridge, "The Stoneman Raid of 1865," 34, 35.

54. Weand, *History of the Fifteenth Pennsylvania Cavalry*, 500.

55. *Official Records*, 49, Pt. 1, 332.

56. *Ibid.*, 332.

57. Weand, *History of the Fifteenth Pennsylvania Cavalry*, 501.

58. Shelby Foote, *The Civil War*, Vol. 3, 905; Davis, 614.

59. Weand, *History of the Fifteenth Pennsylvania Cavalry*, 503.

60. Louis A Brown, *The Salisbury Prison: A Case Study of Confederate Military Prisons, 1861–1865*. Wendell, N.C.: Avera Press [and] Broadfoots Bookmark, 1980, 142–145. The Salisbury National Cemetery contains the largest number of unknown dead of any Civil War cemetery, although the number on the National Monument there (11,700) is probably incorrect, as death records were not available when the monument was erected eight years after the war.

61. This figure was probably inflated since General Bradley T. Johnson, the commander of Confederate forces at Salisbury, had been ordered to Greensboro with his garrison. See Barrett, *The Civil War in North Carolina*, 357.

62. Weand, *History of the Fifteenth Pennsylvania Cavalry*, 504; Barrett, *The Civil War in North Carolina*, 357.

63. Barrett, *The Civil War in North Carolina*, 359.

64. Van Noppen, *Stoneman's Last Raid*, 66.

65. Weand, *History of the Fifteenth Pennsylvania Cavalry*, 504.

66. Brown, *The Salisbury Prison*, 158–161.

67. William Bushong, Co. C, "The Last Great Stoneman Raid," delivered at the Regimental Reunion, Bellefontaine, Ohio, 1916.

68. Van Noppen, *Stoneman's Last Raid*, 65, quoting E.H.M. Summerell to Cornelia Phillips Spencer, September, 1865.

69. James S. Brawley, *The Rowan Story 1753–1953: Narrative History of Rowan County, North Carolina*. Salisbury, N.C.: Rowan Printing Company, 1953, 198.

70. *Ibid.*

71. *Ibid.*

72. Meroney Folder, McCubbins Collection Ms. 9001. Rowan Public Library, Salisbury, N.C. Unsigned document.

73. *Carolina Watchman*, 16 April, 1866.

74. Barrett, *The Civil War in North Carolina*, 360; Van Noppen, *Stoneman's Last Raid*, 70.

75. *Official Records*, Vol. 49, Pt. 1, 324.

76. Van Noppen, *Stoneman's Last Raid*, 70.

77. Weand, *History of the Fifteenth Pennsylvania Cavalry*, 504.

78. *Ibid.*, 505.

79. *Ibid.*, 507.

80. *Ibid.*

81. Barrett, *The Civil War in North Carolina*, 362.

82. *Ibid.*, 363.

83. Van Noppen, *Stoneman's Last Raid*, 78.

84. *Official Records*, Vol. 49, Pt. 1, 335.

85. Sherman, *Memoirs*, Pt. II, 347.

86. *Official Records*, Vol. 49, Pt. 3, 249.

87. *Ibid.*, 277.

88. Sherman, *Memoirs*, Vol. 2, 371.

89. *Official Records*, Vol. 49, Pt. 1, 546.

90. Benjamin P. Thomas and Harold M. Hyman, *Stanton: The Life and Times of Lincoln's Secretary of War*. New York: Alfred A. Knopf, 1962, 406, 407.

91. Weand, *History of the Fifteenth Pennsylvania Cavalry*, 510.

92. *Official Records*. Vol. 49, Pt. 1, 550.

93. Van Noppen, *Stoneman's Last Raid*, 103.

94. Van Noppen, 107; Weand, *History of the Fifteenth Pennsylvania Cavalry*, 512. Weand misspelled Stoneman's name, referring to him as "Stoneham."

95. Weand, *History of the Fifteenth Pennsylvania Cavalry*, 512.

96. Weand, *History of the Fifteenth Pennsylvania Cavalry*, 514.

97. *Official Records*, Vol. 49, Pt. 1, 551, 552.

98. Weand, *History of the Fifteenth Pennsylvania Cavalry*, 517.

99. *The Personal Memoirs of U.S. Grant*, Vol. II. New York: Konecky and Konecky, 646.

100. *Official Records*, Vol. 49, Pt. 1, 616.

101. General Luther S. Trowbridge, "The Stoneman Raid of 1865," 15.

Chapter Eleven

1. James E. Sefton, *The United States Army and Reconstruction, 1865–1877*, Baton Rouge: Louisiana State University Press, 1967, 8.
2. *Ibid.*, 11.
3. Stoneman sometimes referred to his wife Mary as Mollie.
4. George Stoneman, Jr., to his father, June 14, 1865, hereinafter referred to as GS. To GS, Sr., courtesy of Mrs. Frances Pickin Florio, a descendent of George Stoneman's brother, Byron Stoneman.
5. *Ibid.*
6. Tennessee ratified the Fourteenth Amendment in July 1866, under the Radical administration of Governor William G. Brownlow, after a struggle in the legislature. See Thomas B. Alexander, *Political Reconstruction in Tennessee*. New York: Russell and Russell, 1950, 110–111.
7. *Ibid.*, 21.
8. Altina L. Waller, "Community, Class, and Race in the Memphis Riot of 1866," *Journal of Social History*, Vol. 18, 233.
9. Thomas B. Alexander, *Political Reconstruction in Tennessee*, 54; Patrick W. Riddleberger, *1866: The Critical Year Revisited*. Carbondale and Edwardsville: Southern Illinois University Press, 1979, 178.
10. James Gilbert Ryan, "The Memphis Riots of 1866: Terror in a Black Community During Reconstruction," *Journal of Negro History*, Vol. 62, 1977, 244; *Memphis Riots and Massacres*, "Mass Violence in America Series," New York Times, New York, 1969, and Arno Press: facsimile ed. House Report No. 101, U.S. Congress, 1st Session, July 25, 1866. (Hereafter cited as Memphis Riots.) Testimony of Dr. J.N. Sharp, 156.
11. Eric Foner, *Reconstruction: America's Unfinished Revolution, 1863–1877*. New York: Harper and Row, 1988, 262, quoting the *Memphis Argus*.
12. Alexander, *Political Reconstruction in Tennessee*, 57; Ryan, "The Memphis Riots of 1866," 245.
13. Ryan, "The Memphis Riots of 1866," 245 quoting Gerald M. Capers, *Biography of a River Town, Memphis: Its Heroic Age*, Chapel Hill: University of North Carolina Press, 1939, 183.
14. Ryan, "The Memphis Riots of 1866," 246.
15. Memphis Riots. Majority Report, 6. See also testimony of Ellen and Rachel Dilts, *ibid.*, 63–67, 67–68.
16. *Ibid.*, 38. The Minority Report put the figure at 50.
17. *Ibid.*
18. *Ibid.* The Majority Report used the figure of one policemen and one black soldier killed.
19. Waller, "Community, Class, and Race in the Memphis Riots of 1866," 234.
20. Memphis Riots. Testimony of Major General George Stoneman, 50.
21. *Ibid.*
22. *Ibid.*, 52.
23. *Ibid.*, 50.
24. *Ibid.*
25. *Ibid.*
26. *Ibid.*, 360.
27. *Ibid.*, 358, 359.
28. *Ibid.*, Minority Report. 39.
29. *Ibid.*
30. Ryan, 248.
31. *Memphis Riots*. Testimony of George Stoneman, 52.
32. *Ibid.*, testimony of Lucy Tibbs, 160.
33. *Ibid.*
34. *Ibid.*, Majority Report, 25, testimony of Cynthia Townsend, 162.
35. *Ibid.*, testimony by Attorney General Wallace, 314; testimony by Rev. Ewing O. Taade, 89.
36. *Ibid.*, Majority Report, 24; testimony of Walter Clifford, 250.
37. *Ibid.*, 20, 36.
38. Ryan, "The Memphis Riots of 1866," quoting the *Daily Avalanche*, May 5, 1866.
39. *Ibid.*, 53.
40. *Ibid.*
41. *Ibid.*, 23.
42. *Ibid.*, 55.
43. *Ibid.*, testimony of William Hunter, 74, 75.
44. *Ibid.*, Majority and Minority reports, 1–44; Altina L. Waller argues that one-third of the rioters were employed as policemen and firemen, occupations that made them upwardly mobile. Consequently, they were not concerned about losing their jobs to blacks. Many rioters lived outside of the areas where the disturbances took place. Therefore, the riot was a city-wide conflict, based on hostility to black "occupation" of their neighborhoods (Waller, 234–237).
45. *Ibid.*, Majority Report, 3.
46. *Ibid.*, 41.
47. Riddleberger, Patrick, *1866: The Critical Year Revisited*. Carbondale: Southern Illinois University Press, 1979, 181, quoting the *Chicago Tribune*, May 9, 1866.
48. *Ibid.*, 182, quoting *New York Tribune*, May 23, 1866.
49. The *New York Times*, June 29, 1866.
50. *Ibid.*
51. Sefton, *The United States Army and Reconstruction*, 103.
52. Howard K. Beale, *The Critical Year. A Study of Andrew Johnson and Reconstruction*. New York: Frederick Ungar Publishing Company, 1958, 357.
53. Beale, 344, quoting J.B. Bingham to Andrew Johnson, May 17, 1866.
54. Riddleberger, *1866: The Critical Year Revisited*, 218.
55. Riddleberger, *1866: The Critical Year Revisited*, 220; Beale, *The Critical Year*, 366.
56. GS to GS, Sr., December 27, 1866.
57. *Ibid.*
58. *Ibid.* Stoneman was incorrect. George B. McClellan was a Major General of the regular army in 1861. Darius Couch was promoted to Colonel of the Seventh Mass. In June 1861, also in the regular army. John Gibbon (who graduated from West Point in 1847 but was in Stoneman's class), was a colonel in the Seventh U.S. Infantry at the end of the war.
59. Sefton, *The United States Army and Reconstruc-*

tion, 110–111; Cong. Globe, 39th Cong., 2nd Session, 1037.

60. Sefton, *The United States Army and Reconstruction*, 113.

61. John M. Schofield Papers, "Reconstruction in Virginia," Address at Vanderbilt University. Division of Manuscripts, Library of Congress, Washington, D.C.

62. Richard Lowe, *Republicans and Reconstruction in Virginia*. Charlottesville: University Press of Virginia, 1991, 76.

63. Hamilton James Eckenrode, *The Political History of Virginia During Reconstruction*. Gloucester, Mass: Peter Smith, 1966, 67.

64. Maddex, Jack Pendleton, Jr., *The Virginia Conservatives: A Study in Bourbon Redemption, 1869–1879*. Ph.D. diss., University of North Carolina, 1966, 128–129.

65. Otto H. Olsen, Ed., *Reconstruction and Redemption in the South*. Baton Rouge: Louisiana State University Press, 1980; "Virginia: The Persistence of Centrist Hegemony," Jack P. Maddex, Jr. 120.

66. *Ibid.*, 121.

67. *Ibid.*, 122.

68. William T. Alderson, "The Influence of Military Rule and the Freedmen's Bureau on Reconstruction in Virginia, 1865–1870." Ph.D. diss., Vanderbilt University, 1952, 182–184.

69. *Ibid.*, 203.

70. Lowe, *Republicans and Reconstruction in Virginia*, 144; Alderson, "The Influence of Military Rule and the Freedman's Bureau," 203.

71. Lowe, *Republicans and Reconstruction in Virginia*, 144.

72. John Maynard Schofield, *Forty-Six Years in the Army*. New York: The Century Company, 1897, 402.

73. John Robert Kirkland, "Federal Troops in the South Atlantic States During Reconstruction, 1865–1877." Ph.D. diss., University of North Carolina, 1967, 217, quoting Schofield to Grant, April 18, 1868.

74. *Richmond Enquirer and Examiner*, June 3, 1868.

75. *Richmond Dispatch*, June 2, 1868.

76. Stoneman to Schofield, August 26, 1868, Schofield MSS, Library of Congress.

77. Report of George Stoneman, House Executive Documents, 40th Congress, Third Session, Serial 1367, Oct. 31, 1868.

78. Records of First Military District, Vol. 5, Pt. 1, RG 393, Report from Stoneman to Adjutant General of the Army, March 31, 1869, National Archives; Lowe, 159; Alderson, 228.

79. *Ibid.*, Records of the First Military District.

80. *Ibid.*

81. *Ibid.*; Alderson, "The Influence of Military Rule," 228.

82. On December 8, 1868, Congress had passed a bill that authorized an election on the Underwood Constitution in May 1869. The Senate adjourned for the Christmas recess before the bill was considered. See Eckenrode, *The Political History of Virginia During Reconstruction*, 109.

83. Alderson, "The Influence of Military Rule," 231, quoting General Order 61, June 23, 1868, First Military District.

84. Nelson Morehouse Blake, *William Mahone of Virginia: Soldier and Political Insurgent*. Richmond: Garrett & Massie Publishers, 1935, 118.

85. Eckenrode, *The Political History of Virginia During Reconstruction in Virginia*, 117; Blake, *William Mahone of Virginia*, 100, note 188; Maddex, *The Virginia Conservatives*, 48.

86. Schofield to Stoneman, Oct. 12, 1868, Schofield MSS.

87. Maddex, *The Virginia Conservatives*, 66.

88. Otto H. Olsen, Ed., *Reconstruction and Redemption in the South*, Jack P. Maddex, Jr., "Virginia: The Persistence of Centrist Hegemony," 127.

89. Alexander H.H. Stuart, *A Narrative of the Leading Incidents of the Organization of the First Popular Movement in Virginia in 1865 to Re-establish Peaceful Relations between the Northern and Southern States, and of Subsequent Efforts of the "Committee of Nine" in 1869 to Secure the Restoration of Virginia to the Union*. Richmond: W.E. Jones, 1888, 21.

90. *Ibid.*, 20.

91. *Ibid.*, 20.

92. *Ibid.*, 28.

93. *Ibid.*, 29.

94. Stoneman to Schofield, January 19, 1869, Schofield MSS.

95. *Winchester Journal*, March 26, 1869.

96. *Ibid.*

97. Alderson, "The Influence of Military Rule," 240.

98. Lowe, *Republicans and Reconstruction in Virginia*, 169, quoting *Lexington Gazette*, March 31, 1869.

99. Blake, *William Mahone of Virginia*, 103, note 203; Maddex, *The Virginia Conservatives*, 76.

100. Lowe, *Republicans and Reconstruction in Virginia*, 169, note 15; Alderson, "The Influence of Military Rule," 249.

101. *Richmond Enquirer*, April 2, 1869.

102. Lowe, *Republicans and Reconstruction in Virginia*, 170, 171.

103. Otto H. Olsen, Ed., *Reconstruction and Redemption in the South*, James P. Maddex, Jr., "Virginia: The Persistence of Centrist Hegemony," 129; Maddex, *The Virginia Conservatives*, 83.

104. Blake, *William Mahone of Virginia*, 109.

105. Maddex, *The Virginia Conservatives*, 128–129.

Chapter Twelve

1. Constance Wynn Altshuler, *Chains of Command*. Tucson: Arizona Historical Society, 1981, 166; *Drumbeats*, Vol. 4, No. 4, Drum Barracks Civil War Museum, Oct. 1990, 8.

2. Memorial of the Legislature of Arizona asking Protection from hostile Indians, 42nd Congress, 1st Session, Mis. Doc. No. 16, March 20, 1871.

3. *Ibid.* The Legislature of California later passed a similar resolution calling for "prompt and efficient protection to the people of Arizona against the Apache

Indians" (Joint Resolution of the Legislature of California, 42nd Congress, 2nd Session, Doc. No. 161.)

4. James R. Hastings, "The Tragedy at Camp Grant in 1871," *Arizona and the West*, Vol. 2, 1959, 147–148.

5. *Ibid.*, 148.

6. Altshuler, *Chains of Command*, 183.

7. Martin F. Schmidt, Ed., *General George Crook, His Autobiography*, Norman, Oklahoma: University of Oklahoma Press, 1960, 160.

8. Headquarters Department of Arizona, Prescott, May 3, 1870, General Orders No. 1, Department of Library and Archives, Arizona, No. 56024.

9. *Arizona Daily Citizen*, August 8, 1888, "A Stirring Address by Governor Safford on the Troublesome Times in the Early History of Arizona," Hayden File, Arizona Historical Society, Tucson, hereafter cited as Hayden File.

10. *Ibid.*

11. *Ibid.*

12. Altshuler, *Chains of Command*, quoting Stoneman to AG, May 23, 1870, LR AGO, RG 94.

13. General Order No. 4, Headquarters Department of Arizona, May 31, 1870, Department of Library and Archives, Arizona, No. 56027.

14. *Ibid.*

15. *The Weekly Arizona Miner*, Prescott, July 16, 1870, Hayden File.

16. *Ibid.*

17. *The Weekly Arizona Miner*, July 9, 1870.

18. *Ibid.*, July 23, 1870,

19. *Ibid.*

20. *Arizona Daily Citizen*, Tucson, August 8, 1888, Address by Governor Safford, Hayden File.

21. Jay J. Wagoner, *Arizona Territory, 1863–1912*. Tucson: The University of Arizona Press, 1970, 124, 125.

22. General Order No. 5, Headquarters Department of Arizona, June 6, 1870, Department of Library and Archives Arizona, No. 56028.

23. *Arizona Daily Citizen*, August 8, 1888, Address by Gov. Safford; Altshuler, *Chains of Command*, 186,187.

24. J.H. Marion, *Notes of Travel Through the Territory of Arizona*, Ed. Donald M. Powell (Tucson: The University of Arizona Press, 1965), 6.

25. *Ibid.*, 14.

26. Later named Fort Apache and eventually renamed Camp Thomas.

27. J.H. Marion, *Notes of Travel*, 19.

28. *Ibid.*, 25.

29. *Ibid.*, 27.

30. *Ibid.*, 28.

31. *Ibid.*, 38.

32. *Ibid.*, 40–41.

33. Marion called the river the Arivipa.

34. Constance Wynn Altshuler, in her detailed work *Chains of Command. Arizona and the Army 1856–1875*, notes (see p. 187) that Stoneman reported that he finished his inspection on October 9, while Marion gave the date of October 5. There seems to be no explanation for this discrepancy.

35. *Drumbeats*, Drum Barracks, Civil War Museum, Wilmington, Calif. Vol. 4, No. 4, Oct, 1990, 9.

36. General Order No. 1, Headquarters Department of Arizona, January 12, 1871, Department of Library and Archives, Arizona, no. 56043.

37. *Drumbeats*, Vol. 4, No. 4, October 1990, 9.

38. Altshuler, *Chains of Command*, 189, citing Stoneman to Sherman, February 22, 1871.

39. *Ibid.*

40. Hastings, *The Tragedy at Camp Grant*, 149; Dan L. Thrapp, *The Conquest of Apacheria*. Norman, Oklahoma: University of Oklahoma Press, 1967, 80.

41. Hastings, *The Tragedy at Camp Grant*, 149.

42. *Ibid.*, 150, 151.

43. Thrapp, *The Conquest of Apacheria*, 83, 84.

44. *Ibid.*, 84.

45. Hastings, *The Tragedy at Camp Grant*, note 150.

46. Altshuler, *Chains of Command*, 191.

47. Altshuler, *Chains of Command*, 191, citing Thomas Edison Farish, *History of Arizona*. Phoenix: T.E. Farish, 1915, Vol. 2, 269.

48. *Ibid.*, note 33, 191.

49. *Ibid.*, 193, citing Sherman to Schofield, February 2, 1871, 298–1871, LRAGO, R.G. 94, National Archives.

50. *Arizona Citizen*, Tucson, April 1, 1871, Report of Visiting Committee Appointed by the Citizens, Hayden File.

51. *Ibid.*

52. *Ibid.*

53. *Arizona Citizen*, Tucson, "General Stoneman's Report," January 28, 1871.

54. *Ibid.*

55. *Ibid.*

56. Thrapp, *The Conquest of Apacheria*, 86, citing Frank C. Lockwood, *The Apache Indians*. New York: The Macmillan Company, 1938, 176–178.

57. *Arizona Citizen*, Tucson, "General Stoneman's Report," January 28, 1871.

58. *Ibid.*

59. *Ibid.*

60. *Arizona Citizen*, April 15, 1871.

61. *Ibid.*

62. Hastings, *The Tragedy at Camp Grant*, 152.

63. *Ibid.*, 153; Thrapp, *The Conquest of Apacheria*, 89.

64. Hastings, *The Tragedy at Camp Grant*, 153, citing Oury's account, *Arizona Historical Review*, Vol. 6 (1935) 15, 20.

65. *Ibid.*, 154, note 30; Thrapp gives a total of 144, p. 89.

66. Altshuler, *Chains of Command*, 195; Thrapp, *The Conquest of Apacheria*, citing Oury's account, *Arizona Star*, Tucson, June 29, 1879.

67. *The Arizona Miner*, Prescott, May 27, 1871.

68. *Arizona Daily Citizen*, "Address by Governor Safford," May 8, 1888, Hayden File.

69. *Ibid.*

70. *Ibid.*

71. Altshuler, *Chains of Command*, 196, citing Safford to Sec. War Belknap, April 9, 1871, Arizona Archives.

72. *Arizona Daily Citizen*, Tucson, address by Governor Safford, August 8, 1888.
73. *Ibid.*
74. Charles D. Wilson, "George Stoneman: General and Governor. A Biography," master's thesis, San Jose State College, June 1967, citing "Annual Report of the Commander of the Department of Arizona, 1871."
75. Schmitt, *General George Crook*, 162.

Chapter Thirteen

1. Special Order 317, War Department, Adjutant General's Office, August 16, 1871, Service Record of George Stoneman.
2. Special Order No. 322, War Department, Adjutant General's Office, August 19, 1871, Service Record of George Stoneman.
3. *Ibid.*
4. Proceedings of a Board to Retire Disabled Officers, Case of Col. George Stoneman, 21st Infantry, Letter to the Secretary of War, November 2, 1871, Service Record of George Stoneman.
5. *Ibid.*
6. *Ibid.*
7. Charles D. Wilson, "George Stoneman, General and Governor: A Biography," master's thesis, San Jose State College, June 1967, 33, 34.
8. Stoneman to President Garfield, January 23, 1881, Service Record of George Stoneman.
9. *Ibid.*
10. *Ibid.*
11. Attorney General Devens to President Garfield, January 28, 1881, Service Record of George Stoneman.
12. Midge Sherwood, *Days of Vintage, Years of Vision*, Vol. 1. San Marino, California: Orizaba Publications, 1982, 225.
13. *Ibid.*
14. Stoneman misjudged his son. George J. Stoneman attended the University of Michigan and practiced in Seattle, then moved to Honolulu and practiced there. He was elected District Attorney in Globe, Arizona, in 1900 and was a Territorial Railway Commissioner and became a leading attorney in Phoenix and president of the Arizona Bar Association. See *Who's Who in Arizona*, Volume 1, 1913, compiled and published by *Daily Star*, Tucson, Arizona.
15. GS to GS, Sr., May 15, 1872.
16. The deed was registered in January 1872. See Sherwood, 225.
17. Elliot Arnold, *The Camp Grant Massacre*, New York: Simon and Schuster, 1976, has a fictional account of Stoneman running his department from Los Robles, Part Two, 211. H. Brett Melendy and Benjamin F. Gilbert make the same error in their otherwise excellent account of Stoneman in *The Governors of California*, Georgetown, California: The Talisman Press, 1965,, 206.
18. GS to GS, Sr., May 15, 1872.
19. *Ibid.*
20. *Ibid.*
21. *Ibid.*

22. Sherwood, 227, quoting James de Barth Shorb to Maria de Jesus Shorb, February 16, 1872, Wilson Collection, The Huntington Library, San Marino, Calif..
23. Sherwood, 227, 228.
24. *Ibid.*, 473.
25. Newspaper article, "General Stoneman's Home," 1887, name of newspaper and writer unknown.
26. GS to GS, Sr., May 15, 1872. Stoneman was quoting the Old Testament in part, the First Book of Kings, 4:25. "And Judah and Israel dwelt in safety from Dan even to Beer-shebah, every man under his vine and under his fig tree, all the days of Solomon." *The Holy Bible*, Revised Standard Version. The World Publishing Company, Cleveland and New York, 1962, 301.
27. *Ibid.*
28. Virginia Hardisty Stoneman, "George Stoneman, 1822–1894. A Paper on His Life," Submitted to the Los Angeles Historical Society, August 24, 1929.
29. *Ibid.*
30. Captain John C. Fremont, leading a group of Bear Flag insurgents, did not initially recognize the authority of General Stephen Watts Kearny when Kearny's dragoons, including Stoneman, arrived in 1846 to liberate California from Mexico.
31. *Ibid.*
32. *History and Reminiscences, Los Angeles City and County California*, compiled by William A. Spalding, Vol. I. Los Angeles: J.R. Finnell and Sons Publishing Company, 1931, 208, 223, 224, 245.
33. Wilson, "George Stoneman: General and Governor," chapter 4, 39, quoting Robert Glass Cleland, *The Cattle on a Thousand Hills*. The Huntington Library, San Marino, Calif., 1951, 225.
34. Wilson, "George Stoneman: General and Governor," 41.
35. Wilson, 43, quoting the California Transportation Commission, "Report of the Board of Commissioners," Appendix to the Journals of the Senate and Assembly, 22nd Session, 1878.
36. *Ibid.*, 45.
37. *The Governors of California: Peter H. Burnett to Edmund G. Brown*. Georgetown, Calif.: Talisman, Press, 1965, 207; Wilson, 46, note 24.
38. Wilson, "George Stoneman: General and Governor," 50.
39. *Ibid.*, 53.
40. *History and Reminiscences Los Angeles City and Country California*, 182.
41. Colonel James J. Ayers, *Gold and Sunshine: Reminiscences of Early California*, Boston, Massachusetts: R.G. Badger, 1922, 329. Ayers was named state printer by Stoneman after his election as governor. Ayers was responsible for a law requiring the State Printing Office to print textbooks for schools, eliminating exorbitant prices set by private publishers.
42. Wilson, "George Stoneman: General and Governor...," 54, 55; *The Governors of California. Peter H. Burnett to Edmund G. Brown*, 207.
43. *The Weekly Mirror*, 1 July 1882.
44. *Ibid.*
45. *Ibid.*

46. Diary of Mary Oliver Hardisty Stoneman, August 16, 1882. Available through the courtesy of Dr. George B. Stoneman, M.D., great-grandson of General Stoneman. Hereafter referred to as Diaries of MOHS.
47. *The Governors of California,* 207.
48. *Ibid.*
49. Diary of MOHS, October 31, 1882.
50. *Ibid.*, August 18, 1882.
51. *Ibid.*, November 7, 1882.
52. *The Governors of California...*, 207, 208.
53. *Ibid.*, November 8, 1882.
54. *Ibid.*, November 9, 1882.
55. Major General Schofield to the Secretary of War, Service Record of George Stoneman.
56. Diary of MOHS, January 8, 1883.
57. Diary of MOHS, January 16, 1883 and August 18, 1882.
58. *Ibid.*, November 27, 1882.
59. Wilson, "George Stoneman: General and Governor," quoting the *Sacramento Daily Union,* January 11, 1883, 2.
60. *The Governors of California,* 210.
61. *Ibid.*, 213.
62. Newspaper clipping found in the diary of MOHS. Name of newspaper and date was not given.
63. *Ibid.*
64. Wilson, quoting a letter from Stephen M. White to W.W. Moreland, July 18, 1885, White Papers–Correspondence Out, IV, 133.
65. Diary of MOHS, July 18, 1885.
66. *Ibid.*, July 29.
67. Virginia Hardisty Stoneman, *George Stoneman, 1822–1894.*
68. Proclamation, State of California, Executive Department, Sacramento, July 16, 1886, California State Library.
69. *The Governors of California,* 213.
70. Wilson, *George Stoneman: General and Governor...,* 89.
71. George Stoneman to his wife, November 13, 1886, courtesy of Dr. George B. Stoneman.
72. *The Governors of California,* 214.
73. *Ibid.*
74. *Ibid.*, 215.
75. Memorial of George Stoneman to the 51st Congress, April 8, 1890. Service Record of George Stoneman.
76. John M. Schofield to the secretary of war, January 28, 1891, Service Record of George Stoneman.
77. Mary Oliver Hardisty Stoneman to President Benjamin Harrison, unknown date, 1890, Service Record of George Stoneman.
78. *Ibid.*
79. Service Record of George Stoneman.
80. Sherwood, Vol. 1, 318.
81. *Los Angeles Times,* Sunday, December 11, 1892, "The Courts," 14.
82. *Ibid.*
83. Wilson, *George Stoneman: General and Governor,* 93.
84. Colonel James J. Ayers, *Gold and Sunshine,* 329.

Epilogue

1. The Department of Health of the City of Buffalo, Certificate of Death of George Stoneman, September 5, 1894.
2. Information provided by Dr. George B. Stoneman.

Bibliography

Manuscript Sources

Chauker, James M. "Opportunity Lost: William B. Franklin and the Battle of Fredericksburg." M.A. thesis, James Madison University, May 1990.

Diary of Mary Oliver Hardisty Stoneman, private collection of Dr. George B. Stoneman.

Entwistle, Herbert O. "A History of New Berlin: New York to 1907." M.A. thesis, Colgate University, 1953.

General Order No. 1, Headquarters, Department of Arizona, January 12, 1871, Department of Library and Archives, Arizona, No. 56043.

General Order No. 4, May 31, 1870, No. 56027

General Order No. 5, June 6, 1870, No. 56028.

"Journal of the March of the Mormon Battalion under the Command of Col. P. St. George Cooke from Santa Fe New Mexico to San Diego, California." U.S. Government Document, special session, 30th Congress, Senate Document No. 2, Washington, D.C., 1849, October 19.

Kent, William B. *A History of Saltville*, June 1955, available at the Saltville, Va., Library.

Memorial of the Legislature of Arizona asking Protection from hostile Indians, 42nd Congress, 1st Session, Mis. Doc. No. 16, March 20, 1871.

Meroney Folder, McCubbins, J.S. Papers, Ms. 9001, Rowan Public Library, Salisbury, N.C.

National Archives, Washington, D.C., Proceedings of a Board to Retire Disabled Officers, case of Col. George Stoneman, 21st Infantry. "Service Record of George Stoneman."

Peake, Lucy Darrow. *History of the Town of Busti*. Chautauqua, N.Y.: Chautauqua County Historical Society. File 158.001

Pierce, John Edward. "General Hugh Judson Kilpatrick in the American Civil War: A New Appraisal." Ph.D. diss., Pennsylvania State University, 1983.

Report of Brigadier General F.J. Hooker, III Army Corps Headquarters, May 10, 1862, courtesy of the Williamsburg Foundation, Williamsburg, Virginia

Schofield, Gen. John M. "Reconstruction in Virginia." Library of Congress, Washington D.C.

Special Order 317, War Department, Adjutant General's Office, August 16, 1871, Service Record of George Stoneman.

Special Order No. 322, August 19, 1871.

Thiele, Thomas F. "The Evolution of Cavalry in the American Civil War." Ph.D. diss., University of Michigan, 1951.

Wilson, Charles D. "George Stoneman: General and Governor. A Biography." M.A. thesis, San Jose State College, 1967.

Yurtinus, John F. "A Ram in the Thicket: The Mormon Battalion in the Mexican War," Vol. 1, Ph.D. diss., Brigham Young University 1975.

Primary Sources

Adams, Charles Francis. *A Cycle of Adams Letters, 1861–1865*. Pt. 2. Ed. Worthington Chauncey Ford. Boston and New York: Houghton Mifflin Company, 1920.

Arizona Daily Citizen, Tucson, "General Stoneman's Report," January 28, 1871.

_____, "Report of Visiting Committee Appointed by the Civilians," April 1, 1871.

_____, "Address by Governor Stafford," May 8, 1888.

_____, "Address by Governor Stafford," August 8, 1888.

Averell, William W. "With the Cavalry in the Peninsula." In *Battles and Leaders in the Civil War*, Vol. 2. Eds. Clarence Clough Buel and Robert Underwood Johnson. Secaucus, New Jersey: Castle.

Ayers, Col. James J. *Gold and Sunshine: Reminiscences of Early California.* Boston: R.G. Badger, 1922.

The Baltimore Sun. November 22, 1861. Account of the wedding of George Stoneman and Mary Oliver Hardisty.

Bigler, Henry W. *Bigler's Chronicle of the West: The Conquest of California, Discovery of Gold, and the Mormon Settlement as Reflected in Henry William Bigler's Diaries.* Ed. Edwin G. Gudde. Berkeley: University of California Press, 1962.

Busby, Howard A. "With Gillem's Tennesseans on the Yadkin," in *History of the Fifteenth Pennsylvania Cavalry.* Philadelphia: Historical Committee of the Society of the Fifteenth Pennsylvania Cavalry, 1906.

Bushong, William, Co. C. *The Last Great Stoneman Raid.* Delivered at the Regimental Reunion, Bellefontaine, Ohio, 1916.

Butler, Col. Thomas H. "The Stoneman Raid and Why It Was A Failure." Report of Reunion of the Fifth Indiana Cavalry, held at Indianapolis, Indiana, Oct. 10 and 11, 1883. Indianapolis: Hasselman Journal Co. Printers, 1887.

Cadets Arranged in Order of Merit in Their Respective Classes, as Determined at the General Examination in June 1846. USMA Archives.

Carolina Watchman, Report on the Stoneman Raid, Salisbury, N.C., April 16, 1866.

Chaney, Newel. *History of the Ninth Regiment, New York Volunteer Cavalry. War of 1861–1865.* New York, N.Y.: Martin Mertz and Son, 1901.

Couch, Darius. *Twenty-Sixth Annual Reunion of the Association of Graduates of the United States Military Academy at West Point, New York.* Saginaw, Mich. Seenan and Peters, 1895.

Cox, Maj. Gen. Jacob. "McClellan in West Virginia." In *Battles and Leaders of the Civil War,* Vol. 1.

Crook, General George. *His Autobiography.* Ed. Martin F. Schmidt. Norman, OK: University of Oklahoma Press, 1960.

Cullum, Brevet Major General George W. *Biographical Register of the Officers and Graduates of the U.S. Military Academy at West Point, New York,* Vol. 2. Boston and New York: Houghton and Mifflin Company, 1891.

Dallas Herald, "From the Rio Grand," April 4, 1860.

Darrow, Caroline Baldwin. "Recollections of the Twigg's Surrender." In *Battles and Leaders of the Civil War,* Vol. 1.

Denison, Rev. Frederick. *Sabers and Spurs. The First Regimental Rhode Island Cavalry in the Civil War, 1861–1865.* Central Falls, R.I.: E.L. Freeman and Company, 1876.

Douglas, Henry Kyd. *I Rode with Stonewall.* Greenwich, Conn.: Fawcett Publications, Inc., 1961.

Glazier, Willard. *Three Years in the Federal Cavalry.* New York, N.Y.: R.H. Ferguson, 1873.

Gracey, Rev. S.L. *Annals of the Sixth Pennyslvania Cavalry.* New York, Philadelphia: E.H. Butler and Sons, 1868.

Grant, Gen. Ulysses S. *The Personal Memoirs of U.S. Grant.* Vol. 2. New York: Konecky and Konecky.

Hollingsworth, Lieutenant John McHenry. "The Journal of Lieutenant John McHenry Hollingsworth, of the First New York Volunteers. September 1846–1849." San Francisco California Historical Society, 1923–1929.

Hooker, Brigadier General Joseph. Report of Brigadier General F.J. Hooker, III Army Corps Headquarters, May 10, 1862.

Howard, General Oliver O. *Autobiography of Oliver Otis Howard.* New York: The Baker and Taylor Company, 1907.

Hyde, John. *Historical Sketches of Old New Berlin.* Unadilla, N.Y.: Unadilla Valley Historical Society, Vol. 1, 1876. Reprint 1907.

Irwin, Lt. Col. Richard B. Assistant Adjutant General, "Washington Under Banks." In *Battles and Leaders of the Civil War.* Vol. 2.

Lee, Elizabeth Blair. *The Civil War Letters of Elizabeth Blair Lee.* Ed. Virginia Jean Lass. Urbana and Chicago: University of Illinois Press.

Lee, General Robert E. *The Wartime Papers of R.E. Lee.* Ed. Clifford Downey. Boston, Toronto: 1961.

Lincoln, Abraham. *Speeches and Writings: 1859–1865.* Ed. Don E. Fahrenbacher. New York: Literary Classics of the United States, 1989.

Los Angeles Times, "An Ugly Scandal. The Brunson-Stoneman Affair to be Aired in Court," December 11, 1892.

Marion, J. H. *Notes of Travel Through the Territory of Arizona.* Ed. Donald M. Powell. Tucson: The University of Arizona Press, 1970.

Mason, F.H. *The Twelfth Ohio Cavalry in the War of the Rebellion.* Cleveland: Nevins' Stream Printing House, 1871.

McClellan, George B. *The Civil War Papers of George B. McClellan. Selected Correspondence. 1860–1865.* Ed. Steven W. Sears. New York: Ticknor & Fields, 1989.

_____. "The Peninsula Campaign." In *Battles and Leaders of the Civil War.* Vol. 2.

McClellan, H.B. *I Rode with Jeb Stuart. The Life and Campaigns of Major General J.E.B. Stuart.* Bloomington, Indiana: Indiana University Press, 1958.

Memorial of the Legislature of Arizona asking Protection from the Indians. March 20, 1871.

Memorial of George Stoneman to the 51st Congress, April 8, 1890.

Merrill, Samuel. *Campaigns of the First Maine and First District of Columbia Cavalry.* Portland, Oregon: Bailey and Noyes, 1866.

National Archives. Second Cavalry Records. Military History of Officers, 1860.

Official Records of the Union and Confederate Armies.

Official Register, Officers and Cadets of the U.S. Military Academy. 1843–46. USMA Archives.

Parker, Lt. John J. *History of the Twenty-Second Massachusetts and the Third Light Battery in the War of the Rebellion.* Rand and Avery Company Press. Published by the Regimental Association, 1887.

Polk, President James K. *The Diary of James J. Polk, 1845–1849.* Vol. 1, Ed. Milo Milton Quaife. Chicago: A.C. McClurg and Company, 1919.

Price, George F. *Across the Continent with the Fifth Cavalry.* New York: Antiquarian Press, 1959.

Proclamation, State of California, Executive Department. July 16, 1886.

Report of the Joint Committee on the Conduct of the War. Washington: Government Printing Office, Vol. 1.

Richmond Daily Dispatch, May 5 and 6, 1863.

Sanford, W.L. *History of the Fourteenth Illinois Cavalry.* Chicago: R.R. Donnelley & Sons, 1898.

Schofield, John Maynard. *Forty-Six Years in the Army.* New York: The Century Company, 1897.

Sherman, General William Tecumseh. *Memoirs of General W.T. Sherman.* Vol. 2. New York: Charles L. Webster and Co., 1892.

Smith, William F. "Franklin's Grand Division." In *Battles and Leaders of the Civil War*, Vol. 3.

Spencer, Cornelia Phillips. *The Last Ninety Days of the War in North Carolina, 1866.* Reprint. Washington, N.C.: Broadfoot Publishing Company, 1993.

Stoneman, Gen. George. Records of the First Military District of Virginia. Report of Stoneman to the Adjutant General of the Army, Vol. 5, Pt. 1, National Archives, RG 393, March 31, 1869.

Stoneman, Virginia Hardisty. "George Stoneman, 1822–1894, A Paper on His Life." Submitted to the Los Angeles Historical Society, August 24, 1929.

Tarrant, Sergeant E. *The Wild Riders of the First Kentucky Cavalry.* Louisville, Kentucky: A Committee of the Regiment, 1894.

Thomas, Col. Hamton S. *Some Personal Reminiscences of Service in the Cavalry of the Army of the Potomac.* Philadelphia: L.R. Hamersly and Co., 1889.

Townsand, George Alfred. *Rustics in Rebellion: A Yankee Reporter on the Road to Richmond.* Chapel Hill: The University of North Carolina Press, 1950.

U.S. War Department. "Service Record of George Stoneman." Adjutant General's Records, 3414. National Archives, Appointment Commission and Personnel Branch, 1871.

Wainwright, Charles. *The Personal Journals of Colonel Charles S. Wainwright, 1861–1865.* Ed. Allen Nevins. New York: Harcourt Brace and World, 1862.

Watkins, Sam R. *Co. Aytch Maury Grays, First Tennessee Regiment, or, A Side Show of the Big Show.* Reprint. Jackson, Tenn.: McCowat-Mercer Press, 1952.

Weand, H.K. "Our Last Campaign and Pursuit of Jeff Davis." In *History of the Fifteenth Pennsylvania Cavalry, 1862–1865.* Ed. Charles R. Kirk. Philadelphia: Historical Committee of the Society of the Fifteenth Pennsylvania Cavalry, 1906.

Weekly Arizona Miner, July 16, 1870.

_____, July 23, 1870.

_____, May 27, 1871.

White, C.M. "The Prison Life." Believed to have been published in the "National Tribune." Date unknown.

Winchester Journal, "General Stoneman," March 26, 1869.

Secondary Works

Alderson, William T. "The Influence of Military Rule and the Freedmen's Bureau on Reconstruction in Virginia, 1865–1870." Ph.D. diss., Vanderbilt University, 1952.

Alexander, Thomas B. *Political Reconstruction in Tennessee.* New York: Russell and Russell, 1950.

Altshuler, Constance Wynn. *Chains of Command.* Tucson: Arizona Historical Society, 1861.

Battles and Leaders of the Civil War. 4 vols. Edited by Robert U. Johnson and Clarence C. Buell. Reprint. 1887–1888. New York: Castle, 1956.

Barrett, John G. *The Civil War in North Carolina.* Chapel Hill, NC: The University of North Carolina Press, 1963.

Beale, Howard K. *The Critical Year: A Study of Andrew Johnson and Reconstruction.* New York: Frederick Ungar and Publishing Co., 1958.

Bigelow, John, Jr. *The Campaign of Chancellorsville: A Strategic and Tactical Study.* New Haven: Yale University Press, 1910.

Blackwell, Mack J. *The Preston Salt Works: a Vital Link to Southwest Virginia's Industrial Beginning.* Abington, VA, 1992. Published privately by the author.

Blake, Nelson Morehouse. *William Mahone of Virginia: Soldier and Political Insurgent.* Richmond: Garrett & Massie Publishers, 1935.

Boatner, Mark M. *The Civil War Dictionary.* New York: Random House, Inc, 1988.

Boies, Henry L. *History of Dekalb County Illinois.* Chicago: O.P. Bassett, Printer, 1868.

Bowles, Richard Jr. "Shannon Hill Encounter." Goochland County (Va.) Historical Magazine, Vol. 17. 1985.

Brawley, James. The Rowan Story: 1753–1953. *A Narrative History of Rowan County, North Carolina.* Salisbury, N.C.: Rowan Printing Company, 1953.

Catton, Bruce. *The Coming Fury.* Vol. 1. Garden City, N.Y.: Doubleday and Company, Inc., 1961.

Clarke, Dwight L. *Stephen Watts Kearny: Soldier of*

the West. Norman, Okla.: University of Oklahoma Press, 1961.

Coddington, Edwin B. *The Gettysburg Campaign: A Study in Command.* New York: Charles Scribner's Sons, 1984.

Cullen, Joseph P. "The Battle of Chancellorsville." *Civil War Times Illustrated,* 1968. Reissued by Eastern Acorn Press, 1981.

Davis, William C. "The Massacre at Saltville." *Civil War Times Illustrated,* February 1971.

Devoto, Bernard. *The Year of Decision: 1846.* Boston: Little Brown and Company, 1943.

Doty, William J., Ed. *The Historical Annals of Southwestern New York.* New York: Lewis Historical Publishing Co., 1940.

Downs, John P., and Fenwick Y. Hedley, eds. *History of Chautauqua County and its People.* Vol. 1. Boston, New York, Chicago: American Historical Society, Inc., 1921.

Drumbeats. Drum Barracks Civil War Museum, Wilmington, Calif. Vol. 4, number 4, October, 1990.

Eckenrode, Hamilton James. *The Political History of Virginia During Reconstruction.* Gloucester, Mass.: Peter Smith, 1966.

Evans, David. *Sherman's Horsemen: Union Cavalry Operations in the Atlanta Campaign.* Bloomington: University of Indiana Press, 1996.

Foner, Eric. *Reconstruction: America's Unfinished Revolution, 1863–1877.* New York: Harper and Row, 1988.

Foote, Shelby. *The Civil War: A Narrative, Vol. 1: From Fort Sumter to Perryville.* New York: Random House, 1958.

Freeman, Douglas Southall. *R.E. Lee: A Biography.* Vol. 1. New York: Charles Scribner's Sons, 1934.

_____. *Lee's Lieutenants: A Study in Command, Vol. 2: Cedar Mountain to Chancellorsville.* New York: Charles Scribner's Sons, 1944.

Gates, Susan Young. *The Life Story of Brigham Young.* New York: The Macmillan Co., 1930.

Goetzman, William H. *Army Exploration in the American West.* New Haven: Yale University Press, 1959.

Greene, Wilson A. "Stoneman's Raid." In *The Battle and Its Aftermath.* Ed. Gary W. Gallagher. Chapel Hill: The University of North Carolina Press, 1996.

Hall, Clarke B. "The Battle of Brandy Station." *Civil War Times Illustrated.* June, 1990.

The Handbook of Texas. Vol. 2. Ed. Walter Prescott Nebb. Austin: The Texas State Historical Association, 1952.

Harris, Malcolm H. *History of Louisa County.* Richmond: The Dietz Press, 1936.

Hartley, Chris J. *To Restore the Old Flag.* Wilkesboro, N.C.: Old Wilkes, Inc., 1990.

Hastings, James R. "The Tragedy at Camp Grant in 1871." In *Arizona and the West.* Vol. 1, No. 2, 1959.

Hebert, Walter H. *Fighting Joe Hooker.* Indianapolis: The Bobs-Merrill Company, 1944.

Kegley, Mary B. "The Battle of Wytheville." In *Wythe County, Virginia. A Bicentennial History.* Marceline, Mo.: Wallsworth Publishing, Inc., 1989.

Kent, William B. *A History of Saltville.* Saltville, Va., 1955. Available at the Saltville Library.

Kirkland, John Robert. "Federal Troops in the South Atlantic States During Reconstruction. 1865–1877." Ph.D. diss., University of North Carolina, 1967.

Lowe, Richard. *Republicans and Reconstruction in Virginia.* Charlottesville: University of Virginia Press, 1991.

Melendy, H. Brett, and Benjamin F Gilbert. *The Governors of California. Peter H. Burnett to Edmund G. Brown.* Georgetown, Calif.: Talisman Press, 1965.

Memphis Riots and Massacres. Mass Violence in America Series, *New York Times,* 1969 and Arno Press. facsimile House Report No. 101, U.S. Congress, 1st Session, July 25, 1866.

Mohan, Hugh J., E.H. Clough, and John C. Cosgraves. *Pen Pictures of Our Representative Men.* Sacramento: H.A. Weaver's Valley Press Printing House, 1880.

O'Neill, Robert F. *The Cavalry Battles of Aldie, Middleburg, and Upperville.* Lynchburg, Va.: H.E. Howard, Inc., 1993.

Rister, Carl Coke. *Robert E. Lee in Texas.* Norman: University of Oklahoma Press, 1946.

Robertson, Jr., James C. *General A.P. Hill. The Story of a Confederate Warrior.* New York: Random House, Inc., 1987.

Ryan, James Gilbert. "The Memphis Riots of 1866: Terror in a Black Community." *Journal of Negro History,* Vol. 62, 1977.

Sandburg, Carl. *Abraham Lincoln: The War Years.* Vol. 2. New York: Harcourt Brace, and Company, 1939.

Sears, Stephen W. *George B. McClellan: The Young Napoleon.* New York: Ticknor & Fields, 1988.

Sefton, James. *The United States Army and Reconstruction. 1865–1877.* Baton Rouge: Louisiana State University Press, 1967.

Sherwood, Midge. *Days of Vintage. Years of Vision.* Vol. 1. San Marino, Calif.: Orizaba Publications, 1982.

Snedeker, Lenora, A. "Civil War Veteran Makes His Mark." The *Evening Sun,* Norwich N.Y., August 9, 1989.

Spalding, William A. *History and Reminiscences: Los Angeles City and County, California.* Vol. 1. Los Angeles: J.R. Finnell and Sons Publishing Company, 1931.

Stackpole, Edward J. *The Fredericksburg Campaign.* Harrisburg, Pa.: Military Service Printing Company, 1957.

Starr, Stephen Z. *The Union Cavalry in the Civil War. From Fort Sumter to Gettysburg, 1861–1863.* Vol. 1. Baton Rouge, La.: Louisiana State University Press, 1979.

Stegnel, William. *The Gathering of Zion. The Story of the Mormon Trail.* New York: McGraw Hill and Company, 1964.

Thomas, Benjamin and Harold M Hyman. *Stanton: The Life and Times of Lincoln's Secretary of War.* New York: Alfred A. Knopf, 1962.

Thomas, Emory W. *Bold Dragoon: The Life of J.E.B. Stuart.* New York: Harper and Roe, 1986.

Thrapp, Daniel L. *The Conquest of Appacheria.* Norman, Okla.: University of Oklahoma Press, 1979.

Utley, Robert M. *Frontiersmen in Blue.* Lincoln, Nebr.: University of Nebraska Press, 1967.

Van Noppen, Ina Woestemeyer. *Stoneman's Last Raid.* Raleigh, N.C.: North Carolina State College Print Shop, 1961.

Wagoner, Jay J. *Arizona Territory.* Tucson: The University of Arizona Press, 1970.

Waller, Altina L. "Community, Class, and Race in the Memphis Riots of 1866." In *Journal of Social History*, Vol. 18.

Werner, M.R. *Brigham Young.* New York: Harcourt Brace and Company, 1925.

Whan, Vorin E., Jr. *Fiasco at Fredericksburg.* State College, Pa.: The Pennsylvania State University Press, 1961.

Wheeler, Richard. *Sword Over Richmond.* New York: Harper and Row, 1986.

Wilber, Floyd A. "Early Glimpses of the New Berlin Area" and other articles. New Berlin, N.Y.: New Berlin Center of History, Revised Ed., 1964.

Young, Andrew W. *History of Chautauqua County.* Buffalo, N.Y.: Printing House of Matthews and Warren, 1875.

Letters

George Stoneman, Jr., to the Hon. John C. Spencer, Secretary of War, July 26, 1841, United States Military Academy Archives, Special Collections Division.

Samuel A. Brown, George W. Parker, Silus Tiffany, Ossell Cook, and others, Citizens of Jamestown, New York to the Hon. John C. Spencer, Secretary of War, November 13, 1841, USMA Archives, Special Collections Division.

E.A. Dickinson, Headmaster, Jamestown Academy, to the Hon. John C. Spencer, Nov. 17, 1841, USMA Archives, Special Collections Division.

Dr. L. Hazeltine to the Hon. John C. Spencer, Secretary of War, Nov. 17, 1841. USMA Archives. Special Collections Division.

Schofield, Washington, D.C., to Stoneman, Oct. 12, 1868, Schofield Papers, Division of Manuscripts, Library of Congress, Washington D.C.

Stoneman, George, Cadet, USMA, to John Griffith, Oct. 29, 1842, Courtesy of Norman Carlson, Town of Busti Historian, Busti, New York.

Stoneman, Cavalry Camp on the Rio Grande, to Capt. James Cullen, Sept. 28, 1860, USMA Archives, Special Collections Division.

Stoneman to General George McCullum, Supt. Military Academy, West Point. Titled "Etat de Service" (Record of Service). July 5, 1866. Special Collections Division, United States Military Academy Library.

Stoneman to J. Couts, June, 1, 1856, Stoneman Papers, The Huntington Library, San Marino, Calif.

Stoneman to J. Couts, Aug, 27, 1863, Stoneman Papers, The Huntington Library, San Marino, Calif.

Letters of George Stoneman, Jr., to George Stoneman, Sr., courtesy of Mrs. Francis Pickin Florio, descendant of George Stoneman, Jr.'s brother, Byron Stoneman. Letters written from: Knoxville, Tenn., June 14, 1865; Petersburg, Va., December, 27, 1866; San Pasqualito near Los Angeles, CA., May 15, 1872; San Gabriel, CA., Christmas, December 20,1874; Sacramento City, CA., June 1, 1876.

Stoneman to General John Schofield, Aug. 26, 1868, Schofield Papers, Division of Manuscripts, Library of Congress, Washington D.C.

Stoneman to Schofield, October 12, 1868, Schofield Papers. Division of Manuscripts, Library of Congress, Washington D.C.

Stoneman to Schofield, Jan. 19, 1869, Schofield Papers, Division of Manuscripts, Library of Congress, Washington D.C.

Stoneman to President James Garfield, Jan. 23, 1881, Service Record of George Stoneman, National Archives, Washington, D.C.

Attorney General Devens to President Garfield, January 28, 1881, Service Record of George Stoneman, National Archives, Washington D.C.

Mary Oliver Hardisty Stoneman to President Benjamin Harrison (no date available). Service Record of George Stoneman, National Archives, Washington D.C.

Index

Adams, Charles Francis, Jr. 80, 91, 92, 97
Adams, Col. Silas 88, 91, 92, 96, 97
Aldie, Virginia, Battle of 83
Aldrich, Catherine Chaney (GS's mother) 9
Alexandria, Virginia 35
Allen, Capt. James 17
Andersonville Prison 89, 90, 96, 99
Apaches 21, 143, 146, 147, 148
Arizona Citizen 151, 152
Army of the Potomac, V Corps, U.S. 6
Asheville, North Carolina 117, 119
Averell, Brig. Gen. William W. 39, 62, 63, 69, 70
Ayers, Col. James T. 162

Banks, Maj. Gen. Nathaniel P. 43
Barksdale, Brig. Gen. William 57
"Battle of the Bulls," Mormon Battalion 22
Bayard, Brig. Gen. George 56
Bell, Sec. of War, Abe 11
Bentley Cemetery, Lakewood, New York 171
Benton, Senator Thomas Hart 18
Beverly, West Virginia 36
Biddle, Col. James 88
Bigler, Henry 19
Birney, Maj. Gen. David E. 58, 59, 61
Black Codes 123
Brandy Station, Battle of 81, 82
Bronson, Judge A.E. 169
Brown, Joseph F. 93
Buford, Brig. Gen. John E. 63, 77
Burbridge, Gen. Steven E. 101, 102
Burnside, Gen. Ambrose E. 5, 53, 56, 57, 58, 60
Bushong, William M. 114, 115
Busti, New York 9
Butler, Col. Thomas H. 90, 94

California Railroad Commission 161
Camp Cooper, Texas 30, 31
Camp Grant 148, 149, 150, 153
Camp Ogelthorpe 92
Camp Stoneman 84
Canby, Maj. Gen. Edward R. 106, 113, 120, 140
Capron, Col. Horace 88
Chase, Kate 84
Chase, Salmon B. 79, 84
Chautauqua County, New York 8, 9
Christianburg, Virginia 110
Clarke, Cong. Staly N. 12
Cobb, Maj. Gen. Howell 92
Colorado River 23, 24
Columbia, Virginia 72
Cooke, Col. Philip St. George 20–26, 38, 41, 44
Cortinas, Juan Nepomuceno 31
Couch, Maj. Gen. Darius 12, 13, 60
Council Bluffs, Iowa 16, 18
Couts, J. 86
Covington, Georgia 91
Crews, Col. Charles C. 97
Crook, Maj. Gen. George 143, 144, 154, 155
Culpeper Courthouse 55, 66, 67, 69

Danville, Virginia 111
Davis, Lt. Col. Hasbrouck 72, 75
Davis, Pres. Jefferson 29, 111
Drum Barracks 142, 148
Duffie, Col. Alfred 81, 83

18th Massachusetts Reg., U.S. 46
8th Illinois Reg., U.S. 41
8th Michigan Reg., U.S. 88, 97
8th Tennessee Reg. 107
11th Kentucky Reg., U.S. 88, 107, 114

11th Michigan Reg., U.S. 104, 107
Ely's Ford 69
English, Maj. Richard Duvall 96
Ewell, Lt. Gen. Richard S. 82
Exeter, England 7

Fair Oaks (Seven Pines), Battle of 43
15th Pennsylvania, U.S. 107, 109, 120
5th Georgia Reserves, C.S.A. 93
5th Indiana Reg., U.S. 88, 90, 95, 97, 98
5th U.S. Cav., U.S. 44
5th U.S. Colored Artillery, U.S. 103
5th Virginia Reg., C.S.A. 83
55th Virginia Reg., C.S.A. 55
First Cavalry Brigade, U.S. 39
First Div., U.S. 58
1st Dragoons, U.S. 20, 27, 29
1st Kentucky Reg., U.S. 87, 88, 91, 92, 94, 96, 98
1st Maine Reg., U.S. 70, 77, 78
1st Maryland Reg., U.S. 72
1st Michigan Reg., U.S. 35
1st Missouri Mounted Vol., U.S. 15
1st New Jersey Reg., U.S. 71
1st New York, Zouaves, U.S. 35
1st Ohio Reg., U.S. 88, 97
1st Pennsylvania Reg., U.S. 78
1st Tennessee Reg., C.S.A. 91
1st U.S. Colored Artillery, U.S. 101
Fort Magruder, Virginia 40
Fort Monroe, Virginia 39, 47
Fort Whipple, Arizona 144, 146, 148
Foster, Dr. Stephen 21
Fourteenth Amendment 132, 135
14th Illinois Reg., U.S. 88
4th Virginia Reg., C.S.A. 44
4th Michigan Reg., U.S. 120
Franklin, Maj. Gen. William B. 57, 58, 42

195

Fredericksburg, Virginia, Battle of 54–61
Freedman's Bureau 122, 123, 124, 132, 133
Fremont, Maj. Gen. John C. 18, 25, 43

Gaines Mill, Battle of 45, 46
Gardner, Brig. Gen. William M. 113
Garfield, Pres. James 137
Garnett, Brig. Gen. Robert S. 36, 37
Garrard, Maj. Gen. Kenner 88
Georgia State Militia 93
Gila River 22, 23
Gillen, Brig. Gen. Alvin 104, 106, 121, 156
Gloucester Point 74
Gordon, Maj. Gen. George H. 12
Gordonsville, Virginia 65
Grant, Lt. Gen. U.S. 86, 106, 107, 120, 153
Gregg, Brig. Gen. David McMurtrie 62, 72

Halleck, Maj. Gen. Henry W. 118
Hampton, Brig. Gen. Wade 82
Hardee, Maj. William J. 30, 91
Heintzelman, Maj. Samuel P. 31
Hill, Maj. Gen. A.P. 12, 45
Hillsboro, Georgia 94
Hollingsworth, Lt. John McHenry 27
Hood, Maj. Gen. John B. 45, 69
Hooker, Maj. Gen. Joseph 5, 6, 41, 56, 63, 64, 66, 79, 81
Huffman, Lt. Richard 95, 96
Hunnicutt, James W. 132, 133
Hurst, George 162, 170

Indianola, Texas 34
Irwin, Gov. William 161
Irwinville, Georgia 120
Iverson, Brig. Gen. Alfred 91, 94, 97
Ivor, Virginia 75

Jackson, Brig. Gen. Alfred "Mudwall" 102, 103
Jackson, Maj. Gen. Thomas "Stonewall" 12, 13, 14, 43
James River 39, 40, 41, 46, 69, 71
Jamestown Academy 11
Jamestown, New York 8, 9, 171
Johnson, Pres. Andrew 130
Johnston, Col. Albert Sidney 29
Johnston, Gen. Joseph E. 39, 40, 118
Joint Committee on the Conduct of the War 79
Jones, Brig. Gen. William Edmonson "Grumble" 65, 82
Jonesboro, Georgia 89, 91

Kearny, Maj. Gen. Philip 55
Kearny, Brig. Gen. Stephen Watts 15, 17, 21, 23, 27

Kelly's Ford 66, 68, 81; Battle of 63, 64
Keogh, Maj. Myles 94
Key West, Florida 34
Kilpatrick, Col. Judson 63, 72, 74
Knoxville, Tennessee 87

Lakewood, New York 8
La Mesa, Mexico 32
Lee, Elizabeth Blair 48
Lee, Brig. Gen. Fitzhugh "Fitz" 64
Lee, General Robert E. 29, 30, 75
Lee, Brig. Gen. W.H.F. "Rooney" 42, 70, 72
Letcher, Gov. John 36
Leurox, Antione 21
Libby Prison, Richmond 72
Lincoln, Pres. Abraham 5, 6, 39, 53, 54, 67, 78
Lincolnton, North Carolina 117
Little, Jesse C. 16
Longstreet, Lt. General James 41, 69, 75, 76
Los Angeles, California 25
Los Robles, California 159, 160, 161; burns 166
Loudoun County, Virginia 54
Louisa Court House 70, 73
Lovejoy Station, Georgia 90
Lowe, Thaddeus (Aeronaut of the Army of the Potomac) 42

Macon, Georgia 89, 91, 92, 93, 94
Magruder, Brig. Gen. John, ("Prince John") 40, 45
Mahone, Brig. Gen. William 137, 139
Malvern Hill, Virginia, Battle of 46
Marion, John 146, 153
Massaponax River 50
Mayre's Heights 60
McClellan, Maj. Gen. George 12, 13, 35, 37, 38, 39, 46, 52, 53, 54, 55
McCook, Brig. Gen. Edward M. 87, 91, 92, 93
Meade, Maj. Gen. George E. 58, 59, 61
Memphis, Tennessee 123
Merrill, Samuel H. 72
Merritt, Maj. Gen. Wesley 63
Mexican War 14, 15
Middleburg, Virginia, Battle of 83
Milledgeville 94
Monticello, Georgia 91
Mormon Battalion 16, 17, 19
Morrisville, Virginia 66

Nauvoo, Illinois 16
Neese, Sgt. George M. 83
New Berlin, New York 8
New Orleans 123, 129
New York 7, 8, 9 12, 21, 34, 115, 118, 129, 130, 140, 167, 169–170, 171
Nile, Battle of the 8
9th New York Vol. Cav., U.S. 78

9th Reg. U.S. Cav., U.S. 6
9th Tennessee, U.S. 107
9th Virginia, C.S.A. 44, 66, 72
North Anna River 70, 72, 75, 77
North Carolina 2, 69, 101, 102, 105, 106, 107, 108, 109, 111, 112, 114, 117, 118, 119, 121

Ocmulgee River, Georgia 91, 92, 94, 98, 99
119th U.S. Colored Troops, U.S. 112
Orange and Alexandria Railroad 35, 38, 54
Orange Court House 77
Orange Plank Road 77
Orange Springs, Virginia 77
Oregon 29
Oregon Trail 66
Oury, William Sanders 150

Peninsula Campaign 40, 41
Perkins, Mary 8
Petersburg, Virginia 75, 107, 111, 119, 131, 135, 140
Petersburg Index 141
Pettegrew, Pvt. David (Father Pettegrew) 20
Philippi, West Virginia, Battle of 36
Pickett, Maj. Gen. George E. 12, 69
Pit River, California 28
Pleasonton, Maj. Gen. Alfred 50, 52, 62, 63, 70, 78, 81, 82, 83
Polk, Pres. James K. 16
Poolesville, Maryland 49
Porter, Gen. Fitz John 42
Pozo Hondo 25
Prescott, Arizona 144, 148
Price, Col. George B. 19

Raccoon Ford 69, 77
Rapidan River 68, 69, 70, 78
Rappahannock River 5, 38, 39, 55, 56, 58, 61, 66, 68, 77, 78
Reconstruction Acts 131, 132, 133
Reno, Maj. Gen. Jesse 12, 35
Rich Mountain 36
Richmond, Fredericksburg, and Potomac Railroad (RF&P) 69, 74
Richmond, Virginia 6, 39, 40, 42, 43, 44, 45, 46, 51, 54, 55, 57, 58, 59, 64, 65, 66, 69, 70, 71, 74, 75, 76, 78, 79, 80, 86, 87, 107, 111, 114, 116, 118, 133, 135, 136, 137, 138, 140; evacuation 110–111
Rio Grande River 21, 29
Rosecrans, Maj. Gen. William S. 37
Rosser, Col. Thomas Lafayette 83
Russian River, California 28, 29

Safford, Gov. Anson Peacely-Killen 142, 143, 144, 145, 146, 153
Salisbury, North Carolina 101, 112

Index

Salisbury Prison 115
Saltville, Virginia 101, 102, 103, 105
Sanderson, Dr. George B. 19
San Pasquale, Battle of 25
San Pedro River 22
Santa Fe Trail 19
Schofield, Maj. Gen. John 86, 101, 106, 131, 132, 134, 138, 144, 156, 168
Scott, General in Chief Winfield 33, 34
Second Cav. Div., U.S. 29, 44, 88
2nd Dragoons, U.S. 33
2nd North Carolina, U.S. 109
2nd Ohio Heavy Artillery, U.S. 101
Seddon, James A. 75, 77
Seven Days, Battle of 46
17th New York Reg., U.S. 46
Shannon's Crossroads 73
Shenandoah River 54
Shenandoah Valley 71, 72
Sheridan, Lt. Gen. Philip 107, 116
Sherman, Maj. Gen. William Tecumseh 64, 86, 88, 89, 118, 119, 143, 144, 148, 231
Sickles, Brig. Gen. Daniel E. 57, 58, 61
16th U.S. Infantry, U.S. 125
VI Army Corps, U.S. 92
6th Indiana Reg., U.S. 97
6th Pennsylvania Reg., U.S. 82
6th U.S. Cav., U.S. 42, 82
6th Virginia C.S.A., U.S. 82
Smith, Sgt. Albert 22
Smith, Lt. Andrew Jackson 19, 20, 24, 26
Smith, Lt. Elza C. 103
Smith, Pvt. John 27
Smith, Joseph 17, 19
Smith, Gen. Persifor 28, 31
Smith, Lt. Col. R.W. 96
Smith, Maj. Gen. William F. "Baldy" 41, 56, 57, 58
South Anna River 71, 72, 75
Stanton, Edward 118, 119
Star of the West 34
Statesville, North Carolina 116
Stevensburg, Virginia 81
Stocton, Commodore Robert 25
Stoneman, Bertha (GS's niece) 9
Stoneman, Byron (GS's brother) 9
Stoneman, Charlotte (GS's sister) 9
Stoneman, Maj. Gen. George: assumes command of cavalry corps, Army of the Potomac, U.S. 62; Atlanta campaign 88–94; attitude toward prisoner exchanges 99; Battle of Clear Lake, California 28; Battle of Sunshine Church 95; Battle of Williamsburg 40, 41; captured by Confederate cavalry 97; commands cavalry, Army of the Ohio 86; commands cavalry bureau, Washington D.C. 84; commands Dept. of Tennessee 123; commands District of Arizona 142; commands 1st Military District, Virginia 134; commands sub-district of Petersburg, Va. 131; commands III Corps at Battle of Fredericksburg 55–61; death in Buffalo, New York 171; early life 9; education 11; elected governor of California 163; elected Railroad Commissioner 161; established headquarters, Drum Barracks, Ca. 148; exchanged for Confederate Gen. D.C. Govan 100; health 45, 46, 83, 99, 156; leaves California and resides with sister, Mrs. Benjamin Williams 169; on duty in Los Angeles 27, 28; on the Texas frontier with the 2nd Cavalry, U.S. 31; promoted to regular rank of colonel 131; purchases Los Robles 158; raid at Battle of Chancellorsville 65–80; rebuked by Congressional Committee for Memphis riots 129; reinstated and appointed Col. of Infantry by Congress 169; relieved of command, District of Arizona 154; resigns from retirement list 165; Russian River 28, 29; Stuart's Chambersburg raid 49–53; Virginia and North Carolina cavalry raid 101–117; West Point 12, 13, 14; with the Mormon Battalion 16, 20, 21, 22, 23, 24, 26
Stoneman, George, Jr. 8, 9, 10
Stoneman, John (GS's brother) 9
Stoneman, Kate (GS's sister) 9
Stoneman, Mary (GS's grandmother)
Stoneman, Mary Jane "Jenny" (GS's sister) 9
Stoneman, Mary Oliver Hardisty (GS's wife) 48, 163, 165, 166, 167, 168, 169
Stoneman, Rebecca (GS's sister) 9
Stoneman, Richard (GS's grandfather) 7, 8
Stuart, Maj. Gen. J.E.B. "Jeb" 38, 41, 48, 102; Brandy Station 69; Chambersburg raid 49–53; Peninsula Campaign 44; "Ride around McClellan" 44
Sunshine Church 95
"Swing Around the Circle" 130, 131

10th Michigan Reg., U.S. 107, 109, 110, 120, 121
10th New York Reg., U.S. 76
3rd North Carolina, U.S. 101
3rd Pennsylvania, U.S. 41
3rd U.S. Heavy Artillery, U.S. 123
13th Tennessee Reg., U.S. 107, 119
13th Virginia Reg., C.S.A. 66, 69
39th Mass. Reg., U.S. 50
Thomas, Brig. Gen. George H. 30, 105, 122, 143
Thompson's Crossroads, Virginia 72, 73
III Army Corps, U.S. 57
Trevilian Station, Virginia 70
Troop F, 3rd Cav., U.S. 146
Tucson, Arizona 21, 22, 147, 148
12th Illinois Reg., U.S. 75, 82
12th Kentucky Reg., U.S. 107
12th Ohio Reg., U.S. 105, 107, 109, 114
21st Infantry, U.S. 157
24th Indiana Battery, U.S. 88
XXIII Army Corps, U.S. 86
Twiggs, Brig. Gen. David Emanuel 33, 34
Tyler, Sgt. Daniel 17, 20, 24, 26

Underwood Constitution, Virginia 134, 139
Union Mills 38
United States Ford 70, 75
Upperville, Virginia, Battle of 83

Van Dorn, Col. Earl 34
Vaughn, Gen. John C. 104
Vicksburg, Mississippi 102, 113
Virginia Central Railroad 70, 71, 72

Wainwright, Col. Charles S. 66
Warrenton Junction, Virginia 38
Watkins, Sam R. (Maury Grays, C.S.A.) 91
Weand, H. K. 114
Weekly Arizona Miner 145
Wells, Gov. Henry H. 135
West Point 11, 12, 13
Western Virginia (1861), 36
White's Ford, Virginia 51
Williamsburg, Virginia, Battle of 40, 41
Winchester, Virginia 65
Winston and Salem, North Carolina 112
Wool, Maj. Gen. John E. 29
Wyndham, Col. (Sir) Percy 63, 71
Wytheville, Virginia 104, 110

Yanceyville, Virginia 71, 73
Yorktown, Virginia 40
Young, Brigham 16, 19

www.ingramcontent.com/pod-product-compliance
Ingram Content Group UK Ltd.
Pitfield, Milton Keynes, MK11 3LW, UK
UKHW050525150426
5217IPUK00026B/1804